Title:	Seven Secrets of Resilience for Parents
Subtitle:	Navigating the Stress of Parenthood
Author:	Andrew D. Wittman, Ph.D.
Publication Date:	November 2018
Format:	Paperback
ISBN:	978-1-7323568-0-1
Retail Price:	$24.99 US
E-book ISBN:	978-1-7323568-1-8
E-book Price:	$24.99 US
LOC Number:	2018906194
Length:	320 pages
Trim:	6 inches x 9 inches
Classification:	Parenting/Family/Self Help

Media Contact:

Sara Jennings, National Publicist, Annie Jennings PR

Desk: 908.281.5183 Main Office: 908.281.6201 or
sara@anniejenningspr.com

Get Warrior Tough Media

An imprint of the Mental Toughness Training Center, LLC

Main Office: 864.977.1443 or info@getwarriortough.com

If any material is to be quoted, it should be checked against the bound book.

D1416430

Seven Secrets of Resilience For Parents

Navigating the Stress of Parenthood

By
Andrew D. Wittman, Ph.D.

Get Warrior Tough Media
www.GetWarriorTough.com

Get Warrior Tough Media

107 Ambrose Trail

Greer, SC 29650

www.getwarriortough.com

Ordering Information:

Quantity sales. Special discounts are available on quantity purchases by corporations, associations, and others. For details, contact the publisher at the address above, telephone 864-977-1772 or email info@getwarriortough.com

Published by: Get Warrior Tough Media, Greer, South Carolina
Library of Congress Control Number: 2018906194

Publisher's Cataloging-In-Publication Data
Names: Wittman, Andrew D.
Title: Seven secrets of resilience for parents : navigating the stress of parenthood / by Andrew D. Wittman, Ph.D.
Description: First Edition. | Greer, SC : Get Warrior Tough Media, [2018]
Identifiers: ISBN 9781732356801 (paperback) | ISBN 9781732356818 (ebook)
Subjects: LCSH: Parenting--Psychological aspects. | Parent and child. | Child rearing--Psychological aspects. | Resilience.
Classification: LCC HQ755.8 .W58 2018 (print) | LCC HQ755.8 (ebook) | DDC 649.1--dc23

DEDICATION

This work is dedicated first and foremost to my personal Mental Toughness Coach – Kim Wittman. With you constantly shoulder-to-shoulder with me in our endeavor to build a great family, along with three decades of your commitment, love, and partnership, we have raised three AWESOME kids!

To my closest and best friends, Drew, Jack and Mick! You guys ROCK and then some! Thanks for always standing with Mom and me. And thank you for allowing me to enlist you as my test subjects as I crafted, honed, and sharpened the Get Warrior Tough process. I am in awe of each of you and your Resilience! Boo Yah!

Special thanks to Dr. Jon Christiansen - this book would have never happened without your unwavering support and friendship.

To all the parents who agreed to share your stories with me for the book – THANK YOU!

To all my mentors along the way - I'm eternally grateful and will pay it forward.

And to YOU – the Resilient-Minded Parents!

CONTENTS

INTRODUCTION – Leaving a Legacy

Can You Give Anyone Anything You Don't Have?

I have spent large portions of time on five of this planet's six inhabited continents. Regardless of ethnicity, culture, economic status, political or religious ideology, I have observed something common to all humans – parents want their children to have a better life than they have. I've never met a parent who wouldn't do **anything** for their kids. My wife, Kim, and I certainly feel this way. But just being willing to do anything for your child isn't enough, otherwise every child would grow up and enjoy a happy, successful, and fulfilled life. A balanced life. A life filled with harmonious relationships, not ones frayed by hurtful wrongdoings, drama, and embitterment. A life filled with thriving abundance, not one filled with struggle. The enjoyment of a purposeful and fulfilling career they love, not grinding out a job they hate.

It is not enough to love your children. Not enough to want the best for them. There's one and only one thing that is enough. My wife and I have deployed this one essential element in raising our own three happy, successful, and fulfilled children. And continue doing so, even now that they are almost adults. This one thing is resilience.

One definition of resilience is the capacity to recover quickly from difficulties. I call it mental toughness and define it as the ability to take control of your thoughts, feelings, attitudes, and actions proactively, especially under pressure. Resilience is the skill to handle anything life throws your way. It is a mindset that says, "I'm the problem, and I'm the solution. If I have a problem, it's me, but the good news is, I'm also the solution." Resilience says, "I cannot fail, as long as I learn and grow." Resilience operates from a foundation of love, not fear. Resilience turns negative stress into rocket fuel. Resilience taps into internal emotional drivers that enable a person to push past the obstacles, difficulties, losses, and pain to complete any worthy accomplishment.

Even though I am the one writing this book, make no mistake, my wife is the main driver in the discovery, deployment, and installment of mental toughness in our home. When most folks first meet us, they think I'm the driver because of my background: Marine infantry combat veteran, police officer, federal agent, private military contractor, and leadership and mental toughness coach. Kim is by far the more resilient and more mentally tough partner of our thirty-year marriage. She is the citadel, the fortress, and the rock that unwaveringly demonstrated and instilled that resilience in our kids while I was gone for large portions of time, deployed somewhere on those five inhabited continents.

I knew Kimmi was tough, but I had no idea how tough until she became pregnant with our first child. She, being one of those parents who would do anything for her kids, began a massive research project, which continues to this day. She discovered the concept of drug-free, natural childbirth and had us enroll in breathing classes. (You know the kind where we both sit on the floor with pillows and count "Ha – Ha – He's".) When that day in 1997 came, she birthed our firstborn child, Drew, with nothing but mental toughness and a bucket full of ice chips. The medical staff was in disbelief, as offers of epidurals were summarily dismissed. And she did the same for our other two, Jack in 2000 and Michaela in 2003.

It was back in the delivery room that I learned moms are much more resilient and mentally tougher than dads. And that you don't have to join an elite military unit to be resilient and mentally tough. You don't have to be in combat or a fire-fight or almost get killed in a war. If you're a parent, you have it; the trick is to learn how to tap into it and deploy it.

Accessing resilience, or mental toughness, is a skill, and it can be learned, practiced, applied, and mastered the same as any physical skill: tying your shoes, brushing your teeth, or driving a car. Many people I have interacted with over the course of my life have seemed to believe that resilience and mental toughness are almost mystical. Not tangible. Not teachable. Not learnable. I assure you, they are tangible, teachable, and learnable for us parents *and* for our children. We must, however, answer a question first.

Can you give anyone anything you don't have?

If you didn't have a hundred dollars, could you give anyone a hundred dollars? If you didn't have a cup of coffee, could you give anyone a cup of coffee?

It All Starts with Self-Esteem

There are numerous studies with varying statistics in the realm of self-esteem, self-worth, self-regard, and self-confidence, but to make it simple: approximately eighty-five percent of two-year olds have a healthy self-esteem, self-worth, self-regard, and confidence level. They don't know the planet isn't about them. They want what they want, and they want it NOW! We call them the "Terrible Twos," and they have fantastic self-esteem until we drive it out of them.

In her audiobook, *12 Secrets to High Self-Esteem*, Linda Larson says that by age fifteen, the number of those with healthy self-esteem drops all the way down to five percent. That means ninety-five out of one hundred teenagers need help. They don't believe they deserve to have a good life, and with what we know about how the brain works (more on that later), that belief becomes a downward spiral.

Which brings us to these numbers: from about age twenty-four until the grave, only thirty percent of adults have a healthy self-esteem, self-worth, or self-regard. That means seven out of every ten adults need help.

Research from Purdue University shows that the number one fear of all human beings is ostracism or rejection. Cognitive neuroscience has used functional magnetic resonance imaging (fMRI), a tool used to measure brain activity by monitoring changes in cerebral blood flow and neural activation, to show that rejection is registered by the brain in the same way as physical pain. When you and your first crush in high school broke up and it hurt, it was as if it physically hurt.

Conversely, the number one need all human beings are looking to fulfill is unconditional acceptance, also called love. When we look for acceptance externally (from other people), we abdicate our self-worth to others. Remember that old country song, "Looking for Love in All the Wrong Places." Until you internally accept yourself, you are not only abdicating your personal power, but you are also powerless to give that acceptance to anyone else--your spouse, your kids, your family, your friends, your co-workers, etc.

What the statistics bear out is pretty disheartening: seventy percent of adults aren't going to accept you because they haven't accepted themselves. And a *whopping* ninety-five percent of teenagers can't accept you because they haven't accepted themselves. On the flip side, eighty-five percent of two-year-olds accept you just the way you are (all because they completely accept themselves and freely give away that acceptance.)

This reality leaves you with two choices: spend the rest of your life only interacting with two-year-olds or accept yourself. Love you, and then love others. But you must **love you** first – because you can't give anyone anything you don't have.

If the empirical research is to be believed, seventy percent of parents have not internally accepted themselves and are looking for that acceptance from outside sources. Seventy percent of parents, all of whom cannot give anyone anything they don't have, cannot fulfill the number one need of their children: acceptance. No wonder 95% of teenagers, all whom have low self-worth, must go looking outside the home for acceptance. They seek acceptance from external sources like social media, which is stocked full of their peers who also haven't accepted themselves. And the downward spiral is in full effect.

Self-acceptance is the foundational step in navigating the stresses of parenthood because it is the foundation of resilience itself. Our children must know beyond any doubt that they are completely accepted by their parents. How many of us have longed for that acceptance from our own parents and not received it? Alas, they could not give what they themselves did not have.

Two-year-olds are extremely robust and full of boundless energy. Learning to crawl, walk, talk, run, and jump. Mistakes, miscues, and failures are simply part of the process of accomplishment. But at some point, many begin to realize they aren't unconditionally accepted, as parents who have not accepted themselves blur the lines of behavior and identity, expressing disappointment in the child instead of correcting unhelpful actions or behavior. If you have found yourself doing this, don't despair. It's not your fault. It's an imitated behavior, passed down from generation to generation.

Imitation: Monkey See, Monkey Do

Imitation is how we learn. Our children will do what we parents do. They will not do what we *tell* them to do, which we already know. That whole *"do as I say, not as I do"* thing doesn't hold water. If you don't like the way your child is acting, the first place to look is in the mirror. The second place to look is the various influences on your child, i.e. the internet and online content, television programming, family members, teachers, friends, babysitters, etc.

Susan Pinker, a developmental psychologist and journalist, shares her experience during the first Gulf War in 1990. She was working as a clinical psychologist in Montreal and began receiving numerous referrals from pediatricians of children between eight and ten years old suddenly beginning to wet their beds. Others refused to go to school and were afraid to leave the house. After investigating, a commonality was found. Each of the children, though strangers to each other, came from homes that had strong family connections to Israel, which was in the daily news due to Saddam Hussein's missile attacks. The children, although living halfway across the planet from the devastation of war, were mirroring their parents' emotional reactions.

We live in South Carolina. We regularly enjoy fabulous weather throughout the year; however, spring and summer often bring fantastic thunderstorms with awesome displays of lightning. The trees in our yard, both front and back, have been scarred by several crackling bolts of

12

electrostatic energy. The entire house would shake as if we ourselves were under an indirect fire assault. When our children were young toddlers, they would come running into my arms at the first boom of a thunderstorm, crying and hyperventilating, their little bodies shaking with fear. I would scoop them up and calmly whisper in their ear, "Is Daddy scared?"

They would pant, "No, sir."

"Then you shouldn't be scared. When you see Daddy get scared, then you should be scared. But until then, you don't need to be scared. Okay?"

"Yes, sir." And the calming would begin. Crying would stop. Breathing would return to normal rates, as would heart rate, and eventually the fear would dissipate.

In neuroscience, this practice is called *neural coupling*. Studies have shown that human brains, when in the same space, time, and interaction, sync up. Our brains literally begin to mind-meld, and the same regions of the brain fire off in the same sequence in real time. Princeton University neuroscientist Uri Hasson demonstrated the power of this concept in an experiment, which was conducted in two parts. The first phase involved a graduate student, while being brain scanned via functional magnetic resonance imaging (fMRI), telling an unrehearsed story about her high school prom night. Phase two involved twelve other students listening to the recording of the prom story, also while being brain scanned via fMRI. The results showed that the listeners' brains fired off in the same patterns and sequence as each other's and the storyteller's. Along with this finding, further research has shown there is a leader-follower distinction when neural coupling occurs. The leader's brain dictates what is to be mirrored and imitated, and the follower's brain(s) hook in, match up, and fall in line. Therefore, as a parent, modeling resilience and mental toughness is imperative. And secondarily, deliberate and calculated guidance is essential when it comes to other influences, especially the consumption of media content. The producers of any media are by default assuming the leadership position in directing the brain's activity. (I'm actually doing it right now. By reading this, you are thinking about what I am leading you to think about.)

However, before you can model anything, you must learn it and imitate it. Consider this book your field guide to imitating, learning, and modelling resilience and mental toughness. I will give you not only the biopsychology (how the body, mind, and emotions interact) of mental toughness and the cognitive neuroscience (how the brain works), but also real-life examples and illustrations that you can imitate, along with adopting science-based principles.

To that end, I will ask you to wear two hats during our time together. The first hat is that of the **student**. Learning and growing, you yourself becoming resilient and mentally tough. You are gaining control over your thoughts, feelings, attitudes, and actions, especially under pressure. You are learning to handle anything life throws your way. You are adopting a mindset that says, "I'm the problem, and I'm the solution. If I have a problem, it's me, but the good news is, I'm also the solution." You are espousing a philosophy that says, "I cannot fail, as long as I learn and grow." You are operating from a foundation of love, not fear, and turning negative stressors into rocket fuel. You are mastering how to tap into your own internal emotional drivers and push past the obstacles, difficulties, losses, and pain. You are gaining clarity and knowing who you are, where you are going, and why you are going there. You are learning to be rooted and grounded, a citadel and fortress that weathers any storm.

The second hat is that of the **teacher**, the **mentor,** and the **coach**, consistently modeling resilience and mental toughness for your kids. Deliberately and lovingly guiding them to gain control over their thoughts, feelings, attitudes, and actions. Instructing them in creating and discovering their own internal identity and teaching them to solve problems, not complain about them. Being their safety net of growth and learning, allowing them to risk failure. Coaching them on how to turn negative stressors into rocket fuel and mentoring them to find and tap into their own internal emotional drivers so that they can push past any obstacles, difficulties, losses, and pain. Helping them get to know who they are, where they are going, and why they are going there, teaching them to be rooted and grounded, a citadel and fortress that weathers any storm.

SECRET 1 – CRITICAL THINKING & THE BRAIN

CHAPTER 1 – How the Brain Works

The cell phone in my pocket buzzed. It was a text from Kimmi,

"Eric just died. Go to their house now and be with Ruth."

I grabbed my car keys and bolted. During the four-minute drive to Eric and Ruth's house, my brain began to flood my conscious mind with every bit of information about their family stored in my memory. Their oldest child, Justin, and our oldest Drew had been thick as thieves since elementary school, both now one-year shy of graduating high school. They had gone on a trip to Australia together for one of the student ambassador programs, as well as numerous other adventures.

We had a rare friendship with them, a family friendship. They have two boys and a girl, Justin (11th grade at the time), Layla (9th grade), and Miles (7th grade). We have two boys and a girl, Drew (11th grade at the time), Jack (9th grade) and Michaela (5th grade). Eric, a forty-five-year-old entrepreneur, helped me when I started my own firm. He took my boys hunting and fishing along with his boys. Sleepovers. Birthday parties. Movies.

I parked on the street in front of their house and ran up the porch steps. I rang the bell. Ruth came to the door. She was poised and dignified and had tears flowing down her cheeks.

"How are you here?"

I shrugged, "Kimmi sent me."

"He's gone."

"I'm so sorry," I hugged her.

She tearfully began to mutter, "What about Justin's graduation? Who will walk Layla down the aisle?"

"That's not for today, Ruth. Where are the kids?"

If ever there was a situation that called for resilience, this was it. Ruth not only had to deal with navigating the stress of losing her spouse of twenty-two years, but she also suddenly found herself to be a single parent with three teenagers.

The beginning of the road to resilience starts with getting a handle on the how the human machine operates. To do so, we must first understand how the brain works. Nothing that happens in the machine occurs without the brain's input. Nothing. And the human brain is the original search engine. It must answer a question. The answer doesn't have to come out of your mouth, but the brain must search for an answer whenever it is presented with a question. As an experiment to see this fact in action, no matter what I ask you next, do not recall the information.

"What's two plus two?" (Stop answering the question.)

"What color is the sky? (Quit it. Don't think of the answer.)

"In which direction does the sun rise?"

"In which direction does the sun set?"

Ask, and you shall receive. Ask a bad question, and you will receive a bad answer. Ask a good question, and you will receive a good answer. Ask a better question and receive a better answer. A bad question is: "Can being a parent be any more stressful?" A good question is: "How can I survive being a parent?" A better question is: "How can I successfully navigate the stresses of parenthood and thrive?"

That day in 2015, on Ruth's porch, the questions she asked about her sixteen-year-old son's future high school graduation and who in the future would walk her fourteen-year-old daughter down the aisle were both good questions. But on that day, with the starkness of the raw emotion in play, those questions would only increase the stress. On that day, we had to keep our minds focused on getting through each minute, one moment at a time.

Eleven Million Bits

In the last decade or so, through cognitive and behavioral neuroscience research, we have learned enormous amounts about how the human brain works. With functional magnetic resonance imaging (fMRI) brain imaging and brain mapping, we have learned that the brain takes in approximately eleven million bits of information per second. Each of us is a data collecting machine, vacuuming up information at broadband speeds. The cable broadband internet provider in my home has an upload speed of five million bits of information per second and a download speed of sixty-five million bits of information per second. My broadband service downloads information at a rate of thirteen times faster than it uploads. Think about streaming a movie versus uploading the two hundred pictures from your cousin's wedding. Our human brains function in the opposite fashion. We upload information faster than we download it. Far more quickly. In fact, over eighty-seven thousand times faster. We upload eleven million bits of information every second through what we see, what we touch, what we hear, what we smell, and what we taste. How much of that data is downloaded to the conscious mind for action?

The number varies between one hundred twenty-six bits per second all the way down to forty bits per second. For the sake of simplicity, let's stick to the higher number. The human brain takes in eleven million bits of information per second and filters all that data in real time, sending only one hundred twenty-six bits of information per second to our conscious mind for action. We upload at broadband speeds and download at dial-up speeds.

Can you imagine the old dial-up modems? I remember how long it took to download a single image and how much longer it would take to download a single song. Movies and binge streaming shows? Forget about it. When our kids were little, we would go to the Disney website, and it would take over an hour to download a 5-minute Mickey cartoon. It was beyond frustrating. We would find it incredibly intolerable to operate online at those slow speeds. We literally do not have enough time in this life to function at those download rates. Yet that is the rate at which the human brain sends data to the conscious mind for action.

If all we had were dial-up modems to operate online, we would have to be extremely discriminating in selecting the information we wanted to download. Otherwise, we would be completely bogged down, waiting for a download of massive information. Then having to filter and sift through enormous portions of information manually. Then sort that information and finally prioritize it for use. We would be completely unable to function for extended periods of time, waiting for the process to finish.

The human brain, for us to operate in real life and real time, must also be extremely discriminating with the information it selects to send to the conscious mind. Just to function consciously, the brain must filter all the information it uploads, prioritizing the data and finally making its choice of what exactly to transmit to the conscious mind. To understand how the human machine works, to understand truly and accurately how you work and how your child works, you must know how that selection process takes place. The research shows that our thoughts, feelings, opinions, and attitudes are the filter that chooses the one hundred twenty-six bits per second. We literally sift and discard ninety-nine-point nine percent of all that information and focus only on that information that proves and reinforces our thoughts, feelings, opinions, and attitudes. The fancy psychological term for this filter is *confirmation bias*.

To live, function, survive, and even thrive in real life and in real time, the human machine uses a system of mental shortcuts to make snap judgments called heuristics. Think of heuristics as a system of rules of thumb. By default, the human machine acts by uploading those eleven million bits of information per second, assessing a few things that stick out, and projecting an assumption based on experience, prior learning, opinions, and prevailing attitude. Then boom! The choice is made, the action taken.

This system tends to work fairly well most of the time, or so it seems. We run into issues when heuristics-gone-wild show up, called cognitive biases. These little cuties swing into action whenever there is a mismatch between our thoughts, opinions, beliefs, attitudes, and feelings and reality. Which, by the way, is most of the time. Cognitive biases very quickly set up shop and become the default filter of those eleven million bits of information per second, unless we take steps to identify reality objectively. I call it making an honest assessment and metacognition, thinking about how we think.

Geniuses

The human machine is chock-full of cognitive biases. We all deploy some of them far more than others. The more you rely on heuristics and biases, the greater the effect they will have on your life. The important thing is to be aware of their existence. The Resilient Minded person recognizes facts and then uses the knowledge to become a better parent. Average Minded people refuse to acknowledge the facts and stick their head in the sand, because facing facts is uncomfortable, which results in the reinforced use of biases to their detriment. That kind of pretending is not for us. We must become Resilient Minded parents if we are to navigate the stress of parenthood successfully. We face and embrace facts and use this knowledge for our betterment, and we become models, mentors, and coaches and teach our children to do the same.

The bottom line is that you are a genius, whether you consciously realize it or not. Your child's brain knows that your child is a genius. Your brain will never work against your genius self, and your child's brain will never work against your child's genius self. The fancy term for this in psychology is the *personal exceptionalism and illusory superiority bias*.

It works like this: if your child thinks today is going to be an *awesome* day, his or her brain will go to work and find the specific one hundred twenty-six bits of information per second that prove the child to be correct, and today becomes an *awesome* day. However, if your child thinks today is going to be an *awful* day, his or her brain will go to work and find the specific one hundred twenty-six bits of information per second that prove the child to be correct, and today becomes an *awful* day. Your child's thoughts, opinions, beliefs, and attitudes create a medical, electrochemical, and biophysical self-fulfilling prophecy. This consequence is medical science, not motivational speaker mumbo-jumbo.

Building Memories

Understanding how the human memory and memory recall operates is paramount to raising kids. Job number one for the parents who want to enjoy raising their children is the building of wonderful memories.

Fortunately, for Eric and Ruth's children, their father invested heavily in the building of wonderful memories with them. He spared no emotional expense in creating genuinely delightful remembrances with his family. Ruth and the children draw on the gift of those recollections every day for strength, for joy, and for comfort.

Learning and developing all hinges on our memories. The brain connects all the information we have gathered during experiences in life with what is called a schema. Schemas are mental shortcuts that tell us what to expect and make predictions and pre-judgments (opinions and beliefs) when we encounter new information and experiences. The more vivid the memory is, the faster and easier the recall is. Our memories, all based on our experiences, create our thoughts, opinions, feelings, and attitudes (i.e., the filter the brain uses in selecting the one hundred twenty-six bits per second). The more the emotions are involved, the more lasting the memories that are made, and the stronger the opinion, belief, feeling, and attitude about what happened is formed. The greater the emotion of the experience, the longer lasting the memory and the more entrenched the belief, feeling, and attitude.

Think back to your own days in school. How much of that biology class do you remember from seventh grade? Unless you're a biologist, I'm betting not that much, other than possibly the time you dissected the frog. Ewwww, gross! Or Whoaaaaa, cool! But either way, if the exercise evoked strong feelings, you **felt**, and a lasting memory was made. And so was a lasting opinion, feeling, and attitude about cutting open dead creatures. Can you recall the experience or one similar?

When we recall a memory, an experience, we tend to "see" it in our mind's eye playing out like a movie. When we recall a memory, our brains literally reconstruct or reproduce the scene from scratch, gathering the bits of information stored in the various regions of our brains. Literally, a new version of the memory is created each and every time we conjure it up. Often, when similar emotions are invoked during separate experiences, several details of two or more memories merge together. When documented facts are checked and it is revealed that events could not have happened that way, the human machine will still tend to discard the facts and rely on our reconstructed and misremembered version of the memory.

Pain and fear, when mixed with our experiences, create lasting memories and imprint lessons learned that shape our thoughts, beliefs, opinions, feelings, attitudes, and actions. Telling your child not to touch the hot stove and instilling fear of what will happen if they do might work and keep them from ever touching the hot stove. However, a lasting memory is made and learning and conditioning imprinted if the child does not take your word for it and tries it out personally. Pain is suddenly thrown into the mix. A lasting and vivid memory is made. The child just committed what I call a self-correcting error. Along with the pain is the now added factor of the fear of future suffering, and voilá! A new thought, opinion, belief, feeling, and attitude filter is formed.

This pain memory is a double-edged sword. When our oldest, Drew, was first learning to ride a bike sans training wheels, he went with his aunt and cousin for a ride. His cousin is nine months older and had nine months more experience sans training wheels on a bike. The three of them went over to the middle school to ride. A long stretch of the drive was a steeply sloping hill. Drew's cousin took off down the hill. Drew followed. Everything was going smoothly until Drew's bike wobbled. In his inexperience, he overcompensated, and a terrifying wreck ensued. His face was cut deeply and needed stitches. His newly acquired big-boy front teeth were chipped. Blood, tears, pain, and the now added factor of fear of future suffering all helped create a new thought, belief, feeling, and attitude filter: "I'm never riding that bike again!"

Drew was physically scarred for life, but even more impactful would be the mental and emotional scars if we didn't take swift corrective action. As parents, seeing your little darling's face covered in blood and snot and hearing the wailing cry (which gets worse as soon as Mommy and Daddy are in visual range), you may unknowingly tend to ramp up the emotion of the situation with your own panic and fear. This reaction only serves to make the memory more vivid and harder to overcome. Yes, what happened was terrible, and no parents want to see their children bleeding and in pain. If you are freaking out, "Oh my gosh, my baby!" then you are the creator of the mental and emotional wound instead of the healer of it. Every interaction you have with your kids is an opportunity to build and shape memories. Don't waste a single one of those opportunities.

Half the Brain Shuts Down

Fear conditioning, once it sets up shop, is the most difficult obstacle to becoming resilient. Neuroscience tells us that when a human acts from a mindset of fear, anxiety, or even worry (which is just baby fear), that up to half the brain shuts down. If you have ever experienced a fight or flight moment, you know this. The brain uses electrochemical reactions to operate. When we operate in fear, the electrochemical reactions are rerouted to the half of the brain that controls survival. The part of the brain that goes dark and loses power is the creative, problem-solving half that you need to get out of whatever you are facing and overcome it. When we parents allow fear conditioning to embed itself in our kids, we are dooming them to fight the good fight with half their brain, and not the creative half. Fear, anxiety, and worry all point your brain's filter to find the exact one hundred twenty-six bits of information per second that prove your concerns to be correct and discard any bits of information that would you show your genius self to be wrong.

Neurons that Fire Together, Wire Together

I'm the fifth of six children in my family. I was born in 1967 and my younger brother in 1969. All our elder siblings were born throughout the 1950s. Two of my sisters, by default, wrote with their left hands until they

26

went to school. They would have their left hands smacked with a ruler and be forced by the teachers to use their right hands. By the time I was in school, that practice had ceased. I write with my left hand. I also throw with my left hand. Brush my teeth with my left hand.

At age eighteen, I enlisted and was sent to Parris Island, SC for Marine Corps boot camp. A major part of the training process is marksmanship. As a missionary's kid, I had never fired a weapon of any kind. The marksmanship instructor asked me if I was left-handed or right-handed.

"Sir, left-handed, sir!"

"Have you ever fired a rifle in your life, Recruit?"

"Sir, no, sir!"

"Good. You won't have any bad habits to break. As of now, you are a right-handed shooter. It will make your life easier. The rifle and all the gear are set up for a right-handed shooter. You won't need any modified shooting techniques or special gear."

After a week of continual practice holding the rifle and aiming in at the target, my body and brain quickly adopted the new habit of shooting right-handed. Neuroscience definitively shows the neurons that fire together, wire together. Every time you perform a skill or take an action, the brain fires off in a particular pattern. Repeating the same skill or action creates a neuropathway. Think of it this way: the first time you try something, you are a trailblazer. You are in the jungles of the Amazon with a machete, chopping vines, trees, and underbrush. The second time you travel that path, it becomes a little easier. Over time, the more you repeat the skill or action, the more trampled the path becomes. After a few months, the path becomes a dirt road. After a year, you have paved that road. After a decade, it becomes a superhighway, six lanes wide with an autobahn-esque speed limit to match.

We used to believe that once we became adults, the brain's development was complete, and we were stuck with what we had at that time. Researchers have since discovered neuroplasticity. Neuroplasticity is the ability of the brain, no matter the physical age, to change throughout our entire lifetimes. We aren't hardwired. Stop excusing bad attitudes, habits, and behaviors by saying, "I'm just wired that way." You are not.

We literally have the ability, regardless of age or stage of life, to rewire our brains at will. Is it comfortable? No. Comfort comes from the very opposite of rewiring. Default neuropathways are what makes us comfortable. That is why humans are known as creatures of habit. We love to be comfortable, and habits are simply us traveling on the neuro-superhighways we have built, which ensure that comfort. It takes conscious effort to blaze new trails and create new neuropathways.

We activate neuroplasticity and physical rewiring of our brains, creating new pathways every time we learn new information or learn a new skill. An easy way to experience what neuroplasticity feels like is to brush your teeth with your non-default hand. If you normally use your right hand, use your left hand. Practice writing your name with your non-default hand. If you stick with it long enough, as in creating a new neural superhighway, you will become ambidextrous. Not overnight, but it will happen. The more you fire off that set of neurons, the more those neurons bundle together.

You can teach an old dog new stuff, but it takes enduring enormous amounts of discomfort to do so. How long before you switched back to your default hand in the teeth-brushing experiment? The Average Minded person will switch back before completing the task. The Resilient Minded will find a way to power through the discomfort and frustration. As parents, it is much easier to wire healthy behaviors in our kids from the time of birth, which become their default (habits), than it is to correct unhealthy behaviors and detrimental habits when they become teenagers and young adults. That's why it seems easier for children to learn several languages at the same time growing up. It's not actually easier; they just don't know any different. They haven't established a default language superhighway that makes them have to force themselves to build another language superhighway. They build both superhighways at the same time, and they don't realize it's not comfortable.

As parents successfully navigating all the stressors encountered while raising our kids, we must be deliberate, intentional, and even calculating when managing how our own brains are wired. How you handle these types of situations is crucial. You must control yourself and your response. Take as much of the emotional sting out of the situation as possible. Yes, be gentle and tender. Scoop your kids up in your arms and let them feel, as quickly as possible, that this situation is no big thing and that we can handle it, no problem.

WHAT TO DO

1) The human brain must answer a question. The human brain is the original search engine. Ask, and you shall receive. Ask a bad question, and you will receive a bad answer. Ask a good question, and you will receive a good answer. Ask a better question and receive a better answer. The bad question is, "Why can't you get straight A's like your sister?" The good question is, "How can I motivate you to get better grades?" The better question is, "What are the three things you have to dominate, control, and do to raise your GPA?"

2) The brain takes in eleven million bits of information per second but only sends one hundred twenty-six bits per second to the conscious mind for action. The way the brain choses what to send to the conscious mind is by filtering all the data through what you think, what you feel, what you believe, what your opinion is, and what your attitude is. Your brain knows you are a genius and will never go against your genius self. It will find the exact one hundred twenty-six bits of information that prove your genius self to be correct and discard any information that would prove your genius

self to be wrong. Choose your thoughts, opinions, and attitudes wisely; they set the course.

3) Emotional learning is the primary factor in memory construction. What emotions are you bringing to the table? What kind of memories are you building with your kids? How you handle stressful situations is crucial. You must control yourself and your response. Take as much of the emotional sting out of the situation as possible and let them feel, as quickly as possible, that this situation is no big thing and we can handle it, no problem.

4) The neurons that fire together, wire together. Every time you repeat patterns of thought, opinions, attitudes, or actions, you are creating neural pathways which quickly form into habits, and eventually, the pathways turn into superhighways. Be deliberate and purposeful when creating habits, taking actions, or repeating opinions.

CHAPTER 2- Being the Boss of Me

Naomi, a strong-willed, opinionated 8th grader, stood toe-to-toe with her parents, facing off for yet another battle. A rebel without a cause, Naomi had progressed through the levels of the public school disciplinary process. Silent lunches for talking in class had escalated to referrals, detentions, in-school suspensions, and now, a full-blown three-day suspension. Her parents had tried to avoid confronting Naomi because it always ended the same way. Things quickly descended into an emotionally charged shouting match. Today was no different. She knew all the right emotional buttons to push to elicit reactions from her parents. They had no idea what to do with her.

As soon as they questioned her about the circumstances of the latest episode causing the suspension, Naomi fiercely shouted, "You're not the BOSS of me!" Besides the rebellious attitude, she wasn't wrong. The real problem was that Naomi's parents were not only not the boss of Naomi, but they were also not the bosses of themselves. The reason they avoided the confrontations until there was no escape was that deep down, they knew they could not control their own reactions.

We humans instinctively do not like others to "boss" us around. There is a reason for that. The human machine is built to be the boss. But being an effective boss of oneself takes deliberate action.

As of right now, consider yourself to have been hired for the most powerful, prestigious position in the history of all mankind. You are now the CEO of You, Inc. Your job as the CEO of You, Inc. is to get your board of directors to act in concert for your betterment instead of your detriment. Allow me to introduce you to your board of directors. You know them as your Body, Mind, and Emotions.

When you have a board meeting, which director would you say usually wins the vote? Have you ever made an emotional decision? How'd that work out? I was speaking at a large conference in Atlanta and asked the crowd this question. I heard a voice cry out from the back-left side of the room, "Divorce!" The crowd laughed. Almost without fail, in most of the human population, emotions have hijacked our personal boardrooms, and the results have taken us someplace we didn't enjoy.

If emotion running the boardroom wasn't bad enough, the body runs a quick second. The body tends to jump in and take over at any given time. When I enlisted in the Marine Corps, back in 1985, I was 50 pounds overweight. I loved eating, and I hated running. In fact, the only thing on planet earth I hated more than running was more running. What do you do in Marine Corps boot camp? Running. And lots of it.

The first morning we went outside for physical training, we lined up in military formation. The drill instructor gave us the command to face to the right, forward march, and then the dreaded command, "Double-Time March!" We took off running. Three steps later, my body tried to take over the boardroom. "STOP!" it screamed. "We're DYING!" it screamed. Was I dying? No. My body was attempting to take over the boardroom. There are three votes in the boardroom, and the body usually sides with the emotions, only doing those things we "feel" like doing or complaining the entire time we are forced into doing something we *don't* "feel" like doing.

I believe that to be an effective, mentally tough, and resilient parent, the mind should be running the boardroom. Unfortunately, in most us, the mind wields the least amount of power. To gain a majority vote and carry the day, two directors must vote together. WARNING: The mind and emotions are diametrically opposed and will never vote together. It's like the State Department and the Defense Department; they have completely opposite missions. One is diplomatic, and the other is military force. The only chance we have of the mind running the boardroom is to get the body to vote with the mind.

This is great news, because the body is the weakest part of our being and the easiest to dominate. We have all heard the saying, "The spirit is willing, but the flesh is weak." Growing up, I would hear relatives at holiday gatherings use this saying as a humorous way to get away with eating a second piece of cheesecake. "Well, I certainly don't need a second piece…the spirit is willing, but the flesh is weak," as a forkful of yummy yet unhealthy goodness passed through their lips.

What this saying actually means is that our bodies are the weak spot and the easiest to control. Unfortunately for most of us, we stopped dominating our bodies after we stopped wearing diapers. We eat whatever we want and exercise (or not) whenever we feel like it. We go to bed at whatever time the show we are binge-watching is finally at a good stopping point or when the game finally ends. We get out of bed, begrudgingly, to an alarm clock, only if we must. Otherwise, we will get up whenever we feel like it. And on and on. After all, isn't that the point of not having someone "boss" us around and being a "grown-up"? No bedtimes, eat my dessert first if I want to, etc. Our children then learn, imitate, and adopt these practices based on what behavior we parents are modeling for them.

Dominating your body, i.e., self-discipline in sleep, nutrition, and fitness is the baseline entry point for becoming an effective and mentally tough boss of you. And by extension, a resilient parent. Without consistently modeling healthy behavior, it becomes extremely difficult to instill healthy habits in your kids. If you struggle with keeping up with your sleep, nutrition, and finding time for fitness, why do you believe your children won't learn, imitate, and adopt the same struggle?

Since my elementary school days in the 1970s, childhood obesity has tripled to one in every five school-aged kids being classified as obese. Yikes! And the baggage, both short-term and long-term, that comes with being an obese kid is enormous. Overcoming the physical effects are one thing, but overcoming the emotional and social effects are even more difficult. Obese children are targets of bullies, teased, and are more likely to suffer from social isolation, depression, and lower self-esteem. (I don't need to read an academic journal to know this; I lived it.) Research shows that when obese kids enter adulthood, they are at high risk for serious conditions and diseases such as heart disease, type-2 diabetes, metabolic syndrome, and several types of cancer.

I'm not suggesting that we as parents can completely eradicate childhood obesity. We can't outperform our potential. But we as Resilient Minded parents can minimize the risks and model behaviors that endeavor to reach our potential because we know that kids with two obese parents are ten to twelve times more likely to be obese. And children of heavier parents have much lower levels of physical activity and make unhealthy food choices.

The Mind Running the Board Room

We all know instinctively, without anyone having to tell us, when we are making poor food choices. We all know, instinctively, that lying on the couch and avoiding physical activity is not the best choice. Dominating your body is the first step in having the mind run the boardroom and becoming an effective and resilient parent. If the statistics noted above hold true, then making and modeling well-reasoned decisions and life choices will increase your child's chances of success by ten to twelve times. A pretty good head-start.

Step two in having the mind run the boardroom is separating logic from emotion. Emotion is our driver. It is our engine. It is WHY we do the things we do. It is WHY we will do the hard thing. Logic is our steering wheel. We steer with logic, making sound decisions based on facts and evidence so that we can make an actual plan. For the elite soldier, emotional decisions get you or your team wounded, killed, or both. For the business executive, emotional decisions will bring sinus-clearing losses. For the athlete, emotional decisions bring on the humiliation of choking. For the parent, emotional decisions create emotional learning, and not the good kind. Each time we make another emotional decision, we continue to imprint and instill on our children a series of memories, programming, and habits that hurt them instead of helping them.

At first blush, you may think that I am proposing that emotion in parenting is negative and that we should attempt to extinguish our emotions, becoming a robot or android. Not at all. Emotion is equally as important a board member as the mind (logic) and the body. We become Resilient Parents by maximizing each board member's power and keeping each board member in its respective role.

Logic vs. Emotion

Think of it like being an Intercontinental Ballistic Missile (ICBM). Your body is the missile itself and encases the inner workings. Your emotions are the rocket fuel and engine that make the missile fly. And your mind (logic) is the guidance system, aiming and controlling the flight, making the necessary course corrections, and successfully hitting the target. It takes all three components working together to have an effective launch, flight, and hitting of the target. This is resilience. All three components are performing their individual roles, contributing to the success of the mission.

What would happen if the rocket fuel and engine (emotions) took over the job of the guidance system? The missile would blast off and go where? Hurtling through the atmosphere, spinning, and gyrating wildly out of control, the trail of exhaust smoke leaving haphazard spiraling lines in the sky, a testimony to the world of emotion controlling the entire operation. The missile would eventually land somewhere. Without a programmed target into a properly working guidance system (the mind), the missile would most likely hit outside the desired target. If you did happen, by random chance, to hit your desired target, assuming you had clearly defined one, there would be no way to duplicate hitting another again in the future.

Most humans live their lives this way. Emotions are taking over the guidance system as well as being the propulsion system. Flying erratically and unintentionally hitting random targets. Often hurting those closest to the fallout of our emotionally-driven decisions and actions. Other humans, a smaller percentage, live their lives with logic taking over the propulsion system as well as being the guidance system. This analytical imbalance leads to a missile that never gets off the launch pad and goes nowhere, also hurting those closest to the fallout of taking no action at all, only analyzing, re-analyzing, and more analyzing. I've heard it called paralysis by analysis. The key is to separate logic from emotion and deploy both in the roles they are designed to function. Emotion is the driver, why we do the hard thing. Logic is the steering wheel, making reasoned course corrections and adjustments.

Burning House

Imagine that you are coming home from work one day. And it's been one of those days, the kind where you are numb by quitting time. You are driving home, completely on auto-pilot, just trying to decompress. You don't remember getting off the highway on your exit. Passing by the corner gas station didn't even register. You couldn't testify as to whether you stopped at the red light about a mile from your house or not, when you halfway notice some black smoke in the sky.

"Huh. Someone must be burning leaves or something," you mutter.

As you approach the entrance to your neighborhood, you think: *That smoke looks like it's near my street.*

As you approach your street, the billowing column of smoke moves to the forefront of your conscious thoughts: *That smoke looks like it's coming from near my house.*

You turn onto your street, and see your house engulfed in flames. Fire trucks and firefighters everywhere. Neighbors are gawking. As you try to process the scene, it hits you! Your two kids, eight and ten, were home alone! You slam the car to a halt, jump out, and search the crowd for your kids.

You're screaming at the neighbors, "Have you seen the kids? Have you seen my kids!" They are nowhere to be found.

You run towards the fire, full of purpose, shouting, "Someone has to save the kids!"

The fire chief physically stops you and says, "Listen, I've been fighting fires for over 25 years. There's a one in a million chance your kids could have survived. I can't let you go in there. It's too dangerous. I won't even let my people go in. This is now a recovery operation. Please go sit over there until the fire burns itself out, and we'll recover what's left of your babies' bodies."

Decision Time

Do you take the one in a million chance, or do you sit on the curb?

I've been looking for the person that will sit on the curb and haven't found one yet. Almost - I had a guy in New Jersey tell me he wasn't going into the burning house because he didn't have any kids. I asked him, "What if it was your mom?" He immediately said he was going in. (Lucky for New Jersey! I would've told everyone about him. Oops, just did.) If you have kids, you are going into the fire. No question. So, what's the plan?

Run into the flames shouting, "Save the babies!"

That's not a plan. Everyone will die.

First Responder vs. Emotional Reactor

What do we call police, firefighters, and EMS personnel? First reactors or first responders? First responders. What if the firefighters

40

showed up to the scene, saw the flames and smoke coming from your house, and screamed, "OH MY GOODNESS, THAT HOUSE IS ON FIRE!! AAAAAAAHHHHHHKKKKKK!!!!"

Most of us have lived our entire lives as first reactors and continue to be first reactors instead of first responders. Running wildly into the burning house and shouting, "Save the babies!" without a plan is the hallmark of being an emotional reactor.

Have you ever made a 9-1-1 call or seen one on TV? Does the 9-1-1 operator scream, "OH MY GOSH!"? Instead, very calmly, under control, they say, "9-1-1. What's your emergency?"

Then they ask questions, gathering facts and information. Once gathered, they then send that information on to the first responders, who have an actual plan of RESPONSE, not a REACTION.

The question now becomes, "How can we be first responders instead of first reactors?"

Half Your Brain

Remember that we've discovered through cognitive neuroscience, utilizing fMRI brain mapping and imaging, that when a person is in fear or anxiety, half of the brain shuts down? The creative problem-solving half of your brain goes completely dark. Half your brain has no electro-chemical pathways lighting up, no neural net traffic, and no genius creative problem-solving ideas or thoughts generated. All you are left with is fight, flight, or freeze. The part of your brain that you need in order to solve whatever problem you are facing is SHUT DOWN. Yikes!

Before we go any further, I must ask you if you could suspend your disbelief. Let me ask it another way. Have you ever watched a movie that you liked? Congratulations, you have suspended your disbelief. You know movies aren't real; even the ones "based on a true story" are Hollywood-ed up. To enjoy a movie, you override your inner voice telling you that what you see in the film is impossible. I'm not as good as a high-budget blockbuster; so I'll only ask for you to suspend your disbelief for two minutes. I call it the **2-Minute Rule.** Every time you hear your inner voice say things like: *That's impossible. That won't work. That's not right. There's no way. That's crazy talk*, you give yourself two minutes of space. During those two minutes, say this instead: *I know that's impossible, but if it were possible, how would I do it?*

This is how you move from emotional reactors to first responders and give yourself time to separate emotion from logic, giving your mind time to take over the boardroom. Simply asking: *How would I do it?* engages the guidance system of the missile.

Emotion, love for the kids, is the engine and rocket fuel that drives you into the burning house, overriding all fear. But when the fire chief gave his one in a million odds, the resilient parent doesn't argue with the chief, doesn't deny that facts, but says, "Ok, Chief. I get it. A one in a million chance. If I could maximize that chance, how would I do it?"

42

The Result Is not a Plan

The human brain must answer a question. Remember, it is the original search engine. Ask and you shall receive. Ask a bad question, get a bad answer. Ask a good question, get a good answer. Ask: *How would I do it?* and the brain will get you an answer. Now is the time to channel the 9-1-1 operator if there ever was one. Slow your reaction, give yourself some cognitive space, ask good questions, and form a plan. This subtle but huge distinction separates an average parent from a resilient parent. The resilient parent understands that the desired result, "Save the babies," is not a plan. A plan is how to save the babies. It is the step-by-step process, the actions that must be taken to obtain the desired result. Without a plan, the emotions are running the boardroom and hijacking the guidance system.

Does the fire chief know your kids as well as you do? Where would they most likely be? Have you ever had a conversation with them about where to go if there was a fire? In my basement is a giant twelve feet by twelve feet movie screen and high definition projector. Attached to the projector are a surround sound speaker system and video game console. If I wasn't home, no matter what time of day it was, my kids would be in the basement playing video games. Also, in case of an emergency, our family's rally point is under the basement steps.

I'm also going to grab some equipment from the firefighters. I had a firefighter in a conference tell me he would never give his equipment to a parent trying to save his or her children. Silly rabbit! Have you ever seen anyone get between a Mama Bear and her cubs? Of course, she is going to get the equipment! Finally, I'm going jump into one of the fire trucks and drive it into the house right to the spot over the basement steps.

Someone asked me, "You'll drive a truck into your house?"

Yes. The house is on fire, everything is burning. The truck isn't going to damage the carpet and furniture any worse than it already is. I'm going to drive big red right on in, open the doors, grab the kids, and drive out of the flames. Will it work? I don't know, but I do know that a logical, well-reasoned plan is the best way to maximize my one chance in a million. This is what a resilient parent does, separates logic from emotion. Use emotion as the rocket fuel that gets you moving past all fears and deploying logic as the guidance system, with the mind running the boardroom.

Monkey See, Monkey Do

It is essential to be mindful that your child is watching what you do, how you respond or react and do what you do. Humans learn primarily by imitation. With what behavior are you modeling, teaching, and programming your child? Are you modeling the first responder or the emotional reactor to them? Are you raising responders, with the mind running the boardroom, separating emotions, and allowing their bodies to vote with the mind? How proficient are you at controlling your emotional reactions? How about when someone cuts you off in traffic? Steals your

44

parking spot at the store during a rainstorm? When your little darling spills a full glass of milk?

Events happen. Your response or reaction dictates what happens next, the outcome. You cannot control anything external to you. You cannot control the weather, the traffic, the economy, society, or what other people think, say, or do. You can only control how you respond or react. Resilient parents don't try to control anything external, including their children. They focus on controlling the only thing they can control: their response.

What is it called when you keep responding the same way to the same external factors and expect to get a different result? Insanity. When I first accepted my job as a federal officer at the U.S. Capitol Police, my family and I moved to Bowie, Maryland. We lived fifteen miles, door-to-door, from the Capitol, the seat of democracy and the beacon of the free world. No matter what time of day I left the house for work, the commute would take at least forty-five minutes. Being by default a type-A person, I would just about have a stroke every commute. My blood pressure was through the roof. Every day, I was in a bad mood when I got to work, and every night, I was in a bad mood when I got home, grouching at everyone that came into my space until the traffic tension finally subsided.

I was setting the tone, atmosphere, and environment in my space. I could get away with it at work. After all, the average person is in a bad mood because of traffic. However, at home, it was a glaring issue. I was truly happy to see my kids when I got home. Why was I allowing the ancient phenomenon of traffic rob me of the joy of walking in the door after work? The truth is, traffic wasn't the problem. The problem was my emotional reaction to the traffic. In the words of Captain Jack Sparrow, "The problem isn't the problem; the problem is your attitude towards the problem."

If I had kept reacting in the same manner, I would have stroked out, had a heart attack, alienated my kids, and ended up in divorce court or, worse, stuck in a miserable marriage. Stupid traffic! Wrong. Stupid Andrew! (The definition of stupid is knowing the right thing to do but continuing NOT to do it.) If I wanted a different result, I had to control what I could control and change my emotional reaction into a well-reasoned response. I had to get my body to vote with my mind and get emotion out of the pilot's chair.

For my commute, I bought a bunch of cassette tapes (it was the 1990s; now I Bluetooth media files from my phone) of college lectures on leadership talks, communication skills, psychology, history, economics, and attitude. I would pop in a lecture, and before I knew it, I was at work or back at the house. My commute became a time of growth, learning, and development and quickly became the favorite part of my day. I would get to work *too* quickly, before a lecture ended. I would sit in the parking lot to finish before going inside. One day I realized that I always seemed refreshed, energized, and bursting with positive energy when I walked in the door. Now that's what I want my kids to learn and implement.

Putting it Together in the Real World

My entire family went to the elementary school carnival, the yearly PTA fundraiser. We ran across Christopher, a 5th grader with a fantastic mind for science. He and his parents were like a lot of families, doing well enough financially to miss qualifying for any government assistance but not well enough to afford anything extra. The kind of situation where the price of a gallon of gas mattered.

During our conversation, we learned that Christopher had been invited to a STEM (science, technology, engineering, mathematics) summer program at Wake Forest University. His parents were so proud of him but a little sad as well.

"We can't swing the cost of the camp. He just can't go. We just can't do it," his dad told me. Christopher was working very hard to look stoic. He understood, but that didn't make it sting any less.

"I completely understand, Tom," I said, "That's a really tough one. But if it were possible that Christopher could go, how could we raise the money?"

An almost uncomfortable silence ensued. The subtle insertion of the 2-Minute Rule was beginning to work its magic. The brains of Christopher's family were searching for the answer to a better question. Within seconds, Christopher's mom offered, "Christopher, Aunt Jacquie has been asking you to help her clean out her garage and has offered to pay you."

"Yeah! And I could ask Mr. and Mrs. Sheets about raking up the leaves in their yard," Christopher excitedly squealed.

"Well, I have been thinking about selling my big speaker system," Christopher's dad chimed in.

As parents, we don't need an emergency to feel overwhelmed and stressed. Something as delightful as our child being invited to a STEM camp can cause a pressure-filled crisis. Whenever you find yourself in the position of acting as an emotional reactor, slow everything down by channeling the 9-1-1 operator and deploying the 2-Minute Rule. This strategy will give you the cognitive space to be the CEO of You, Inc., letting the Mind assert itself over the Emotions in your boardroom and putting yourself in the position of acting as a first responder.

WHAT TO DO:

1) Become the CEO of You, Inc., and get your board of directors to act in concert for your betterment instead of your detriment. Your board of directors is your Body, Mind, and Emotions. The Mind should be running the boardroom.

2) Dominate your body. Exercise self-discipline in sleep, nutrition, and fitness as the baseline entry point for managing stress and becoming a candidate of an effective and resilient parent.

3) Separate Emotion from Logic. Emotion is the engine and rocket fuel, the driver. Logic is the guidance system and steering wheel. Never confuse the two.

4) Channel the 9-1-1 operator and become a first responder versus an emotional reactor by controlling the only thing you can control: your response to external factors or events. Slow your thinking down and be as calm as an emergency dispatcher.

5) Suspend your disbelief and deploy the 2-Minute Rule. When you hear the voice of resistance that says: *It's impossible; we can't; I don't know how*, say, *I know we can't, but if we could, how would we do it?*

CHAPTER 3 – Thinking: A Physical Skill

Respect the Game

Kaleb, a happy-go-lucky seven-year-old, is like most kids of his generation, he knows his way around a smartphone and video gaming console. Where he is different, is how well he knows his way around a basketball court. His dad is a high-school basketball coach and middle school baseball coach. Kaleb loves basketball as much as video games. He lives several houses down from our family home, and on any given day, at any given time, I see Kaleb shooting hoops in his driveway, working on ball skills and footwork. He's three feet and five inches tall and can crush me (six feet and five inches tall) in a game of H-O-R-S-E at any time, in any weather. Over and over, he practices the physical skills of basketball. His older sister, Kylie, does the same with her sport of softball.

When I asked Kaleb and Kylie's parents about how their kids came to be consistent practitioners of the fundamental skills of their chosen sports, their father, Keith, said, "We teach them to respect the game. If you don't stay sharp on those skills, the game can take you out on any given day." He went to explain how his baseball team had lost a game to a team they should have easily beaten, but sloppy execution of the fundamental skills had sabotaged their success.

Caitlyn, an eleven-year-old who is not athletic, practices the piano in the same manner. She daily trains, over and over, the physical skills of hand position, rhythm, and scales until her hands deftly fly over the ebony and ivory keys, producing melodies and harmonies. She respects the music the way Kaleb and Kiley respect the game.

Both of my sons, Drew and Jack, wrestled in high school, and my daughter, Michaela, plays lacrosse for her high school program. They each came home from practice with study sheets and video links of moves, counter-moves, techniques, and step-by-step processes for every part of their respective sports. Their results on the field of play or the mat were directly related to how skillful and well-practiced they were in what to do, how to do it and when to do it, executing sport-specific, physical skills in real time. To be an effective parent with the mind running the boardroom, it is essential to respect the game of parenting and to practice the process of thinking and making decisions continually, just as athletes practice their physical skills on the field and musicians practice their physical skills on the stage. I encourage you to look at thinking in the same manner as you view any performance activity (sports, music, dance, etc.)

Once I began to see thinking as a physical skill, I could finally hone my thinking skills. To get good, you must work on conditioning, techniques, skills, and execution, and you must train daily. Successful athletes and musicians put in massive amounts of time and effort over the course of years in preparation for game days and performances. Interesting thing about any new skill - humans are awful at it at first. Humans again learn mainly by imitation, and we need a model, a coach, a teacher, and a mentor to assimilate any new skill. As a parent, your child will imitate your thought process.

When my kids started their sports, they had coaches and more mature athletes to model, coach, teach, and mentor them. They knew nothing. Their bodies could not perform the movements. They quickly grew frustrated. They stayed with the discipline long enough to gain at least minimal ability to perform. They continued to learn and practice and began to enjoy small successes and leveraged those into larger, more fulfilling successes. The younger they started their sport, the easier the process seemed.

I say all this to make you aware that building the skill of thinking, for you the parent, may seem frustrating and difficult at first, but stick with it. It will be as herky-jerky as when you first learned to drive a car as a teenager. Or how you felt during those foreign language classes in high school.

In paving the way to success, it's important to understand the hierarchy of thinking of the human machine, broken down for simplicity into four levels. The four levels of thinking are auto-pilot, negative, positive, and critical thinking.

Autopilot Thinking

Most of our day is spent on autopilot, with our conscious minds disengaged from the tasks at hand. Which sock and shoe do you put on first, left or right? How many life-and-death decisions do you make during your commute to work without realizing it? Remember, we take in eleven million bits of information per second, but only one hundred twenty-six bits go to our conscious minds for action. So an enormous portion, ninety-five to ninety-nine percent of all cognitive activity, happens outside of our consciousness. Autopilot thinking is neither good nor bad; it just is. Welcome to being human. The point is to understand how the machine works and to use it to our advantage.

Have you ever been to Times Square? I was there on a recent trip to the city and noticed autopilot thinking taking place on a large scale. As the crowds approached an intersection and crosswalk, I noticed that everyone stopped, not according to the traffic light, as most folks were looking at their phones, but because the person in front of them stopped. The entire crowd proceeded to cross the street whenever one person at the front stepped into the street. Everyone, without conscious thought or risk assessment, followed like a herd of cattle, regardless of oncoming traffic or what the walk/don't walk signals were displaying. What I saw is a classic example of autopilot thinking in action.

While operating at this level of thinking, the Body is running the boardroom. Your body is driving the car, without conscious thought. Brushing your teeth without conscious engagement is a common example. Humans are creatures of habit. Our habits are literally our brains on autopilot, which is why programming ourselves and our children with habits that help instead of hurt is so vital.

Negative Thinking

The next level up is negative thinking. The negative thinker, while standing in the crowd of people in Times Square waiting to cross the street, refuses to cross the street. The negative thinker says, "A million people can cross the street without getting hit, but if I even step off the curb, I'll be the one in a million that gets hit." While operating as a negative thinker, Emotion is running the boardroom and all the baggage that comes with it. While negative thinking is not optimal, it will ensure your survival. But surviving isn't the same thing as living, and it's certainly not thriving.

Negative thinkers are plagued with thoughts that are detrimental to their mindset, opinions, and beliefs, leading to constant worry and anxiety, all producing a myriad of emotional and physical ailments. According to the National Science Foundation, our brains produce as many as 50,000 thoughts per day. A full ninety-five percent of these thoughts are repeated daily, and they reflect our mindset, opinions and beliefs. Remember, the filter of the eleven million bits per second to the one hundred twenty-six bits of information per second to the conscious mind is our mindset: what we think, our opinions, beliefs, and attitudes. Negative thinkers are in survival mode and are limiting their potential. Think of all the potential opportunities across the street in Times Square that will never be realized due to the paralyzing worry of being the one in a million that gets struck by a car attempting to cross.

Behavioral psychology research has shown that as high as seventy-seven percent of everything we think is negative, counterproductive, or working against ourselves. At the same time, medical research shows that as much as seventy-five percent of all illnesses are self-induced, and eighty percent of all ailments are stress-related.

A 2007 study out of the University of Arizona found that, on average, women speak 16,215 words per day, and men speak 15,669 words per day. Humans, regardless of gender, tend to speak 16,000 on average daily, and think 50,000 thoughts in the same period. The evidence of your thoughts is found in your words. If you aren't sure whether or not you are acting as a negative thinker, listen to your own words. Are you saying things like: "I can't; that won't work; I'm just not good at that; I'm always late; I can never get organized; I'm awful at remembering names; I'm tired; I'm stressed; nothing ever seems to go right; I'm just not creative; I'm so out of shape; we'll never be able to afford that; I never catch a break; I always get sick this time of year; etc."?

The more you repeat these things, the more they become a reality in your life and in the lives of your children. Remember, neuroscience demonstrates that your thoughts, opinions, beliefs, and attitudes become medical, electrochemical, and biopsychological self-fulfilling prophecies.

Positive Thinking

55

Conventional wisdom tells us to think positively. I'm personally not a fan of positive thinking. Positive thinking will get you killed quicker than negative thinking. The positive thinker, in Times Square says, "I can lay down in the street, and the drivers of oncoming traffic will stop or swerve. Nothing bad will happen to me." Yikes! Danger is a fact. It's real, and no matter how positive a spin one puts on it, danger can and will, if ignored, kill you. At no time, during any of my eleven deployments into high-threat environments, did I ever walk up to the bad guys and ask if we could hug and make it all better. Positive thinkers quickly fall into the trap of deluding themselves, and suddenly emotion has hijacked the boardroom. Then any semblance of a well-reasoned, evidence-based, logical decision goes out the window. That is not for you. And not for your child.

If it sounds as if I'm advocating for negative thinking, reread all the awful results that come from negative thinking. Both positive thinking and negative thinking are areas where emotion is running the boardroom, and the best option is for the mind to be running the boardroom. Resilient Minded people, both parents and children, are not positive or negative thinkers. They are critical thinkers.

Critical Thinking

When you see or hear the term "critical thinking," it doesn't mean that we are judging others, being harsh, unforgiving, cold-hearted, or unkind. Critical thinking is a deliberate way of thinking our thoughts. It's the use of reflective reasoning about our opinions, beliefs, attitudes, and actions. It comes from Socrates and is based on his methodical process of thinking, known as the Socratic Method.

The critical thinker gathers as much information and evidence as possible, then evaluates the known facts and makes decisions based on those evaluations. The critical thinker takes risks based on specific rewards. Not on winning-the-lottery-type rewards (positive thinking). And not the worst possible outcome, no matter how improbable (negative thinking). In Times Square, the critical thinker takes notice of the walk/don't walk signals, the oncoming traffic, and cross-traffic vehicles that may be turning into the crosswalk, and that thinker crosses the street for a specific reason, not just because the crowd is crossing. Critical thinkers know their destination and the purpose why they are going there. Destination and purpose are the hallmarks of the resilient-minded.

There are enormous amounts of chatter about "critical thinking" out there, mostly in the fields of science, academia, and law. However, most who ascribe to critical thinking cannot lay out a specific step-by-step, articulable, and duplicable process. Those academic papers and texts that do lay out the critical thinking elements are unwieldy, making it impractical to use them in real life and in real time. So, I created my own process that takes the most important and usable concepts of the Socratic Method and turns it into a step-by-step, decision-making formula.

Thinking Like C.R.A.P.

There are four simple steps to being resilient-minded, mentally tough, and effective as a parent and as a human being. These articulable and duplicable steps are the culmination of centuries of empirical evidence, combined with the latest scientific research and over three decades of personally battle-tested perfected practice. I call it thinking like C.R.A.P. That way you can't forget it. If you think all your thoughts like C.R.A.P., your life will be exponentially transformed.

C.R.A.P. stands for clarity, relevance, accuracy, and precision. I took the most useful elements of critical thinking and ordered them for maximum impact. If you run every thought through the filter of each of these elements, in order, you will capture the biggest bang for your critical thinking buck! Thinking like C.R.A.P. is how thinking is transformed into a physical skill that you can practice.

The Golf Swing of Thinking

My day job is mental toughness coaching, and I coach a lot of golfers. Golfers attempt to put a little ball into a very small space, far, far away. I also train snipers, and similar to the golfer, the sniper is attempting to put a tiny projectile into a very small space, far, far away.

Both marksmanship and golf have a physical process to every shot. For the marksman, it's grip, stance, body position, breath, and trigger control. For the golfer, it's grip, stance, body position, and the mechanics of the swing. When a golfer first starts out in the sport, learning to swing the club for the first time, everything is conscious and herky-jerky. The novice is trying to push the new skill through his or her one hundred twenty-six bits per second filter. That's a very small funnel and slow. The skill still takes conscious effort. Soon, with training and commitment, the skill becomes a talent and moves into the non-conscious (which covers the unconscious, the subconscious, and anything else that is outside of conscious thought) – the rest of the eleven million bits per second.

It's like driving a car. When a person first starts learning to drive a car, everything is herky-jerky, conscious, and over-deliberate. Soon enough, too soon if you have teenagers, the driver begins to make hundreds of life-and-death decisions behind the wheel without conscious thought.

Thinking like C.R.A.P. will also be herky-jerky and cumbersome at first. But stick with it by making a commitment to practice, and soon you will be thinking every thought automatically through this process. You will begin to be a critical thinker via auto-pilot. This is the target: to be a critical thinker by habit without conscious thought. Every thought, when making all decisions, filtered through Clarity – Relevance – Accuracy – Precision.

Clarity – What's the Target?

Imagine walking up to Tiger Woods and asking, "What's the target?"

Now imagine that he replies, "See that sand trap over there?"

"Yes," you say.

"That's not it."

"Right, but what's the target?"

"Do you see that pond over there?"

"Yes."

"That's not it either. Those trees aren't the target, and neither is parking lot or the clubhouse."

This seems ridiculous, but this is seemingly how most people approach life. They are great at identifying what they don't want but have a difficult time identifying what it is they do want. The Resilient Minded, critical thinking parent relentlessly employs clarity, clearly defining the desired target, not performing what I call target elimination.

We came by our confusion honestly. Our parents raised us that way.

"Look both ways when you cross the street."

"Why?"

"So you don't get hit."

Is that the target? No, the target is to arrive on the other side of the street safely. The way the brain works is this: if you say "don't," the brain chops off the "don't," and whatever is left becomes the new target. I have found that more times than not, we tend to phrase things negatively. For example, when my daughter, Michaela, was younger and she would help set the table for dinner, my wife, Kimmi, would make the deliberate effort of phrasing instructions positively. When Michaela was carrying a glass of milk to the table, instead of Kimmi cautioning her with, "Don't spill that," she would say, "Remember to look to where you are going, and you won't spill a drop."

On the surface, this doesn't seem like a big deal. However, negative phrasing has a nasty way of changing the focus and of assaulting our inner dialogue and self-talk. The way we speak to ourselves, the language and phrasing we use when we think our thoughts, has an enormous impact on our focus, attitudes, behaviors, and actions, and on the choices we make.

Don't think about a clown. What did you just think about? A clown!

It seems like a subtle and simple shift, but the results are profound. Stop yourself whenever you catch a "don't" coming out of your mouth. "Don't hit it into the sand trap. Don't spill your milk, Johnny. Don't hit your sister. Don't be mean. Don't be selfish. Don't put your feet on the furniture." These negative warnings all become the new target. Instead, we must clearly define what it is that we DO want. What our target is, not what the target is NOT. Ask yourself: *What is the outcome that I really want? What am I trying to accomplish? What do I want to happen? What is my target?* Get crystal clear on your target first and foremost. Without clarity, the entire critical thinking process is over before it starts, and the mind has no chance of running the boardroom.

Relevance – Is This a Sand Trap? Is This Helping or Hurting Me Hit the Target?

Once clarity is gained and the desired target, outcome, or result is clearly defined, the resilient-minded thinker turns to the filter of relevance. The human brain must answer a question. Ask a bad question, and you get a bad answer. Ask a good question, and get a good answer. Once the answer to "What's my target?" is ascertained, "Is this relevant?" is the very next question to ask.

For the golfer, is the sand trap, the water obstacle, or the trees relevant? What's the target? The hole. The sand trap is not relevant to the target. Don't hit it in the sand trap. Where's the ball going? Don't hit it in the water. Where's the ball going? Gah-Bluuuuush!

Let's take it to the kitchen table. Have you ever called a family meeting to talk about getting the chores done that got off target and ended up in the sand trap of complaining about all manner of offenses (from who's hogging the bathroom, to who's eating all the good breakfast cereal), for two hours? Hours of your life you can never get back?

Without a clearly defined target, knowing exactly what we **do** want, we have a difficult time identifying the sand traps, those things that are not relevant. Things that do not help me hit my target. Things that hurt me and delay me from hitting my target. Things that take me off course, veering into detours or worse.

Don't rat me out, but I have people in my life that I have nicknamed "Sand Trap". They are not relevant to getting me to my target. In fact, they hurt me and get me off course, causing detour, delay, and even derailment. They bring their drama and emotionally-charged thinking into my boardroom, and next thing I know, I'm furiously whacking away with a sand wedge, trying to get out of the bunker. Most often, it takes enormous amounts of mental, emotional and physical energy to get back onto the course. Effort, energy, and resources that should have been helping me instead of hurting me. Here is the secret to graceful and unforced management, coaching, and mentoring, i.e. good parenting. Ask, early and often, "Is this helping or hurting?"

A few years back, my speaking schedule was brutal; I spoke to over 200 audiences that year. I would leave Sunday afternoon for the week and return home on the last flight Friday night. I did this month after month, for almost the entire year. One week, I didn't make it home until Saturday evening due to flight delays. I walked in the front door and got my hugs and kisses from my wife and daughter. "Where are the boys?" I asked. It was weird they weren't in the middle of the welcome home party. The custom in our house is that when one of us walks in the door from school, work, or wherever, we all stop what we are doing, jump up, run to the door, and give a mini-welcome home party, lavishly plying the returning family member with hugs, kisses, I-Love-Yous, and So-Glad-You're-Homes.

"Your boys," (whenever they are "your boys," I know they are messing up) "are in the basement with their friends and have been playing video games for over nine hours. Can you do something about it?" my wife replied.

I went downstairs, where the twelve feet by twelve feet screen, high-definition projector, and gaming console are, to find a half a dozen teenage boys engrossed in simulated combat. Sigh.

"Hey guys! I'm home."

"Daddy!" they screamed, and then they jumped up and plied me with my second welcome home party. Hard to be mad at them when they're heaping tons of love on you.

"Mommy said you guys have been playing for nine hours. Is that about right?"

"Yes, sir."

"I don't care who is over here; you guys can't play video games for nine hours straight. Now, tell me what I just said so I know you understand."

My youngest son, Jack, piped up and put us in a sand trap, "You said you don't care who we have over to play video games."

Sigh. I did say that. I wasn't clear in my communication, clearly defining the target. Who they had over to the house wasn't relevant to the target of limiting the time of video game play. Also, not playing for nine hours wasn't a clearly defined target. What if they played for eight hours and forty-five minutes? See how fast we parents can get into sand traps of our own making?

I performed an after-action review of this scenario and made the course correction. Enter the secret (and magic) of graceful and unforced parenting, asking early and often, "Is this helping or hurting?" All my kids have ultimate targets, which I detail later on, but suffice it to say they have plans for what they want to do when they grow-up. Each of them desiring college degrees from excellent colleges. Armed with that knowledge and the secret magical question, all future scenarios of too much screen time went like this:

"Whatcha doing?"

"Playing video games."

"How many hours have you been playing, do you think?"

"I don't know."

"Are you still planning on going to college and get your degree?"

"Yes, sir."

"Do you think hours on end of gaming is helping you hit your target or hurting you?"

"Sigh," head drops, shoulders slump, and then mumbling.

"I'm sorry, I didn't hear you. What was that?"

"Hurting. I'm turning it off."

We don't want to inflame situations and put others on the defensive emotionally. It's most likely not the best approach to shout out, "THAT'S NOT RELEVANT". I have found it to be a benefit all around to ask a series of questions (starting with myself):

How does that statement or action help us with the issue at hand?

How is this idea connected to achieving the desired result?

How does that issue bear on the discussion?

How does this train of thought relate to what I'm trying to accomplish?

How does your question or statement pertain to what we are dealing with?

Usually irrelevant ideas (sand traps) come into the conversation from having either no clearly defined target, a misunderstanding the issues, a misdirection from owning bad behavior (*Johnny's parents let him do it, and he doesn't get in trouble*), or from someone who simply allows their emotions to run rampant in the boardroom (i.e. not thinking like C.R.A.P.).

Accuracy – Is This a Fact or a Truth?

Once we have clearly defined our target (Clarity), and have identified the sand traps (Relevance), we must drill down further to Accuracy. Be accurate in your assessment of the situation. Here's the question to ask yourself: "Is this a truth, or is it a fact?" The trick to being accurate in our thinking and our communication lies in separating facts from truth.

Facts and Truth are two completely different entities. A fact is merely information, neutral, independent, and objective. As a police officer investigating a crime, I was always in search of the facts. If and when a case went to court, facts were entered into evidence, but the witnesses would swear to tell the truth. The "truth" is our internal perception of the facts and circumstances that make up the experiences of life. We know, for a fact, that eyewitnesses are unreliable at best.

For example, it's a fact that it's 68 degrees outside. The truth is, that after three years of living in Hawaii, 68 degrees feels downright cold. However, it is also a truth, after spending a winter in Serbia and Kosovo, that 68 degrees is heat-stroke territory.

Facts cannot change; they are unalterable. Truth, on the other hand, is pliable. Knowing this, we can take the facts of any circumstance and perceive them from any angle we want, creating for ourselves a truth or truths. Truths make up the foundation of beliefs; we take action on our truths. Almost everyone knows the medical fact that fast food isn't good for you, but for most of us, the truth is that "it tastes good." The fact is that the fast food industry does billions of dollars in sales each and every year. And it's a fact that 1 out of 10 deaths is related to obesity.

As Naomi stood toe-to-toe with her parents and shouted, "You're not the boss of me!" her parents responded with, "Stop disrespecting us! We are your parents and will not tolerate your disrespect!"

Is disrespect a fact or a truth? It is a truth; like beauty, it is in the eye of the beholder. As critical-thinking parents, we must accomplish two things: 1) move truths into the fact column, and 2) own our truths. When we do this, we put the Mind in control of the boardroom, instead of the emotions. Notice the difference in the stress levels when Naomi's parents become First Responders, using logic versus the default mode of Emotional Reactors.

"You're not the boss of me!"

"Naomi, when you shout at us with your hands on your hips, while toe-to-toe with us *(moving truth into facts by stating facts of the behavior)*, we feel disrespected *(owning their truth instead misplacing it with an accusation)*. Can we, at least, agree to show each other respect?"

Neuroscience – Turning Facts into Truths

The human machine operates in truths, not facts. There is no exception, no way around it. It is a scientific fact that the brain and emotions are designed and built to operate solely based on truths. The hardware that turns facts into truth is called the Reticular Activating System (RAS), a section of the brain the size of your pinky finger, located near the spinal column.

The RAS controls our attention, awareness, and focus. It filters all information gathered by what see, hear, and touch, and it regulates our wakefulness and sleep transitions. It cannot tell the difference between real events and synthetic events, which is why dreams seem so real at the time, even when we experience events in them that bend the laws of physics.

The RAS filters how you perceive your circumstances and environment. It converts each stimulus, all situations, and every set of facts into a truth. Simply, it interprets facts and tells your conscious mind whether to see the twelve-ounce glass with six ounces of liquid in it as half-empty or half-full. Herein lies the key to turning circumstances, whatever they may be, to your advantage.

Your programming and training (and remember, your child learns primarily by imitation, as they will do what you do) dictate whether you will perceive the lower truth of half-empty -- choosing to focus on what resources you don't have, imagining negative outcomes, and producing worry, anxiety, and stress. Or conversely, whether you will perceive the higher truth of half-full, choose to focus on what resources you do have, and imagine how to use them to your greatest advantage.

We must collect as many unbiased, objective, evidence-based facts as possible to make logical, well-reasoned, clear decisions. We must also perceive the facts in a way that elevates us and puts us on the path to success and fulfillment, even in the face of the bad news. Whenever you do receive bad news, separate out the facts. Recognize, acknowledge, and evaluate those facts. Understand that every set of facts has lower truths and higher truths associated with it. Viewing the glass as half-empty (lower truth) is true. Viewing the glass as half-full (higher truth) is also true. The level of truth you choose depends on which director is running the boardroom: Mind, Body, or Emotions.

Here's a real-world example from the Wright Brothers, the innovators of flight. Behold, the bad news of the law of gravity, a fact that cannot be changed or altered. If you step off a building, you will fall to the ground. Unalterable, and to the person who wants to soar, this seems to be bad news. However, the Wright Brothers, having recognized, acknowledged, and evaluated the fact of the law of gravity, elected to focus on the higher truth that they would fly, ostensibly defying gravity.

Their higher truth drove them to the discovery of a subsequent fact, the law of lift and thrust. Their desired outcome, their target, was: "We will fly," and their chosen and deliberate "half-full" response eventually led to the discovery of these additional facts: typical takeoff airspeeds for jetliners are 150–180 mph, while light aircraft, such as a Cessna 150, take off at around 63 mph. Ultralights have even lower takeoff speeds. And flying is statistically one of the safest ways to travel.

How you deal with "bad news" depends solely on how you perceive and interpret facts, how you choose the level of truth that helps you instead of hurting you.

The next time your child sasses you, before you shout back, stop for a second and ask yourself, "Is sass a fact or a truth?" The hallmark of a truth is that it means different things to different people. What might be sass and disrespect in your home might be a standard operating procedure in someone else's.

As the CEO of Me, Inc., with my mind running the boardroom, I move truths into the fact column. I understand, all the while, that since I enjoy having my own truths (opinions and beliefs) and perceptions of the facts, I should be generous enough to allow others that same enjoyment. Separating fact from truth is a game-changer in controlling your thoughts, feelings, and attitudes and transforming that pesky and destructive emotional reaction into a well-reasoned, kind response.

Again, the human brain must answer a question. The input of bad questions equals bad answers out. The input of good questions equals good answers out. Here are a few examples of good questions in determining accuracy:

What truths are you using as "facts" in your decision making? *(For example: The coach is a total jerk; so my child is not going to keep playing on that team.)*

What truths are you manufacturing that put you on the path of fear, worry, depression, or defeat? *(For example: That teacher has the reputation of being really hard; I hope you pass her class.)*

What new truths can you create by changing your attitude, perception, and level of awareness that will put you and your children on a path to confidence, fulfillment, and happiness? *(For example: I'm with you; the coach does raise his voice sometimes. But he is usually doing it to make you all perform better.)*

Precision – Can This Fact Be More Exact?

The final step in the critical thinking process, once we have clarity (identified the target), relevance (remove the sand traps), and accuracy (moved truth into the fact column), is precision. Precision is processing facts that can be drilled down to be more exact.

Imagine you get the little league email with the upcoming schedule for the season. All the dates of the games and the opponents listed, all facts, with "TBD" listed for locations. Precision is nailing down the locations. Precision is the difference between overdrawing your bank account or not. Like that time I thought there was $1500 in the account and wrote a check for that amount. Then the bank charged me $45.00 overdraft fees. Upon verifying the precise balance, I found the fact of $1500 was more exactly only $1499.97. That three-cent imprecision cost me forty-five dollars.

A common occurrence and an excellent example for parents volunteering at school, is when the PTA fundraising chairperson drops one more thing on your plate and says, "I need this ASAP!" Is "ASAP" a fact or a truth? Is it BIG ASAP or little asap? ASAP might be five minutes for one person and five days for another. Here's how the critical thinker handles this ticking time-bomb of miscommunication.

"Madam Chairperson, when do you need this?"

"I need it by Wednesday, this week."

Truth has now been moved into the Fact column, and now we ask ourselves, "Can this fact be more exact?" Yes, it can. Wednesday is a big block of time.

"What time on Wednesday do you need this?"

"By the close of business." (Is the close-of-business a fact or truth? It is a truth; do you always go home the same time every day? Have you ever had to work late? Does the school close business the same time as the grocery store? Just that fast, we have fallen back into the truth column.)

"What time exactly do you need this?"

"By 5:00 PM Eastern Time."

Now we are cooking! If you think every thought like C.R.A.P. (clarity, relevance, accuracy, and precision), your entire life will transform, and your mind will begin to exert control of your boardroom consistently. Magic will happen when you begin to see and decide that thinking is a physical skill and daily practice the process of how to think your thoughts. Like Kaleb practicing basketball and Kaitlyn practicing piano, thinking like C.R.A.P. must be trained over and over and over and over again, and then trained some more – until it becomes a habit. The target is to train your brain to think every thought like C.R.A.P. automatically, in the same way you automatically drive the car, without conscious effort.

Putting It Together in the Real World

My high school son needs your prayers. He has to make the hardest decision of his life by Tuesday. He had tryouts today for his club soccer team. He played at the highest level last year and wants to play with them again. He also played high school JV basketball this year, too. He is talented at both sports.

The soccer coach told him he had to decide between club soccer and basketball if he wanted to play on the National Premier League team. Unfortunately, they overlap, as soccer goes into January. The basketball coach thinks there is only one sport, basketball. If my son makes varsity this year, he will get limited playing time, if any, due to the quality of rising senior players.

Basketball is my son's favorite sport. But he is probably more talented at soccer. He doesn't like to sit on the bench or lose. Both coaches can be jerks. My son could play both sports if he plays down in soccer but wouldn't have the level of competition he desires. So it's not life or death but not a clear decision for a 16-year-old. Say a prayer for him as he makes his decision.

I found the above post on my social media timeline. Clearly, the parent is stressing out and once again, like Christopher being invited to STEM camp, turning something good, an opportunity, into a stress-filled crisis. Many parents like this one do not have a process by which to make decisions. And therefore, they don't have the tools to lead their children through deciding. Instead, stress levels sky-rocket as we leave the fate and future in the hands of the social media prayer-chain. All the unpleasantness could be eradicated by merely applying the C.R.A.P. process.

Primarily, what's the target? Does he want to play in college? Get recruited and win a scholarship? If so, soccer seems to be the obvious choice. The rest of the post is not relevant; it's a sand trap. Decision made. Problem solved.

If the target is to enjoy playing, the parent needs to move the truth of "basketball is his favorite sport" into the fact column. What makes it his favorite? The teammates and friends? Less running than soccer? More profound enjoyment of the game? And more precisely, if it's enjoyment of the game, which aspects? Offense? Defense? Strategy? Once drilled down, the picture becomes more evident, and by employing the process of C.R.A.P., stress levels decrease because we are now using the guidance system of logic to reach a decision instead of the rocket-fueled engine of emotion.

This parent also added to the stress levels by including such sand trap truths as "both coaches can be jerks" and "the basketball coach thinks there is only one sport, basketball." The final statement is not even a true truth. There is almost no possibility of a basketball coach acknowledging no other sports exist. This truth could be more accurately stated as the basketball coach strongly desires commitment from the players on the team.

WHAT TO DO:

1) Begin to take notice of what level of thinking you are using at any given time when dealing with your child. The Four Levels of Thinking are: Auto-Pilot (*old habits like Naomi's parents, being emotional reactors*), Negative Thinking (*thinking the worst of your*

child, "I know you're hiding something"), Positive Thinking (thinking "Not my child, they would never act that way"), and Critical Thinking (identifying the outcome you want and the sand traps, then moving truths into precise facts).

2) The Critical Thinking Parent sees thinking as a physical skill, the same way a golfer views the mechanics of swinging the club. Practice your thinking skills every day, even if only for thirty minutes a day.

3) Practice the four-step critical thinking process when dealing with your child (thinking like C.R.A.P.)

    a. Clarity – What's the target? What is it we are trying to accomplish?

    b. Relevance – Is this a sand trap? Is this helping or hurting me hit my target?

    c. Accuracy – Is this a fact or a truth? (Move truths into the fact column)

    d. Precision – Can this fact be more exact? (Drill-down as precisely as possible.)

SECRET 2 – INTERNAL IDENTITY

CHAPTER 4 – Being a Parent Isn't Who You Are

On March 27, 2015, Ruth lost her husband of twenty-two years and the father of their three children. When Eric passed away, she also lost her identity as Eric's wife. During the aftermath of Eric's passing, she didn't have the time or the mental and emotional capital to process the loss of her identity and the way her role as mother had just changed to *single-mother*. Included in this paradigm shift was a doubling of the parental duties, as well as becoming the sole breadwinner in the house. Fortunately for Ruth, she had always seen herself as a strong person, someone who didn't hide under the covers, someone who got up and took care of what needed to be done. She intuitively utilized her internal fortitude as her new identity.

Struggling with the loss of a loved one is shocking and painful, but it can be devastating when you lose your identity at the same time. People often try to identify others by the roles they play in life. For example, "That guy is a cop; he's a janitor; she's a doctor," etc. Because we tend to label others in this fashion, we also have the tendency to label ourselves as well. Not only do we take on labels based on our professions, "I'm a medical device sales rep; I'm the regional director for XYZ Bank; I run the production floor for ABC Manufacturing; I'm a digital branding manager," but we also apply and assume external labels like, "I'm a mom; he's a family man; she's Baptist; he's Catholic; he's an Alabama football fan;

she's an Auburn fan; he's an outdoorsman; she's an animal lover," and on and on. The problem with labels is that they describe roles you play, not who you are.

If you happen to be serving in the law enforcement (LE) profession, you already know this: most law enforcement officers (upwards of 80%) die within 3 years of retirement. Shocking to those outside of the LE community, this statistic is just a fact of life to those who do the job. Since the human brain has to answer a question, let's ask this question: Why is that? Is it all the free Pancake-N-Waffle Hut food we've been eating? Well, that certainly didn't help. But no, it is that the badge and the gun form a large part of most cops' identities. And when we retire and no longer have the badge and gun, we lose that identity and purpose and very quickly wither.

I've seen it happen many times over, across various industries, professions, and walks of life. In many families, parents take on the role of mother or father as an identity. That's why I wince a little whenever I hear someone say, "I'm a Mom," knowing that when the kids are adults and out of the house, a difficult transition period is most likely going to occur. To be a resilient and effective parent, you must come to terms with who you truly are and who you want to be. Not externally, not taking on the label others give you, not labeling yourself with your career, hobby, spouse, or parental role, but internally.

Taking on an identity based on external labels and roles is much easier, requiring less mental energy and introspection. It's the path of least resistance. This is why people throughout history have sought to make labels for themselves and others. I remember reading about Michael Jackson during the concert prep the day before he died. He was completely distraught that he couldn't perform the moonwalk and dance at the level he could in his prime. His identity as the King of Pop was based on externals, and when the external began to fade, well, you know the rest. Sadly, he over-medicated himself with the help of a hired physician.

Race, ethnicity, country, clan, job title, professional title, academic title, cleric title, the bumper sticker on the car, the fan gear, the brand names we wear, the religious denomination, the political party, and on and on. These are Band-Aids on bullet holes. They are counterfeit identities, shortcuts to doing the hard work of deciding who you want to be.

Who Are You, and Who Do You Want to Be?

Creating an internal identity and building an identity statement is by far, hands down, the single *most important* thing you can do to as a parent, second only to teaching your children to create an internal identity and then guiding them in building their own identity statements. Taking complete control of your board of directors (Mind, Body and Emotions) requires that you have a clearly defined and stated internal identity, an identity based on inner strengths, sustainable qualities of distinction, and steadfast character.

Start by listing the traits that you want to embody and that you desire to pass on to your children and grandchildren. Consider those long-lasting, durable qualities that evoke admiration and respect. Here are a few to prime the pump of your genius mind: excellence, integrity, honor, dedication, compassion, loyalty, loving kindness, strength, fortitude, mental toughness, resilience, tolerance, creativity, innovation, diplomacy, generosity, gratitude, consistency, self-discipline, open-mindedness, appreciation, courage, smarts, sincerity, fairness, and honesty.

An internal identity leads to being rooted and grounded. It is the anchor that keeps you from being blown off course or even from drowning when the storms come-- and come they will. It is the moral compass that always guides you along the way. Once you make the decision of who you are, all the choices in life are simple and already made for you.

For instance, my internal identity and corresponding identity statement are: "I'm a man of excellence who always keeps his word." Once I made the decision that this statement embodies who I am, the choices in my life become simple and even pre-made. This statement dictates every action I take. It is my foundation. It keeps me rooted and grounded. It is the anchor that preserves me from being blown off course, viciously tossed, or from drowning when circumstances in life turn into a tempest. It highlights the internal strengths and virtues by which I want to define myself. It highlights the inner qualities of steadfast character that I aspire to assimilate and embodies those traits I wish to pass on to my children and grandchildren. My identity statement is the needle on my moral compass that always points to true north, keeping me from losing sleep or anguishing over a moral dilemma.

Because I made the decision to be a man of excellence, I must give my absolute best effort in everything I do. No half-stepping, no minimum output, or doing just enough to get by. Not settling for mediocre performance or effort in any area of my life. I give maximum effort, sustained excellence, in everything I do or put my hand to, including rest and relaxation. When I watch a movie or TV, I give maximum effort to watching that movie or TV show. I don't watch aimlessly or half-heartedly, and I am very deliberate and calculating as to what I watch. I give maximum effort to my nutrition, fitness and sleep. To my work. To my clients and customers. To my family. To myself. I am consistently striving to reach my genetic potential in every area of life. This way of being allows me to fail and still go to sleep at night knowing I did my absolute best. I will certainly continue to work diligently to get better and improve, but if I come up short, it's not a failure. It's a learning and development experience.

Because I made the decision to aspire to keep my word always, no matter what (even if it costs me time, money, or pain), I am very guarded, calculating, and deliberate when giving my word. In simpler terms, every time I'm a faced with the choice of giving my word, my decision gives me permission to say, "NO." If I always keep my word, I also must also be very selective of when and to whom I give it. The choice not to have to give into guilt or pressure has been premade.

During the same year when I spoke to over 200 audiences and was only home for thirty-six to forty-eight hours each weekend, I had a particularly brutal week. My trip entailed a multi-state swing that had me zig-zagging across the country. I was in a different city and state every day of that week, and I had no idea what time zone I was in by Friday. My connection was delayed, something to do with a bird in the engine and no maintenance tech on duty. I missed the last flight home on Friday night by minutes. The plane was still sitting at the gate, but the door was closed. Ugggghhh! I went to the customer service desk and collected my new ticket for a Saturday morning (6:30am) flight and my voucher for a hotel room. I followed some aircrew folks to the hotel shuttle, all the while doing controlled breathing exercises.

After finally making it home and walking in the door, I hugged and kissed my gorgeous wife and kids; put on my sweatpants, hoodie, and bunny slippers; grabbed a mug of espresso; plopped down on the couch; and propped my feet up on the coffee table (what I call "assuming the position") to watch the end of College Game Day and a slate of football games.

DING-DONG!! DING-DONG!! DING-DONG!! Three rings of the doorbell in quick succession. I didn't even blink. I sipped my coffee and kept gazing at the screen. More ding-dongs. More sipping and gazing.

More ding-dongs. More sipping and gazing. One of the kids ran down the steps from the second floor and opened the door. I faintly heard some muffled voices and kept sipping and gazing. I had had a hard week, and the ding was probably one of the neighborhood kids seeing if one of mine could come out and play.

"Dad, Mr. So-and-So is here!" (Name withheld to protect the not necessarily innocent).

Mr. So-and-So has lived in the cul-de-sac longer than any of us. He's an original owner, and a decent, quiet neighbor, but is Eeyore from Winnie the Pooh. Bless his heart, as grandma would say. Sigh.

"Hey bud! How's it going?"

"Well, we're moving," (in Eeyore voice).

"Oh. Wow. Is that good or bad for you?"

"Well, it's good, I guess. We're downsizing." (They have two adult sons and a grandchild.)

"That's fantastic!"

"Well, we have a rental truck. My sons were supposed to come help us load up, but they can't make it. And we had some friends from church coming, but they aren't going to be able to make it, either. So I'm asking around to see if anyone can help. The Smiths said they would try to help us...."

Enter my internal identity and identity statement. The Smiths, not having an established internal identity and corresponding identity statement, felt the social pressure and guilt of saying they would "try to help." Did they help? Not much if at all. They didn't want to feel the pain of rejection by saying, "No."

I immediately said, "I won't be able to do that, but you can call Two Men and A Truck, and they can help you." There was no way I was going to be pressured or guilted into giving up a chunk of the thirty hours I had at home for the entire week to someone whose own kids wouldn't give their time to their father. I had permission to say, "No," because if I must keep my word, I just don't give it that often. That's who I am.

My kids loved this when I said we were going to Disney World. Why? Because, having given my word, I would make sure that we were going to Disney World, and we did. The kids don't like it that much when I say, "You're grounded for three weeks." Why? Because that means they're grounded for three weeks; there is no wavering after one week.

Trying Is Lying

Why did my other neighbors tell Eeyore they would "try" to help? Have you ever had a backyard BBQ, and you invited someone to come who said they would "try to make it"? Did they come? No. Why did they say they would try to make it? So you wouldn't feel bad? Well, how did you feel when they didn't show up? Badly. They didn't care one thing about you and how you would feel. They were protecting themselves from the pain of rejection they anticipated they would feel from you if they said "No" outright.

Previously, in chapter one, we touched on acceptance as the number-one need of all humans. I believe it bears repeating: *The number one fear of all human beings is rejection.* Cognitive neuroscience and fMRI brain-imaging have shown that rejection is registered by the brain the same way as physical pain. Humans instinctively avoid pain, and when we get any kind of inkling we are about to be rejected (i.e. feel pain), we immediately raise our defenses. Therefore, conflicts happen. Two people who fear rejection are in the same space.

Conversely, the number one need all human beings are looking to fulfill is acceptance. When we look for acceptance from other people, we abdicate our self-worth to others. There's an old country song called "Looking for Love in All the Wrong Places." Until you internally accept yourself, you aren't only abdicating your personal power, but you are powerless to give that acceptance to anyone else: your spouse, your kids, your family, your friends, your co-workers, etc. Remember, you can't give anyone anything you don't have. If you didn't have a hundred-dollar bill, you couldn't give a hundred-dollar bill to anyone.

How Beliefs Are Formed

To change our results, we must change our actions and behaviors on a long-term or even a permanent basis. As a coach, I can tell what a client believes simply by looking at the behaviors and actions that they practice day in and day out. We all act and behave based on what we believe. For example, I believe that cars and trucks can hurt me badly; therefore, I always look both ways before I cross any street.

In between our beliefs and results are a few contributing factors that affect our actions, our feelings, and our attitudes. We act a certain way based on how we feel about something, and our feelings come from our attitude about that thing.

Before I enlisted in the Marine Corps, I was fat and very unfit. My actions -- eating chips and lying on the couch -- were activities (or lack thereof) that I felt very good about doing, or more accurately, that made me feel good and comfortable. I had a bad attitude about physical activities and vegetables, and I didn't feel good and comfortable running and eating healthful foods.

My drill instructors quickly changed my attitude, which eventually changed my feelings, my actions, and finally my results. But my drill instructors first attacked the root cause. They changed my beliefs about fitness and nutrition permanently by changing what I believed about myself. I entered boot camp believing I was the fat kid that always got bullied. I exited as a lean, green, fighting machine.

My drill instructor accomplished this transformation by changing the language I used about myself. Each night before lights out, we recruits would stand at attention in front of our bunk beds. The drill instructor would give the command to get into bed. When this happened, the entire platoon would say the following indoctrinating program about ourselves: "Devil

Dog, Shock Troop, Blood-sucking War Machine, Ready to Fight, Ready to Kill, Ready to Die, but Never Will!"

Gruesome? Maybe, but the DIs were creating and building professional warriors, the ones who run towards the guns, not away from them. The ones who destroy the enemy by fire and maneuver so that our fellow citizens and their children can sleep soundly. Was the training effective? Well, after 30 years, that *program* is still running so strongly that I can quote every word, and my behavior certainly shows the change. Ask my wife and kids.

Identity Statement

Write out who you are now and who you want to be, what I call an identity statement. An identity statement, once ingrained, makes every decision, every choice, every action, every behavior, and every habit a NO-BRAINER! You literally take the conscious mind out of the equation. The identity statement is the autopilot, programmed belief that must be built, installed, and constantly running inside your eleven million bits per second to filter and choose the one hundred twenty-six bits of information per second that is sent to your conscious mind for action. It literally changes your perspective and your point of view of the world around you. The identity statement is the way to train your reticular activating system (RAS) to transform facts into truths that help you instead of hurting you.

The identity statement is a statement built in this format, "I am this who does that." A simple sentence. Not long. Not flowery. Pithy. Short. Concise. Powerful. To build your identity statement, ask yourself:

1) Who do I want to be?

2) What are the internal qualities by which I want to define myself?

3) What strength do I want to highlight?

4) What virtue do I aspire to?

Here are a few examples of identity statements built by some of my coaching clients. (I add these to prime the pump of your genius self.)

"I am a man of great ideas who builds long-lasting relationships."

"I am a woman of integrity who maintains a balanced and effective life."

"I am a risk taker who fearlessly manages risk and works through any outcome or consequence."

"I am a strong woman who remains calm and always does the right thing."

My business partner, Harold "Dutch" Coleman, Jr. has as his identity statement, *"I am a man of God who loves people."*

Kimmi, my stunning wife, has as hers, *"I am a powerful woman who makes things happen."*

Because imitation is the surest way to learn, I want to spend a little time explaining what went into my own discovery and adoption of my internal identity. The catalyst came in May of 1989. I was a twenty-two-year-old corporal when I was transferred from Hawaii to Camp Geiger, NC, and assigned to Weapons Company, 3rd Battalion, 6th Marine Regiment. Coincidentally, a twenty-nine-year-old captain, John E. Folchetti (now a retired lieutenant colonel), was taking command of the unit at the same time I was joining it. We were slated to deploy to the Republic of Panama on an operation leading to the capture of General Noriega.

As John officially accepted command of the company during the change of command ceremony, he gave us an introductory speech to set the tone of his tenure. It was short, to the point, and simple to understand. He said, "Gents, ride hard, shoot straight, and never lie." That speech was an epiphany moment for me, and his words were forever etched in my brain. It was years before I began to fully understand them, internalizing and assimilating the timeless principles therein contained. To this day, when asked what the best advice is I've ever been given, I respond with Lt. Col. John Folchetti's words: "Ride hard, shoot straight, and never lie."

Riding hard is all about maximum effort in every task we take on. Reaching our genetic potential requires focus and energy. As my Mama used to say, "You have to use some elbow grease!" It's a simple concept, but not easy. The concept is a four-letter word, W-O-R-K.

To many people, you might as well have just cussed them, especially when you tell them that success, fulfillment, and happiness require exertion, effort, and work on their part. I have observed people look at others' success and say, "Well, they just got lucky." They didn't just get lucky, and they are not an overnight success. They may have caught a break, but they had to do the preparation and work to be ready to execute and capitalize on that break. If you don't ride hard, you're going to have a long wait to enjoy the fruits of your genetic potential. In life, if you want to realize success, fulfillment, and happiness, you are going to have to put your back into getting it.

Sustained commitment to giving your best effort always is one of those internal qualities I really wanted my children to adopt. So I knew I had to model that behavior consistently as a parent. Presto, the first ingredient of my identity and statement. Effort alone won't get it done though.

Enter shooting straight. Shooting straight doesn't really have to do with rifle marksmanship; it's more about being skillful. What I really wanted for my children to adopt was an identity of sustained excellence. Sustained excellence is a mix of riding hard (maximum effort) and practiced, polished, honed execution of a skill set.

It's not only the skills to do our specific job, but what some have called "soft skills." I hate to call them soft skills. Leadership, mental toughness/resilience, critical thinking (like C.R.A.P.), etc., are hard skills in which to be competent, let alone polished and honed. Shooting straight, hitting the target and using good marksmanship skills, is all about achieving the results you want. The marksman's goal is the bullseye of the target; the Resilient-Minded parent and child set out to do the same. Applying the correct techniques on a consistent basis to hit the target requires shooting straight. Presto! The second ingredient of my internal identity and statement: "I'm a man of excellence."

The never lie element isn't talking about when your significant other asks you, "Does this outfit make me look fat?" ("No, your fat makes you look fat," is NOT the appropriate response.) Never lie is talking about your integrity and your character. When you tell somebody that you are going to do something, follow through and do it. Keeping your word is so rare today that, if you do this one thing, you will rise to the top. You will garner respect and credibility simply by doing what you say you will do.

And make no mistake: for your children to receive course corrections from you, they must respect you and see you in a credible light. I cringe whenever I hear parents threaten ridiculous consequences while attempting to correct a child's behavior. Everyone knows that the parent is not going to follow through with the threat, which results in no behavior change, loss of credibility, and loss of respect, making it even more difficult

91

the next time the parent attempts to correct the child. For instance, threatening that your child will receive no birthday presents this year if they don't shape up. Or the old go to, "I'm not going to tell you again to brush your teeth, clean up your room, eat your vegetables, etc.!" Of course you are going to tell your kid the same thing again and again and untold numerous more times.

I may seem harsh, but I have to say that these are lies. Never lie, especially to your kids. Presto! The final ingredient of my internal identity and statement, "who always keeps his word."

Guiding Your Children in Building Their Own Identity Statements

Once you have your own internal identity statement hammered out and refined, it's time to guide your child in discovering his/her own internal identity and creating his/her own statement. The science of learning demonstrates that our offspring learn best by imitation. The most impactful action you can take in guiding your child is to be and model the internal traits that you would like your child to adopt as his or her internal strengths.

I can't ever remember sitting down formally and guiding my children to discover, construct, and articulate their internal identities. Throughout their lives, they have listened as Kimmi and I have taken teachable moments to highlight those internal strengths and character traits we wished to pass on. I have explained the structure of the sentence,

"I am.... who is...." I have mostly concentrated on modeling my own identity and allowed natural learning, imitation, to take its course.

While writing this chapter, I was traveling out of state. I sent out a family group text and asked whoever had an identity statement to text it to me. Considering the ride hard, shoot straight, and never lie epiphany of mine, let's look at my children's self-written identity statements, which I had never asked of them before.

Drew, my twenty-year-old son, has as his, "*I am a man of greatness who never gives up.*"

Jack, my seventeen-year-old son, has as his, "*I am a man of commitment who always strives for excellence.*"

Michaela, my fourteen-year-old daughter, has as hers, "*I am a hard-working young lady who dominates and is devoted.*"

I can clearly see the influence of Lt. Col. Folchetti's directive in each of their identity statements. Their statements are another real-world example of the applied science working and producing results. Seeing them is encouraging to me and hopefully to you as well. Once the parents know who they are and who they aspire to be, all that remains is consistently living out who you say you are and who you say you want to be. Nature will run its course, and your child will imitate, discover, and adopt your example.

WHAT TO DO:

1) Take the time to discover your internal identity by asking yourself:

a.   Who do I want to be?

b.   What are the internal qualities by which I want to define myself?

c.   What strength do I want to highlight?

d.   What virtue do I aspire to?

2) Build an identity statement that clearly and accurately articulates who you are and who you aspire to be, built in this format, "I am this who does that." A simple sentence. Not long. Not flowery. Pithy. Short. Concise. Powerful. Keeping in mind that who you are should not be confused with a role or label.

3) Guide your children to discover and create their own internal identities simply by living your own identity and modeling those traits you want to pass on to them. Then have real conversations about building those internal strengths and character traits you wish to pass on.

CHAPTER 5 – Peer Pressure, Clicks, Bullies, and Backstabbers

Phillip seemed happy and well-adjusted all throughout elementary school. His parents noticed a shift once he entered the fifth grade. He began dragging his feet in the mornings and leaving later and later. Often, he begged his parents to let him stay home. Initially, his mom and dad thought his behavior was just pre-teen and "normal." As time passed by, Phillip increasingly showed signs of hating school and began to shut himself off from friends and family.

One day, Phillip's mother found some scraps of paper in his backpack. There were notes scribbled on the scraps. They contained messages like:

"You don't have any friends."

"NO ONE likes you."

"You don't deserve any friends."

"You should kill yourself, you are such a loser!"

When Phillip's mom asked him about the notes, he finally confessed that a kid at school had been bullying him, and the torment had been getting progressively worse. Now the kid was pushing Phillip on the playground. Phillip's parents sat down with him and asked him what his response was to this kid. Phillip was a rule follower and didn't want to get in trouble; so he kept everything to himself.

Phillip's mother emailed the teacher but got no response. Like Phillip, she didn't want to make matters worse, but the stress of the situation was becoming unbearable. Worrying. Fretting. Losing sleep. Finally, she and Phillip's dad sat down with Phillip and told him to stand up for himself. If the bully pushed Phillip, he should push back and defend himself. They assured Phillip that he would never get in trouble at home for defending himself against a bully.

Sure enough, within days, the bully pushed Phillip to the ground during recess. Phillip, with full assurance from his parents, shoved the kid back. A scuffle ensued; Phillip was undoubtedly getting his point across by the time two teachers broke it up. Suspensions were handed out, but true to their word, Phillip's parents stood by their son. After that day on the playground, bullies never bothered Phillip again.

We all sympathize with Phillip in this story; however, what about the other kid and his parents? In all honesty, bullying is behavior we all hate to see our kids receive, but we are often blind to the truth when our kids are acting in the role of the bully.

As veteran parents will attest, our little darlings begin to turn into quite the challenge during the pre-teen and teenage years. One day we wake up, and our little angel, who was loving and wanted our attention, wants nothing to do with us. Being seen anywhere near a parent, for the middle schooler, becomes an immediate embarrassment and pointedly NOT cool. As parents, we are a little hurt and tend to become alarmed when our precious progeny begins taking actions on our grandparents' bad behavior checklist - smoke, drink, cuss, or chew, and go around with those who do - while at school or when hanging out with their friends.

When parents are faced with evidence or reports of these behaviors, we are tempted to become delusional, stick our heads in the sand, and pretend nothing has happened instead of dealing with the offense. Resilient and effective parents must teach their children how to navigate the minefields presented by in groups and out groups, commonly known as cliques, and the peer pressure that is inherent in the human search to meet that all-important need of acceptance.

On the flip side of the coin are the bullies and backstabbers, who are trying to inoculate themselves from the pain of rejection. They act on the belief that the best defense is an aggressive offense. The middle school environment (a gathering of youngsters thrown into a churning sea of hormone-raging, survival-minded youths all thrashing to avoid the fear of rejection and frantically seeking the illusion of safety via the feeling of acceptance), is fraught with peril for unprepared children and parents alike.

The stakes are higher than you think when it comes to unconditional acceptance of yourself and your offspring. If you cannot accept your children because you haven't accepted yourself, you are causing them physical pain as their brains register the rejection. We instinctively know that emotional wounds are more difficult to heal than physical wounds, and yet we continue to inflict them repeatedly on our descendants. Yes, descendants. The risks and rewards are multigenerational.

No pressure, but how you parent will influence the next two to three generations. I believe it would be helpful to look at a couple of case studies as examples of how what you do today leaves a legacy, whether you want it to or not. The issue is acceptance of yourself and your children and the effects of not doing the work to forge your own internal identity. The following examples illustrate two extremes of parental approaches to coping with the vacuum of internal identity and the results on the children.

Case Study One

This story begins with the ringing in of the New Year in 1929 in the city of Philadelphia. The U.S. economy was booming. Five days later, Fredrick Russell Wittman, my father, was born. By October of that year, the stock market crashed and brought with it the Great Depression. Difficult times that are difficult to imagine and understand.

My father's childhood happened to occur smack dab in the middle of it and ended with sixteen-year-old Fred working on a dairy farm in Pennsylvania as his contribution to World War II. During the harsh years of his upbringing, my father was frequently told by his father that he was a mistake, an unwanted child, and a drag the family's limited resources. These declarations were accompanied by some outlandish treatment that would be certain to get a visit from social services these days.

With a way of meeting the number-one need of acceptance nowhere to be seen, replaced instead with outright rejection, Fred sought that acceptance outside the home. He believed he found a place with a group of old-school Christian fundamentalists. He attended the only nearby Bible school, which was more moderate in its views, where he met my mother.

My mother's family had emigrated from Denmark, and feeling the pain of being the out group, they immediately began assimilation. In an attempt at acceptance, they only spoke English, even at home. My mother never learned Danish.

My parents were married and immediately entered the ministry, holding tent meeting revivals, planting small churches, and eventually beginning missionary work in the West Indies, Australia, and China.

My dad hated the pain he felt from the rejection of his parents and vowed never to inflict that pain on his six children. But making a vow and keeping it are two different things. It's like that time I ate too much peanut butter chocolate cake and got a tummy ache. I felt so bad that I swore off sweets and vowed never to eat cake again – until the tummy ache wore off.

My parents always attempted to make us feel wanted. However, my parents, to this day, still have no clear internal identity and have not accepted themselves. To cope with the rejection, instead of creating an internal identity of inner strengths and qualities that they aspired to pass on to their children, they adopted the external identity of a religiously dictated set of behaviors NOT to do. To secure acceptance of the in group, their particular denomination, they had to "abstain from the appearance of evil." Whatever the powers of that in group decided appeared to be evil must be avoided, and any who engaged in those behaviors would be "shunned." (That's a thing, a formal act, turning your back on someone, never again to speak their name or acknowledge that they even existed ever again.) The ultimate rejection.

My parents, to cope with the pain of rejection and attempt to fulfill the need of acceptance, adopted this set of rules. Instead of accepting themselves and deciding who they were and who they wanted to be, they subjected themselves and their children to a system that doled out acceptance as a reward for NOT doing things. It went further than don't cuss, drink, smoke, chew or go out with those who do. It was stuff like: women, don't wear pants, shorts, or dresses that show a knee when sitting down, and don't even think about wearing makeup or polishing your nails. Don't go to the movies, even G-rated movies. Don't drink soft-drinks out of a bottle. Don't fight back. Don't join the military. Don't vote.

My parents spent their entire lives with an identity predicated on NOT doing a list of behaviors in order not to feel the pain of rejection. All the while, ironically, they kept doling out judgmental abhorrence, inflicting the pain of rejection on any who they deemed to violate the sacred list of acceptable behavior and continued acceptance of the in group, especially their children and grandchildren. The cascading effect of my grandfather's outright rejection of my father would continue to have fallout on me and would have reached my children if I allowed it.

Of course, with the threat and fear of being shunned dangling ever before them, my parents were strict disciplinarians when it came to be obeying the "Don't" checklist. Remember, neuroscience has revealed that the brain chops off the "don't" so that whatever is left is the new target. "Don't touch that!" in the brain becomes "Touch that!" It's not rebellious; it's how the human brain works. Don't drink. Don't smoke. Don't go out with girls that wear makeup. Don't go to the movies. Because the entire premise of their external identity was based on "Don'ts," discipline had to be extremely harsh, swift, and painful.

My parents' extra discipline has served me well, and I'm extremely grateful for it. In psychology, it's called a desirable difficulty. One example that is indelibly etched into my memory was an occasion when I didn't obey fast enough for my dad. My mom had the teapot going on the stove brewing some tea. My dad jumped up, grabbed the teapot of boiling water, came from behind the chair I happened to be sitting in, and poured it on me. It's certainly not what I would wish for myself or wish on anyone else, but these types of incidents put me on the path of resilience, acceptance of myself, allowing me to accept others, and the discovery of the power of internal identity.

When horrible things happen in life, you can either become bitter or become better. The resilient-minded choose to become better and refuse to let bitterness take root. The resilient-minded reach for post-traumatic growth (PTG) instead of allowing post-traumatic stress (PTS) to take over. My dad could get his belt unbuckled, off, and in motion towards my backside in less than a second. My mom had a wooden spoon and big wooden old-timey hairbrush that she would deploy with equal dexterity.

My quest for acceptance necessitated me walking on eggshells, mistaking approval for acceptance. And like most humans, I became addicted to the approval of others. First my parents, then my peers (the other kids at school), then teachers, and ultimately my Marine Corps drill instructors. I was well-behaved when I was seeking approval, but alas, I could never seem to achieve acceptance. After all, my parents' entire existence was proudly being part of an out group. This was fine in elementary school, but once I entered the seventh grade, the whole out group and proud motif set me up as a target. I didn't fit in with any clique, the upside being that peer pressure wasn't an issue, because I feared repercussions at home more than the ridicule at school. But this separation from peers translated into my becoming easy prey for bullies.

My first beating came after school one day, early in the year. I just curled up into a ball and cried like a baby, sobbing during the entire incident, in front of the huge crowd that had quickly formed. One of the big "Don'ts" was "don't fight back;" no physical defense was allowed. After that first beat down, beatings became a regular occurrence. I increased my eggshell walking, living in fear of triggering a beat down at school and at home. By the time I entered the eighth grade, I had turned to food as a coping mechanism for the fear and rejection. I over-packed my five-feet three-inch frame with one hundred and eighty-five pounds of fat, elevating my out-group status to new heights, only to reach astronomical heights when we moved to Wagga Wagga, New South Wales, Australia when I was fifteen. The town, whose aboriginal name means "Crow, Crow" or place of many crows, was filled with 30,000 Australians and Aborigines and four Americans (my parents, me, and my younger brother) back in 1983.

Tripling down on my out-group rejection, I was a religious fundamentalist, a fat cry-baby, and a bloody Yank. The Aussies smelled fear and immediately dubbed me "Beach Ball" and "Chuck," Peppermint Pattie's nickname for the Charlie Brown. And on cue, I was the target of bullies, to whom I responded with my usual blubbering and crying. Then everything changed. Two knights, not in shining armor but in school uniform, had mercy and compassion on me. They ran off the bullies, protected me, and befriended me. For the first time in my life, I felt safe, but I felt something more: acceptance. Unconditional acceptance.

Both of my benefactors were planning on entering the Australian Royal military, and they introduced me to the warrior culture. We studied World War II battles mostly, but we also looked to a full complement of military history, including biographies of generals, tacticians, heroes, and villains alike. These new friends introduced me to that all-important part of Australian culture, football. (They have four different sports classified as "footy": Aussie Rules, Rugby League, Rugby Union, and Soccer.)

Rugby League seemed the most similar to American football, called Grid Iron in Oz; so I began to practice with the school team. Then I hit puberty full on, and in a single six-week period I shot up to six feet four inches and two hundred thirty-five pounds. I was the biggest kid in the school and prop-forward on the rugby team. My bullying problem ceased. I stopped fearing the bullies' beat downs and stopped fearing my dad's.

Two years after we moved to Wagga, one of my sisters who was thirty at the time came to Australia. She was on a mission to rescue me and bring me home to the States to graduate high school. My parents, although they agonized over the decision to send me home with her, allowed it. Staying in Australia kept me around the pro-military influence of my friends. Their plan was for me to graduate and then go to Bible college. My plan was to join the United States Marine Corps. I knew that the Marines had what I needed and would teach it to me. I didn't want to live my entire life with fear and anxiety. So my two eldest sisters and my older brother, all in their thirties, took part in getting me through my senior year of high school.

Within weeks of landing back in the States, I went to the Marine Corps recruiting office. I waited four hours for the recruiter to get back to the office, refusing the offers of the Navy recruiter so many times that he eventually gave up. When the Marine recruiter, Staff Sergeant Aldrich, finally walked into the office, I told him, "I want to enlist in the infantry for the longest amount of time I can." The Staff Sergeant informed me that since I was still at the tender age of seventeen, my parents would have to travel to the U.S. embassy in Canberra, Australia and sign the paperwork giving me permission to enlist. That phone call did not go well.

Remember, parts of the "Don't" checklist included don't fight, and don't join the military. My parents did what they were taught to do, shun those who egregiously violated the forbidden behavior directives. They literally told me I was going to hell if I enlisted, and we didn't speak for several years after that. (We have a great relationship nowadays; reconciliation was had by all.) They didn't sign, and I had to wait until my eighteenth birthday, when I enlisted in the infantry for six years. I passed through the gates of Parris Island Marine Corps Recruit Depot on November 4, 1985 and started the practice of my lifelong obsession with mental toughness and resilience.

Case Study Two

This case begins in 1969, in the middle of the sexual revolution, just outside of Washington, DC. Two youngsters were in love, got married, and had the first of three daughters at the age of eighteen. The other two girls were born within a few short years. Soon after the arrival of the third child, the father left the wife and daughters to pursue a spectacular career in getting and staying high on marijuana. The eldest daughter, my wife Kim, was seven at the time of that most poignant of rejections, abandonment. Her mom worked two and three jobs, had wonderful support from her parents and her brothers' families, but to say that life as a single mom was a struggle is an understatement. Divorce and single-parent homes were stigmatized in the 1970s and into the 1980s. But emotional wounds cut deepest, and even when the girls visited their father, his actions made it clear that his priority was more along the herbal, self-medicating lines and not so much their well-being.

Having a drug or alcohol addicted parent is more common than a hardline religious fundamentalist parent. Both end up being abusive to themselves and their offspring. Adults in the position of being a parent struggle to cope with life without an internal identity or self-acceptance.

These two cases are two sides of the same coin. One case is adopting impossible codes of behavior and voluntary castigation to make themselves feel better about their inabilities to measure up and handle life. The other, self-medicating with their drug of choice to make themselves feel better about their inabilities to measure up and handle life. Yet the results are the same: children who are afflicted with the pain of rejection, or at least feeling the void of not being unconditionally accepted.

Fortunately for my wife and her sisters, her maternal grandfather stepped into the gap and provided that unconditional acceptance. But the wound was such that to this day, my wife is vehemently opposed to marijuana usage, and during her pre-teenage years she shunned drugs, blaming them for the cause of her pain. In the same way that she has shunned drugs and abandonment, I have shunned conditional acceptance of my children.

The Greatest Gift

As we now know, the number-one need of all human beings and all social animals is acceptance. The greatest gift you can give anyone is your attention. Giving your undivided attention screams pure, unadulterated, unconditional acceptance. Ignore someone, and you are inflicting the pain of rejection. Especially in this age of smartphones and unlimited options of places to give your attention, I am grateful to every person who gives me the gift of attention.

The same holds true for every one-on-one interaction with anyone, anywhere, at any time but especially with your children. When I listen to my kids, I pay attention to what they are saying and how they are feeling. I imbue in them a sense of validation. I simultaneously fulfill their number one need, acceptance, and alleviate the pain that comes by way of their number-one fear, rejection. Because they know they have my attention and validation, my teenagers drop their defenses, become open to me, feel safe around me, sense love in me, and can receive love from me. They become pliable: easy to persuade, teach, mentor, and mold. This reciprocal relationship causes my cortisol (the stress hormone) to maintain a normal, healthy level.

107

Stephen R. Covey first introduced his concept of five levels of listening in his book, "Seven Habits of Highly Effective People." I have applied a slight spin to his work. His lowest level is ignoring. I believe that's not listening at all and is a form of rejection.

Let's start the listening continuum with the Pretend Listeners. These people are looking at their email or social media feed, playing on their phones, or otherwise attempting to split their attention. They say stuff like, "Uh-huh, uh-huh, right, really, uh-huh." They are faking it. They may have heard every word, but they weren't listening.

Who does that response frustrate? It's frustrating for both the speakers and receivers. The speakers are frustrated because their message isn't getting through, and the receivers wish the speakers would shut up so they could fully concentrate on that social media meme. If your teenagers are operating as pretend listeners while you are speaking to them, take a breath before you get upset, and remember that humans learn by imitation.

The second level contains the Selective Listeners. They tune in and out of conversations based on things that catch their interest or not. My Dad was a master at this level. My kid brother and I would be talking about a pet rabbit having bunnies, and my Dad would chime in, "Who's pregnant?" That's how rumors get started; go back to watching *Perry Mason*, Dad.

Third comes the Active Listeners. These people are actively engaged in the conversation, but only to the extent that they are thinking of what they are about to say as soon as the current speaker takes a breath. On a recent family road trip, the boys and I were talking about hunting and fishing. As soon as there was a slight lull in the back-and-forth talk, Michaela, my fourteen-year-old daughter, seemingly randomly said, "Meatball subs are my favorite subs."

The rest of us said, "What? We're talking about hunting and fishing."

She replied, "Well, I didn't want to think about what you were talking about; so I was thinking about what I wanted to think about and saying what I wanted to say." At least she was upfront and honest about it.

The fourth level is made of Interactive Listeners. This level should be our default listening mode. The listener is paying attention and asking clarifying questions. There is no magic here. What the speaker says reminds us of something happening in our own lives, and we relate to the ideas expressed based on our own experiences. For example, if the discussion at the dinner table turns to how awesome Jack's science grade is, Mick and Drew immediately begin thinking about their own awesome (or not) science grades.

The final and ultimate level is reserved for the Empathetic Listeners. This level is where the magic happens. Empathetic listening takes enormous amounts of mental, emotional, and physical energy. The listeners must box up their own thoughts, feelings, attitudes, opinions, and agendas, putting them in the back closet of their being. Empathetic Listeners give pure, unadulterated, unfiltered acceptance and attention. The listeners make a massive effort to put themselves in the place of the speaker and to see, hear, and feel what is being conveyed from the speaker's point of view. No judgment. No criticism. No opinion. No solution. No advice. Just empathy.

This level is where the resilient and effective parent can work massive magic, because you are fulfilling the speaker's (your child's) number one need, acceptance, and removing their number one fear, rejection. Your validation of your child's feelings will become like a drug. Your child will feel so good that you will find the little guy coming back for more and more and more. Humans don't remember what was said as much as they remember how they felt when they were saying it to you.

Each of us has, at one time or another, operated at each listening level. The key here is to be aware. At a minimum, when you are with your child, ramp up to the interactive level. Life happens, and stressors come and go. So don't expect perfection. There will be times that you catch yourself operating as a pretend listener because an urgent email just came in from work. If you are aware and make a deliberate effort to improve your listening levels, the kids will pick up on it and appreciate it. Make it a practice to set aside some time to listen empathetically, especially if your child is having a challenging day or crisis.

I have made it a practice never to turn away one of the kids from sitting on my lap, no matter how big they have gotten. I want them to feel safe and unconditional acceptance. Our home is a sanctuary from all the junk and stress from cliques, bullies, backstabbers, and peer pressure. Kimmi and I foster an environment where there is no fear of us revoking our unconditional acceptance and putting performance conditions on it. We cannot accept our children any more than we already do, and nothing the kids do or don't do will change that.

This is important. If your kids fear rejection and consequences for their actions, they will raise defensive shields, and communication will suffer. Practice being a non-judgmental listener. We'll cover how to do that in greater detail in a later chapter. For now, practicing unconditional acceptance in your home is an effective method for neutralizing the effects of peer pressure and cliques (those seeking acceptance) and bullies and backstabbers (those seeking inoculation from the pain of rejection) in your child's life.

WHAT TO DO:

1) Make a deliberate, purposeful effort always to make your child aware of your unconditional love and acceptance, and never place performance stipulations on that love. Remember, the stakes are

high. The effects of your acceptance or rejection of your child are multigenerational.

2) Understand that peer pressure and cliques are all about human beings seeking fulfillment of the need for unconditional acceptance, and they will gravitate to wherever they feel they find it. If you don't provide it to your children, they will look elsewhere to find it, often with a group whose values you might not share.

3) Bullies and backstabbers are merely fellow human beings who are seeking to inoculate themselves from the pain of rejection, most often experienced at home first. Be intentional in the home never to model the behaviors of bullies and backstabbers. That includes the cessation of gossiping and speaking ill of others.

4) When you catch yourself operating as a listener who is pretend, selective, or active (saying what you want regardless of the conversation) when your child is speaking to you, commit to upgrading your level of listening to interactive or empathetic.

5) Consistently giving your children your undivided attention coupled with empathetic listening will make them feel unconditionally accepted and loved. In addition to fostering a close-knit relationship with your child, you both will enjoy the byproduct of the normalization of cortisol (stress hormone) levels.

CHAPTER 6 – Rivalries

Sibling Rivalry

Leah and Naomi were sisters, though never close growing up. Leah, two years the eldest, was a rule-following, well-mannered, straight-A student with perfect attendance. Naomi was the younger, outspoken, opinionated rebel looking for a cause. Naomi usually found herself toe-to-toe with her parents, shouting "You're not the boss of me!" Her parents' default reply was, "Why can't you be more like Leah?" To add further injury to the insult, the parents would turn to Leah and accuse her of not being a good enough example for Naomi to follow. The sisters have confessed that they didn't get over the rivalry until well into their thirties, and even now, another decade later, some of the old wounds still haven't healed.

Frenemies

Maggie and Shavon were the best of friends all throughout elementary school, middle school, and into high school. Then they both began to compete for the same space on the school varsity soccer team. While still clinging to the BFF title, they slowly but surely became rivals. During the team banquet at the end of their junior year, awards were given, accolades received, and the seniors honored. The festivities ended with the announcement of next year's varsity team captains. Shavon's name was called along with two others. Maggie's was not. Maggie shot straight up from the banquet table, knocking over her chair, pointed at Shavon, swore at her, and stormed out of the hall.

Dueling Grandparents

Jessica and Ben, a couple in their early thirties, have a 4-year old boy and a 2-year-old girl. The children are blessed to have two complete sets of grandparents that love to be involved in their grandchildren's lives. Jessica's parents are a few years older and have only the two grandchildren. Ben's parents, while younger and more active, have other grandchildren from Ben's siblings. These circumstances have created a bit of slant in the amount of time and resources spent by each set of grandparents. During a springtime birthday party, Jessica's mom had the time to devote to making the cake, decorations, and invitations. She really went all out in her efforts. Ben's mom, while understanding she hadn't the same amount of time to commit to the party, still had feelings of being second fiddle. She wanted to be the favorite grandmother.

At the family Fourth of July picnic, Ben's mom planted her holiday flag, claiming both Thanksgiving and Christmas dinners to be hosted at her house. Birthday parties might not have been her forte, but holiday dinners were her domain. Details were planned and executed flawlessly, leaving Jessica's mom feeling like Ben's mom had during the birthday party. She wanted to be the favorite grandmother. The grandparent rivalry was formed, and while not usually mentioned in a book on parenting strategies, it caused stress for the parents just like any other rivalry involving their children.

Defining Rivalry

The concept of rivals derives from the Latin "rivus" meaning stream. Latin "rivalis" means a person using the same stream as another. In other words, two people vying for space on the same journey. As a parent understanding this concept, I ensure that the stream my family is journeying has plenty of space for all of us. Issues arise when we shrink the size of the stream. Each of us needs to feel there is plenty of space, resources, and unconditional acceptance for everyone in the family. When the kids (or the grandparents) get the feeling that there is only room on the stream for a single-file line, that's when jockeying for position in line produces jealousy, anger, and eventually contempt. Once contempt takes root, it's a quick spiral to vengeful, underhanded tactics to sabotage each other. Ambition rears its ugly head, and the standard operating procedure becomes tearing down others to raise one's own position. As this jockeying continues, siblings may even come to hate and resent one another well into adulthood, with the hope of reconciliation eluding them altogether.

Marcus Aurelius, a philosopher and one of the great emperors of Rome, said, "A noble man compares and estimates himself by an idea which is higher than himself; and a mean man, by one lower than himself. The one produces aspiration; the other ambition..." The old maxim that "a little competition is a healthy thing" breeds ambition instead of aspiration. Ambition looks downward with the sole purpose of outdoing others, pushing others down to raise oneself up. Aspiration, on the other hand, looks upwards with the purpose of achieving higher personal performance, behavior, and character. Those who opt for aspiration only compete against themselves, comparing current personal performance, behavior, and character against past personal performance, behavior, and character. Aspiration seeks both to find role models and to be a role model for others.

Rivalries of all types can increase stress for the parents and the entire family. Whether it's the dueling grandparents, the frenemy at school or on the team, or a sibling competing for the same space in life, left unmanaged a rivalry can cause physical and emotional suffering.

The human machine is a blank slate when it enters the world, and programming immediately begins. Recalling that imitation is the bedrock of that programming and learning, we must be mindful that children do and imitate what we as parents do. My wife and I don't compete with others, and we don't compare ourselves to others. We don't have rivals; we don't keep up with the Joneses or anyone else. We run our own race. We focus our energies on what we can control, our own performance, behavior, and character. We don't allow the grandparents, aunts, uncles, or cousins to compete with each other for "most favored" status. We don't allow our children to compete with others, but especially not each other. We have fostered a climate of competing only with one's self.

Rivalry Is the Symptom, Not the Disease

Jealousy, anger, contempt, and sabotaging others are symptoms of the disease of not having accepted oneself internally, operating in fear of rejection, and dealing with those pesky, underlying self-esteem/self-worth issues. Parents must first accept themselves, then give that unconditional acceptance to each one of their children, and finally lead their children down the path of self-discovery of their individual internal identity and internal self-acceptance. When each of these elements is present, the foundation is laid for a durable, loving, and close relationship between your child and anyone they choose. As a friend of mine says, "All relationships require work: work on yourself," as in work to be devoted to the well-being, success, fulfillment, and happiness of all the others.

What I'm saying may sound like pie-in-the-sky type stuff, but if you adopt and practice the principles of being a first responder instead of the emotional reactor, thinking like C.R.A.P., and accepting yourself along with an internal identity, the improvement will all happen automatically. Most parents attempt to fix all the sibling infighting by attacking the symptoms, which often exacerbates the problems. Screaming, "Don't hit your sister!" translates into "Hit your sister!" as you know by now that the brain chops the "don't" off and leaves what is left as the new target.

Success Strategies

There are several strategies to deploy to develop the skills of cooperation and collaboration between siblings and/or frenemies (yes, even with the grandparents) and help them work through conflicts in productive ways.

First and foremost, **be a selfish parent, and play favorites**. I'm selfish as a parent. I want to be part of every child's every accomplishment, milestone, and achievement, as often as I possibly can. And I play favorites. Each one of my kids is my favorite. And since each is my favorite, I naturally prefer, desire, and choose to be as much a part of their lives as I possibly can. I don't have any issues with leaving the office to be at important events in my children's lives. My kids are my favorite, and they know it. I don't make it to every event, but they are a priority.

Second, **don't mistake fairness for equality**. My parents confused these two concepts. As missionaries with six children, they believed that in order to be "fair," what they did for one child they had to do for all the others. It may seem like a good idea, but in practice, it's a disaster. If the oldest got music lessons, everyone had to get music lessons, whether we wanted them or not. If one got souvenir dish towels from a foreign land, everyone got souvenir dish towels from that foreign land. If they couldn't see how they could possibly afford to give something to all six children, everybody got nothing, which, being a missionary family, seemed to be the default mode.

My oldest son had an opportunity to travel to Australia with a student ambassador program. The total cost was approximately six thousand dollars. Under my parents' plan, a trip for Drew would never even be considered, because even if they could find the six thousand dollars for him, they couldn't possibly do that for all six kids. Permission denied. Permission not even considered. Don't even bring it up. Instead, as parents, we took the lead in celebrating Drew's fantastic opportunity, figured out how to make the finances work, and demonstrated to his other siblings that when they had fantastic opportunity arise (not necessarily a trip to Australia), we would all celebrate it with them and figure out the financing. This decision is fair but not equal.

Jack, the younger brother who didn't get to go to Australia, loves shooting, hunting, fishing, and all things outdoors. He had an opportunity to enter the sport of competitive fishing as well as competitive shooting for his high school team. He bought all of his rods and reels, his tackle, and he even paid for all his practice and match ammunition. However, once he progressed in each sport and wanted to take his performance to the next level, he realized that borrowing core equipment wasn't getting it done. He needed access to his own kayak from which to fish and needed a quality match-grade target rifle. We celebrated his adventurous endeavors and figured out how to make the financing work for the purchase of a quality kayak and a top-of-the line target rifle. Fair, not equal.

Third, **give each child individual time and attention**, early and often. Building wonderful memories is Job #1 for resilient-minded and effective parents. So be deliberate, and build some great, personalized memories. My kids know that they each are my favorite, and I demonstrate that reality by setting aside one-on-one time and attention for each of them. The memory I'm focused on building is how they feel when we are together, not necessarily what we are doing. Whatever "fun" activity we do together is just the vehicle to make them feel unconditionally accepted, loved, and an amazing person. I listen and listen some more. I pack up my own agenda, any stressors, distractions, thoughts, and feelings, ramping up to the empathetic listener level. This means I don't offer advice, solutions, opinions, or course corrections until they ask me for it. Don't worry. They will ask you for guidance, and when they do, they will receive your message. Forego the temptation to ramrod your thoughts, especially once they hit the "tweener" stage.

During these individual sessions, I make maximum effort on my part to see, hear, and feel as much as possible from their perspective. This is a long-term strategy, setting up the tone and tenor of the relationship during the tough teenage years. Kim and I have purposely and deliberately fostered a default mode of non-judgmental, non-critical, loving acceptance. The practice of early-and-often individual time and attention have paved the way for honest and open communication, navigating some pretty tough issues like drugs, alcohol, and sex. The reason kids don't talk to parents is that the parents have established a pattern and habit of not listening empathetically.

The fourth success strategy is to **realize each child is completely different** from any sibling(s). All three of my kids have different personality styles, passions, natural abilities, preferences, desires, and communication styles. One size does not fit all. At no time have my wife and I said to any of our kids: "Why can't you be more like your brother or your sister?" Each child also has a particular motivational driver. What motivates one child to take action will not necessarily motivate the others. When parents grasp the variance in each child's style and approach, they can adapt the style and approach to match each individual child. This practice neutralizes the tendency to compete, compare, and jockey for position amongst the siblings.

Widening the Stream

Whether dueling grandparents, siblings, or frenemies are all vying for the same space in the stream, the result is a rivalry filled with jealousy, stress, and worse. As a parent navigating the stream, one of the most effective ways to defuse a brewing rivalry is to widen the stream. Create a more extensive space, allowing all the people in the room to be themselves. A simple way to do this is to view personality as a person's style, not as who they are. Once you recognize personality as the packaging and not the product, you tend not to internalize affronts as rejection.

Several years ago, I was deployed to Amman, Jordan. Because I needed to do some laundry, I went to the local Jordanian version of Walmart, seeking detergent. When I was growing up, my mom always used Tide detergent. I loved the way it smelled, and so far from home and away from family, I decided to get some Tide and capture the comforting feeling that accompanied the scent. As I stood in front of the shelves of laundry detergent, I couldn't find Tide, or any detergent I recognized. However, my eyes were drawn to a package that had Tide colors, orange and blue, but the colors were reversed, blue and orange. The label was in Arabic; so I have no idea what brand it was. But I picked it up and turned the package over in my hand. Lo and behold, in the fine print in the bottom corner was the Proctor and Gamble logo! Finally, something familiar. I purchased it and went to do my laundry. I opened the package, peered inside, and inhaled tentatively. Wait! Could it be? I inhaled deeply....ah. It was Tide! I was flooded with the comforting feeling of being at home watching Saturday morning cartoons with my kid brother.

The packaging was completely different. Different label. Different brand. Different language. Same product. I think of personality as packaging. It's a style and approach to dealing with the outside world. But personality is not identity. Your personality is not who you are; it's not your internal identity. And your children's personality is not who they are; it's not their internal identity. The frenemy's personality is not who that person is, and neither is the grandparents' personalities. Personality is how we humans externally present ourselves. We all tend to gravitate towards, prefer, and feel most comfortable around those who share the same style and approach. The old adage that "birds of a feather flock together" isn't wrong. To overcome that tendency, parents must understand primarily that when it comes to their children, the personality style they most enjoy is not relevant. As a parent, what I like and how I feel about a particular personality style is a sand trap. The target is to widen the stream and allow everyone space, not to force others to stay inside your personal-style comfort zone.

I've long had an opinion, a truth, that the human personality is ever changing and not permanently hard-wired. I hated personality assessments and tests. Results seemed to be used as a justification not to learn and grow and not to attempt to get along better with others, and worse still, as an excuse for being a jerk. "Well, here's my test results. It's just how I am wired; so get over it." Sigh.

Intuitively I knew I was correct, but I didn't have any empirical data or research to back my theory. That all changed in 2012 when psychologists at the University of Edinburgh in the United Kingdom completed the longest-running study in the history of human personality. The study, which started in 1947, established personalities of more than twelve hundred fourteen-year-olds and tracked them over the next sixty-three years, when participants were seventy-seven years old. "The younger-self and older-self seemed to bear no resemblance to each person. It was as if the second tests had been given to different people," the study's authors noted. The research points to "personality-plasticity," a term meaning that personality changes and will change. Because our style and approach are pliable and will change, why not deliberately guide them in a direction that helps you connect better with your children?

Personality Styles

The study of personality styles first emerged in 400 B.C. and was introduced by Hippocrates in ancient Greece. Hippocrates offered four basic types of personality or temperaments based on bodily fluids. The temperaments weren't inaccurate, even if Hippocrates' theory about where they originated was. The four fundamental temperaments are **sanguine** (enthusiastic, active, and social), **choleric** (independent, decisive, goal-oriented), **melancholic** (analytical, detail-oriented, deep thinker and feeler), and **phlegmatic** (relaxed, peaceful, quiet).

Research in this area has continued to evolve and develop. There are multitudes of personality tests, assessments, and models. There are four-type models, five-trait models, six-dimensional model, all the way up to and including a sixteen-trait combination model. As designators some use letters, some colors, others use animals, and others still subscribe to Hippocrates' original model.

In my work as the CEO of the Mental Toughness Training Center, our instructional design team has developed an integrated and simplistic four-style model based on a combination of the DISC assessment and the work of Carl G. Jung, a protégé of Sigmund Freud. We created this tool simply as way help leaders grasp the variance in each employee's style and approach and then adapt their own leadership style and approach to

124

match each individual. Laying out a path to cooperation and collaboration instead of competition and rivalries. And most importantly, operating from an understanding that personality is not a permanent, genetically imposed, hard-wiring of your being. It's simply your default mode of communication and approach.

The first style in the Mental Toughness Training Center model, we call the Dominator. It's just like it sounds. This style is fast-paced, clear, blunt, quick, and to the point. The mantra of Dominator is "Accomplish the Mission!" If you have ever watched an episode of "Survivor" on television, you saw Dominators in action. On the first day when the Survivor teams are marooned, and no one really knows each other yet, the Dominator happily starts barking orders and assuming command. This style angers all the other members of the team who are not Dominators.

I'm a recovering Dominator. We Dominators are happy to fill any vacuum in leadership, management, or power, whether asked to do so or not. We don't care about hurt feelings; we care about getting the job done. Achieving our goals, hitting the numbers, accomplishing the mission: that's our priority, not the fact that you feel like we barked at you, and you took it personally. Your perception is not my problem; my problem is that you aren't doing your job up to standard or fast enough. We Dominators don't mean to come off as arrogant and brash; we just never thought about how we appear. We're too focused and busy working to spend the time or energy worrying about pleasantries.

The opposite style of the Dominator is what we call the Comforter. The Comforter is slower-paced, people-oriented, considerate, and agreeable. The mantra of the Comforter is, "Let's hug it out." They have a strong need for inclusion. The Comforter has an equally strong need to feel valued as a human being.

If you've seen the movie *Elf* with Will Farrell playing Buddy the Elf, you have seen a Comforter in action. Buddy is the quintessential Comforter. He very much wants to feel valued and included, especially by his dad, Walter, played by James Caan. Buddy's dad is completely repulsed by Buddy's style and approach. That is because Walter is a Dominator. Dominators and Comforters together are like mixing oil and water. If you are a Dominator and your child is a Comforter, you must modify your default communication and personality style if you want to connect with your child.

A more conducive style to the Comforter is the Headliner. Headliners move at a fast pace, display passion and excitement about new ideas, and hate details. They find kinship with Comforters in that Headliners are very tolerant and accepting of people. The mantra of the Headliner is, "It's all about the big picture!" Don't bog down a Headliner with the details; just give them the headline. I liken them to the one-minute manager who comes up with a grand idea and scoots off to the next grand idea, leaving the planning and execution to others. They can't be anchored down with minutiae and specifics. They love new ideas for the idea's sake.

Taking action is not their priority. Another new idea is much more exciting than executing the last one. They flit around like a hummingbird from one person to another person, sharing each exciting new concept until the novelty wears off.

The opposite style, clashing majorly with the Headliner, is the Scientist. The Scientist is much slower-paced, which is part and parcel of their methodical approach to life. The mantra of the Scientist is, "It's all about the details." They love to dig into the details and minutiae of everything in an attempt to gather and analyze as much information as possible before making a decision. They completely distrust anyone who is not process-oriented and is only interested in the flash and sizzle of a concept (i.e. the Headliner). They don't enjoy people; they enjoy processes. They have little time for pleasantries and can be seen as arrogant and brash, similar to the Dominators. They do everything by the book, live by written policy and the letter of the law, and shun any nonsense about the spirit of the law, exceptions, and unwritten rules. They hate daydreamers, pie-in-the-sky-types, winging it, spontaneity, and flying by the seat of your pants.

Connecting with Each Style

When Kimmi and I were first married, I was a twenty-one-year-old Marine infantry corporal. I was as extreme a Dominator as possible. I tested off the charts. My wife was a Comforter. They say opposites attract. Soon after the honeymoon period wore off, I came home from work one afternoon and apparently started barking at Kimmi in an unacceptable manner. She stood her ground and declared, "You're not talking to me that way! I'm not one of your Marines. You have to go to sleep sometime. I have a cast-iron skillet, and I'll use it." We laugh about it now, but I thought she was serious and so began my quest to drive to the center.

The center is the hub that connects each style, and in the center resides balance. Imagine possessing all of the best qualities of each style and jettisoning all the undesirable qualities. That's the center, and I was headed there because I wanted to be with Kimmi more than I wanted to be right. I have observed many people in similar situations react with, "Well, that's just the way I'm wired; so deal with it." That's not a recipe for a loving, healthy, and lasting relationship, whether with your partner or your children. I began the process of dominating thoughts, feelings, attitudes, and actions. Though it hasn't always been easy and I'm still not dead center, I'm really close.

Deliberately changing your personality and communication style so that it connects credibly with every other style is an effective way to reach each member of the family, wherever they are currently. If you practice the principles laid out in this book so far, you will automatically drive to the center. But I believe it would be helpful if you knew exactly how relationships work in this arena.

Both the Dominator and Scientist styles are very close-minded. Dominators believe that they know best what to do and that their way is the best way to do it. The old "my way or the highway" axiom. No arguments, no debates, no discussion, and no one asked you for your opinion. The Scientist does everything by the manual, policy, procedure, and the letter of the law, no exceptions. If the process is to do A first, B second, C third, and D last, don't even think about doing D before C, even if it makes sense. In order for both Dominators and Scientists to drive to the center, they need to open their minds. And the human machine becomes open-minded by thinking like C.R.A.P. (clarity, relevance, accuracy, and precision). Both premises, "My way is the best way," and "This is the best practice," are truths, not facts. When we get to the accuracy step, "Is this a fact or truth?" the critical thinker sees the "truths" and moves them into the fact column. The fact is that there are many ways to bake a cake. And the fact is that when we say "best practice" we shut down our genius brain from continuing to filter the eleven million bits of information per second that may discover a better practice.

Both the Comforter and the Headliner are very open-minded. These personality styles buy stuff from the ads on their social media timelines at two o'clock in the morning. "Oooooh, I need that! And look at all the features, and only three easy payments of $34.99." Because Comforters and Headliners love people, inclusion, and tolerance and are so open-minded, it's rather easy to take advantage of them. For these styles to drive to the center, they need to close their minds. And the human machine becomes more closed-minded by thinking like C.R.A.P. "I need that" is a truth. When moved to the fact column, it becomes, "I am being dazzled by marketing tactics" and adds enough skepticism to draw Comforters and Headliners towards objective reality and the center.

Concerning communicating across the various styles, the Headliner and Dominator are both very direct in their language and messaging; some might even call them blunt. For example, your teenager keeps doing that thing that annoys you to no end, and you say, "Stop doing that!" The teenager may obey, but the change of behavior, of course, only lasts thirty seconds, max, when the behavior resumes, causing you shout, "WHY ARE YOU DOING THAT?" The behavior stops, but only because your teenager avoids being around you because you yell so much.

On the other hand, the Comforter and Scientist are very indirect, softer, and less clear in their language and messaging. For example, when your teenager keeps doing that thing that annoys you to no end, you say…. nothing. Indirect communicators often avoid any confrontation, which of course, only exacerbates the problem. The behavior continues and becomes a pattern and a habit, and eventually you reach your breaking point and go nuclear.

For direct communicators, driving to the center entails softening your language and tone. Instead of screaming, "WHY ARE YOU DOING THAT?" try a different tactic that is less inflammatory. For the indirect communicators, driving to the center entails asserting yourself and confronting the issue instead of ignoring it or letting others walk all over you. In either case, driving to the center in your communication could look something like this: "Hey, I'm sure you have your reasons for doing that; do you mind me asking what they are?" Remember that the human brain has to answer a question, and chances are, your teenager has never thought about the reasons for the behavior that annoys you and may well have not even been aware of the behavior. Either way, you have interrupted the action with a reasonable question that doesn't put your teenager on the defensive. (We'll take a more in-depth look at communication in a later chapter.)

Navigating the Rapids

When the space of a riverbed narrows, the water flow speed and power increase, creating a hazard that we call the *rapids.* For anyone on the river, encountering rapids increases stress, because one wrong move can have devasting consequences. Rapids are a perfect picture of any rivalry: two or more people trying to occupy the same space in the river at the same time. As the channel narrows, the pressure increases. Learning how to communicate with each type of personality will smooth out the ride through rough waters and help all parties involved (parents, siblings, frenemies, and even the grandparents) to decrease the emotional toll of any personality struggles.

WHAT TO DO:

1) Replace competing with others and ambition with competing with oneself and aspiration. Remember that ambition looks downward

with the sole purpose of outdoing others, pushing others down to raise oneself up. Aspiration, on the other hand, looks upwards with the purpose of achieving higher personal performance, behavior, and character.

2) Be aware that rivalries of any nature occur when two or more people are trying to occupy the same space in the stream of life at the same time. Widen the space with unconditional acceptance of all parties, give individualized attention to all parties, and strive for equity, not equality.

3) Know the various personality styles; understand that personality is packaging, not who the person is; and drive to the center, the hub that connects each personality style where you model all the best qualities of each style and jettison all the undesirable qualities.

SECRET 3 – MINDSET MASTERY

CHAPTER 7 – The Mindset Incubator

Ashley, a competitive and street-smart 5th grader, is the daughter of two entrepreneurial parents, the kind of power couple that is continually seeking out new business opportunities and turning them into successful ventures. Ashley is also a talented artist with high standardized test scores in math, science, and reading, and as such chose to enroll in a charter school. During an assigned project on budgeting, she demonstrated that her parents' attitudes, opinions, and approach to life, while not formally taught in the household, were passed down.

Students had to choose a career, learn about the budget based on the earnings in their chosen field, and set up their lives accordingly. Ashley decided on being a doctor. With her allotted earnings statement, she bought a very modest house and sublet to a roommate to cover her mortgage. Then the eleven-year-old purchased the least expensive reliable transportation she could find, forgoing the status-displaying cars of her peers. When asked her reasoning for such a basic lifestyle, she responded with an entrepreneurs' principle. Wasting money on frills would rob her of setting aside money to invest whenever a business opportunity happened across her path. Astonishing! Not so much: her mindset was merely a byproduct of her environment.

There are thousands of levels of consciousness. Thousands of nuanced and variable ways in which to perceive the world. For the sake of simplicity, I use five substantial categories of consciousness, or what we call performance mindsets in our Get Warrior Tough program. A performance mindset is a person's established set of opinions, beliefs, feelings, and attitudes that form the basis for their worldview. Different people's performance mindsets predetermine their personal responses to circumstances, situations, and the world at large and their interpretations of those factors. Your mindset directly affects your levels of stress. Stress is a truth, and like beauty, it lies in the eye of the beholder. How you percieve the circumstances of parenthood is within your control, and herein lies the third secret of resilience: mindset mastery.

The lowest performance mindset and worldview are what I call *The Defeated*. The Defeated have a worldview and a belief that they have already lost, even before they have begun. The Defeated believe that life is awful and then you die. The Defeated are completely beaten: beaten down in life, beaten down by circumstances, beaten down by the weather, and beaten down by economic and political conditions. There is no use even trying. Those who share this mindset tend to make up approximately five percent of the population in the developed world.

The next level of performance mindset and worldview up from the bottom is the *Survival Minded*. The Survival Minded tend to make up approximately ten percent of the population of the developed world. Those who adopt and share this mindset do just enough to have just enough, living from paycheck to paycheck, whenever those may come. They only want to know when payday is, when the next break is, and when the next day off is. They don't seek any resources or corresponding responsibilities beyond doing just enough to survive. Life is always a struggle, and enjoyment is derived only from small pleasures, taken rarely, when possible.

The mid-level performance mindset and worldview are the **Average-Minded**. The Average-Minded don't want to be rich; they just want to be comfortable and have job security. Those who adopt and share this mindset tend to make up approximately seventy-five percent of the population of the developed world. These folks play not to lose. They don't ever want to lose whatever comfort and illusion of security they believe they have amassed. Playing it safe, they have an employee mentality. Never would they bet their own money on their own abilities and performance, but they expect employers to bet the company's money on them. Many spend most of their time avoiding getting fired, all the while complaining about the company who is paying them.

The next level of performance mindset and world-view is **The Tyrant**. Tyrants are looking out for number one! They will mow you down and run you over. They tend to get results and obtain a certain level of success and higher performance. However, they also tend to burn almost every relationship they have on the way to the top of the mountain and will most certainly push down everyone else on their way up. They love ambition and loathe aspiration. Those who share this mindset tend to make up about ten percent of the population of the entire planet, in the Third World or the developed world. There always seems to be no shortage of Tyrants. They are like the farmer who burns an entire field of crops to get rid of the one weed in the middle of the field. This mentality is the choice of many narcissists, bullies, and backstabbers.

The highest level of performance mindset and world-view, the one we all should aspire to achieve (why else would you be reading this book?), is the **Resilient-Minded**. The Resilient-Minded person plays to triumph in life and is a class act, operating from a core value belief that, "I'm the problem, and I'm the solution." The Resilient-Minded person knows that if he or she has a problem, he or she _is_ the problem. But the good news is that he or she _is_ also the solution to that problem and every other problem. Those who adopt and share this mindset tend to make up less than five percent of the human race.

The Resilient-Minded person operates out of a perspective of love and abundance. All of the other mindsets operate out of a perspective of fear and scarcity. Oh, and did I already mention that cognitive neuroscience, through fMRI and brain mapping, has discovered that half the brain shuts down when you operate out of fear, anxiety, or even worry (which is just baby fear)? Let that sink in for a moment. When you worry about your children, you are shutting down half of your brain. The creative, problem-solving half of your brain, your creative genius self, the part of your brain you need in order to get out of trouble and solve whatever problem you are facing, goes completely dark.

Mindset and Consciousness Are Contagious

The scientific research unequivocally shows that you will become most like the people you spend the most time with. If you have a friend that is obese, a study published in the New England Journal of Medicine found that you have a fifty-seven percent chance of also being obese. It also found that if you identify an obese person as a strong and close friend, the percentage rockets up to a one hundred seventy-one percent chance you will be obese. Mindset and consciousness are contagious, and not just with obesity. Growing up, many parents tell their children, "I don't like you going around with those kids. They're a bad influence on you." And then there's the old saying, "Birds of a feather flock together." Fortunately, we humans can change our mindset by changing flocks. Or better yet, get the best feathers from the beginning by being in the right flock. The first flock we each join, and the source of our initial mindset is our parents.

My target, as a parent, has always been to give my kids the mindset and consciousness to set them up for success and to handle deftly anything life throws their way.

Missionary Mentality

It took decades for me to dig myself out of the survival mentality of being raised with an old-school, fundamentalist missionary mindset. My sisters' names are Joy, Hope, and Faith. My father thought it was funny to tell everyone, "We have Joy, Hope, and Faith, and are living on charity." It got some laughs for sure, but that mindset was pervasive.

Everything we had was usually second-hand, third-hand, or the cheapest available. My parents never took any government assistance. They never voted either. They believed both to be outside the scope of their religious convictions. Growing up, we always had just enough, never going hungry, never without shelter, never without clothes or shoes. However, the shoes we wore only fit us about a third of the entire time we wore them. The few times we got new shoes, they would be too big, allowing room to grow into them. And once you grew out of them, my parents would look at them and say, "There's plenty of wear left in them. Back in my time, we would just put cardboard in the bottom if the soles wore out." To their credit, they were raised in the 1930s during the Depression; that background coupled with the missionary mentality instilled a mindset that set us all up for a life of struggle.

As kids, we didn't suffer. How we lived was normal, and we didn't know any different until we hit middle school. When you show up wearing hand-me-down clothes from No-Name-Mart and everyone else is wearing normal brand-name clothes, the other kids tend to point it out in a not-so-nice fashion. The haircuts my dad gave us didn't help much, either. What other kids did and said to us was devastating but was not the most damaging. The most damaging thing was creating a mindset that programs you to think that you can't ever afford something, so don't even dream about it. (Notice the difference from Ashley's upbringing. Her parents didn't waste resources on frills, either, but they were working on being able to afford anything they dreamed of in the future.) And since you don't even dare dream about a nicer life, you never can see how it could ever be better than what you have. Just be glad you have what you have. Half a loaf is better than none. Don't ever think that an entire loaf is better than half. How dare you be ungrateful and greedy!

My parents scrimped and saved to take us to Bethany Beach in Delaware, a two-and-a-half-hour drive from my childhood home in Wilmington. We would spend the day at the beach, and after 6 pm, we would go to the Indian River State Park to get showers. We waited until after 6 pm because the parking attendant went off duty then and we could get in without paying. Afterward, as a treat, we would go to the boardwalk at Rehoboth Beach, where all the attractions and amusements were. We would just walk on the boards, and our treat was to watch all the other kids riding the rides and playing the games. Honestly, it would have been better not to go at all than to go watch other kids having fun.

To this day, I won't take the kids anywhere if we don't have the finances. I go earn more and put the extra towards the outing. Once the funding is in hand, we go, and we go BIG! When we went to Disney World, I had enough budgeted so that I never had to say "No" to anything the kids asked: snacks, souvenirs, trinkets, toys, rides, restaurants, whatever. Remember that Job #1 of the Resilient parent is building wonderful memories. We had a grand time, and the kids will never forget it – just as I will never forget watching the other kids have fun.

When I was first married, between my missionary mentality upbringing and my Marine Corps infantry "everything-I-need-is-in-my-rucksack" mentality, I proudly believed and stated, "I can live in a tent. That's all I need." I made the mistake of saying this in front of someone with some sense. That person looked at me and said, "Is that all your wife needs? What about if you have kids? Is that all they'll need? Do you want them to be raised the way you were?" It was as stinging as a slap in the face. Tears welled up in my eyes. My goodness! I was repeating the cycle. The Marine Corps gave me the mindset to control my body. It helped me for sure, but I traded one brand of survival mentality for another brand of survival mentality. I had to figure out how to take the warrior mindset of mission accomplished and apply it to every area of my life.

Different Mindset in Different Areas

I learned that you can have different mindsets in different areas of your life. For example, I was Resilient-Minded when it came to fitness and combat, but I couldn't scrape up enough extra money to buy lunch out of a vending machine. I began seeking solutions to this epic fail on my part. In my search, I ran across an Albert Einstein quote that gave me a clue: "A problem cannot be solved at the same level of consciousness at which it occurs." In other words, if you have a Defeated-Minded problem, like, "We can't afford for you to go to college; so don't even think about it," a

Defeated mindset cannot solve it. If you have a Survival-Minded problem, like, "We will never get ahead enough to take a vacation," a Survival mindset cannot solve it. If you have Average-Minded problems, like, "The cost of repaying student loans is crushing us," they cannot and will never be solved if you continue to operate with an Average mindset. And I don't really want to become a Tyrant; so let's just go straight for the Resilient-Minded mindset. Any time you believe resources are scarce or you are fretting about anything, you are operating at a mindset level that is lower than the Resilient-Minded one. Unless, and until, you raise the level of your mindset, you cannot and will not solve that problem. Ever.

Self-Limiting Beliefs

Raising your consciousness starts with recognizing your self-limiting beliefs. I was oblivious to my own, deeply-programmed, self-limiting beliefs until that day I was asked about my wife's needs and those of my unborn children. Since that day, I have vetted every single one of my beliefs and have discarded or upgraded any belief that was self-limiting. Once I started looking, I found legions of them.

Here's the first few dozen I found coming out of my mouth:

"I can't. I have to. I'm just not good at that. I've never been good at sales. My desk is always a mess. I hate my job. I'm just not cut out for that. I get a cold this time every year. You can't trust anyone anymore. Nobody wants to pay me what I'm worth. I just can't seem to get anything done. I'm awful at remembering names. I'm tired. I'm stressed. If only I had more time. If only I had more money. If only I could catch a break. That's impossible. Whatever. I don't know. I don't know what to do. I don't know how to do that. Nothing seems to go right for me. I don't have the patience for that. There's always more month at the end of the money. I can't afford that. I'm just not creative. That won't work. It's going to be another one of those days."

Mindset Mirror

I found it helpful in my life to hold up what I call the mindset mirror and take an honest assessment of exactly what my own mindset actually is, not what I want to think it is. To make things simple, let's drill down to people with only two mindsets, Average and Resilient.

Average   vs.   Resilient:

Controlled by external factors vs. Control themselves and their responses

Avoid risk vs. Attack risk head-on and manage it

Live in delusion   vs. Live in objective reality

Do anything to stay comfortable   vs. Purposely leave comfort zone

Practice a skill until they get it right vs. Practice until they can't get it wrong

Long for security vs. Don't believe that security exists outside their own abilities to handle whatever life throws their way

Average   vs.   Resilient:

Sacrifice advancement for safety vs. Sacrifice perceived safety for advancement

Operate out of fear vs. Operate with confidence from preparation

Focus on the score/results vs. Focus on execution of the process

Shift blame and make excuses vs. Take complete personal responsibility

Focus on the problems vs. Focus on solutions

Get tired and frustrated and give up vs. Always find a way to stay in the fight

Think they know enough vs. Crave fresh knowledge and more training

Believe in victory only when they see it vs. Know they will see victory after believing

Speak the language of fear and defeat   vs. Speak the language of love and confidence

Believe they are doing the best they can vs.   Know   they   can always learn and do more

If, after looking in the mindset mirror, you are satisfied with your reflection, please skip the rest of this chapter. If, however, you wish to upgrade your mindset, keep reading. I will lay out a simple process of mindset mastery in the following pages.

Commitment

In 1519, Hernán Cortez embarked on a quest to capture the world's greatest treasure at the time: Aztec gold, silver, and jewels. He manned an armada of eleven boats, sixteen horses, and six hundred men and landed on the coast of Mexico. He was up against one of the superpowers of the ancient world: thirty thousand Aztec and Mayan warriors. For six hundred years, others had tried and failed to conquer this empire. All of the native warriors were fighting to save their homes, wives, children, and family members. Cortez' band was fighting for gold. Who had the advantage? Who was going to fight harder? Who was all in? Who was committed? The Aztecs were committed to their families and their homes. Cortez' group was fighting for money.

Cortez knew that six hundred men versus thirty thousand wasn't the issue. Commitment was the issue. So Hernán threw a beach party for his troops. During the clambake, legend has it, Cortez sent his lieutenants back to the boats and set them afire. With the boats up in flames, Cortez evened out the playing field. Now everyone was committed.

The command to burn the boats left the Spaniards with only two choices — win or die. We know today how the Cortez decision to burn his boats turned out. Hernán Cortez became the first man to conquer the Aztec and Mayan empires successfully. His only resource? Securing the commitment to win or die trying from his men. There was no exit strategy, no "Plan B" in place to save the lives of his men.

144

This is commitment. You must "burn your boats" in order to succeed. If you have a Plan B, you have already lost; it's just a matter of time. As soon as the going gets difficult, you will cut and run. Plan B is really Plan A and has been all along; you are just deluding yourself. The point isn't which side is right or wrong; it is which side is committed.

Attaining a Resilient Mindset requires commitment. Effectively navigating the minefield parenthood can be and living a successful and balanced life requires commitment on your part, not mere involvement. To illustrate the difference between commitment and involvement, I like to use the breakfast plate. Imagine sitting down to a wonderful breakfast, complete with a plate of eggs and bacon. I love breakfast food, and I love eggs and bacon, but especially bacon. Bacon is so good! One day, while enjoying a plate of bacon and eggs, it dawned on me that the chicken was merely involved in my breakfast by supplying the eggs. And while the chicken's contribution was good, it wasn't my favorite. Bacon was my favorite. Bacon was the pig part of my breakfast. And the pig was committed, not merely involved.

That's a perfect picture of commitment versus involvement. If we take a second to think about it, involvement never brings forth the results we are seeking. Only commitment produces lasting, sustainable results. When I was dating my wife, I was involved with her. However, once I committed, I married her. No Plan B. No annulment or divorce option. No getting involved with other women. I burned my bachelor's boat. When I had children, to be an effective and resilient parent, I had to commit, not merely be involved in rearing them.

There are no levels of commitment. Either you are committed, or you are not committed. It's like being pregnant: you are or you're not. Make the commitment to think like C.R.A.P.; be a responder, not a reactor; accept yourself and your kids unconditionally; craft an internal identity statement; and raise your mindset and level of consciousness to Resilient-Minded. No other option. No excuse. Just do it.

Consistency

As a coach, one of the saddest things I see is watching a client do great for several weeks, practice critical thinking skills, keep commitments, achieve goals, look great, see their countenance change for the better, and then stop doing all the things that produced their success. Sometimes that client will try to "get back on the wagon" of good habits, actions, and behaviors, only to stop again after a few weeks. Then they enter a cycle of succeeding on again and off again, with downward spiraling results, and eventually they find themselves in worse shape than at the beginning.

The on again/off again inconsistency in performance is one of the biggest killers of success I've ever come across. Doing well for a few weeks, then coasting … then feeling bad enough to start doing well again for a few weeks, then backsliding some more. Over and over, the only thing consistent is their inconsistency.

146

Yes, the routine is boring sometimes. When I feel bored being consistent, I remind myself of the time I was flying in a corporate jet with an ex-fighter jerk, I mean jock, as the pilot. He decided he was bored with consistent flight and started doing some "Goose and Maverick" stuff. The boss wasn't on the plane; we were dead-heading back home, only an aide, me, and Mr. Ex-fighter (and soon to be ex-corporate aviation) jock. Fuel was burnt; stuff was launched across the cabin; coffee spilled; suit jackets stained; and oxygen masks dropped ... but hey, the jock wasn't bored. Nor was he consistent. I like consistency, a lot.

Can you imagine an inconsistent commercial pilot? There's a news story for you. What about an inconsistent surgeon? Any volunteers to be his or her next patient? Most of us get torn up if the garbage pickup isn't consistent, if the mail runs late, or if the cell signal goes in and out. Power outage? Water heater dead? How about inconsistent cable, satellite, or streaming TV during a big game? We don't tolerate anything less than a consistent performance from our entertainment service providers, not to mention our favorite franchise quarterback who is prone to throwing the Fourth Quarter interception. But we're usually okay with inconsistency in our own performances.

Once you have committed as a parent to be effective and Resilient-Minded, next is consistency. Parenting and workplace management are similar: commit to your charges, and act consistently. As parents, that means consistently keeping promises made to your child and also applying the consequences and correction to bad behavior, i.e., keeping your word. It also means consistently listening and being present. The fact that the boss was a jerk and you had a bad day at work doesn't excuse you taking your frustrations out on your spouse and children. The worst bosses I've ever worked for were Jekyll and Hyde types. Nice one day, nuts the next. I was never sure which person was going to show up, Jekyll or Hyde. Unfortunately, many parents behave in the same manner; the kids are not sure who is coming home, Jekyll or Hyde.

No Excuses

This leads to the third step in the process of becoming Resilient-Minded: stop all excuses. There is a pandemic out there of excuses. It's infectious and contagious. It spreads quickly, and the infected are entrenched throughout the globe. Excuses are everywhere. They are pervasive. Even society's leaders have succumbed to their contagion.

You can rise to the top, almost instantly, wherever you are, in whatever organization you find yourself a part, by simply not allowing yourself to excuse yourself. So, too, can you become an effective and Resilient-Minded parent if you ditch the excuses. There are reasons for a lack of consistency and commitment, and those reasons should be discovered and corrected. However, there is NEVER an excuse. I'm brutal with myself. No butt chewing from any Marine Corps Gunny ever came close to the level of correction I give myself. I hold myself to a higher standard than anybody else expects of me, and in doing so, I rise above the cesspool of inconsistency out there.

Take notice of how those around you deflect personal responsibility for their actions and behaviors. Take notice of yourself and ask yourself, "Am I excusing my own substandard performance?" If so, why? Is it just out of habit? Or is it that we cannot face ourselves objectively and own our results? Why do excuses pour from our lips? Is it easier to blame others, blame the economy, blame the bosses, blame the teachers, blame the school system, blame our parents, or blame the weather? Of course it's easier, but that is a downhill run to mediocrity and worse. Make today the day you stop blaming the dog for eating your homework. If you forgot to do your homework, ask yourself, "Why?" If you didn't do it because you were lazy or chose something more enjoyable, then put on your "Big Girl Pants" or your "Big Boy Pants" (as my wife says) and own your choices. Own your feelings. Own your thoughts. Own your behavior. Own your character. Own your work ethic. Own your results. Own your life. Own yourself.

Here's a clue: Kids can spot excuse-making and a blame shift a mile away. They can uncover a hypocrite like nobody's business. And don't be fooled; they adopt this behavior almost faster than any other, because it works on you. Humans hate to be seen as hypocritical, and the children instinctively know this truth and will use excuses if you do, knowing all the while that you have no ground to stand on if you try to call them on it. Kimmi and I don't allow excuses from ourselves in our parenting, nor do we allow them from our children. We also don't nag them to clean their rooms if ours is a mess. What up? Right.

Environment

Our environment is made of the voices we allow to have a platform. We must pay attention and be mindful of what we hear, what we see, what we read, what we feed on, and where it comes from, and we must place a measure on it. I give minimal value to what I see on TED Talks or the television news, what I hear on talk radio and sports radio, or what I read in newspapers, blogs, religious media, business books, and even self-help books -- *until* I vet, examine, scrutinize, assess, investigate, and verify every voice and source. I absolutely refuse to allow any voice unrestricted access to my environment and my family's environment. Any unauthorized TV, talk radio, sports radio, music, gossip, complaining, fearmongering, any voice that spews: "The world is about to end; we are going to hell in a handbasket; and the global financial collapse is scarier than WWIII, which of course, could also happen any second now; and did you hear what so-and-so said or did on *Dance Wives* and *Real House Moms*?" Oh, and let's not forget social media feeds. All of these voices are given fighter jet escorts out of my family's environment. The first step in identifying the voices is assessing the language used and emotions evoked by each voice.

Language is the key. The language we use creates images and visualizations in our minds, which in turn form our truths and beliefs. Those truths produce feelings and attitudes, which spur our actions and behaviors. Actions and behaviors produce our results, and our results produce our success, fulfillment, and happiness. Therefore, the root cause of success, fulfillment, and happiness is the language we use.

The first written languages appeared in the Near East at the beginning of the Third Millennium B.C. – the Bronze Age. A very limited number of languages are verified from before the collapse of the Bronze Age and the rise of alphabetic writing. They are the Sumerian, the Egyptian, and the Semitic (Aramaic) languages. When I researched the originally-defined usage of the concepts of human language that would produce Resilient-Minded success, fulfillment and happiness, I found a mirror image of fifteen categories to help quickly identify the language and emotions of every voice in the world. For ease of use, I created two lists so that I could quickly assess a fear and scarcity mentality and a love and abundance mentality. I call them the Evil List and Good List.

The Evil List is the playbook of fear and scarcity. It comprises fifteen categories that we should red flag and shut down, along with any negative emotions they evoke, and do so immediately inside our airspace. Let's break them down:

EVIL LIST

ANXIETY/DISTRESS - The feeling of worry or anxiety about an event or events (this is the most preferred destructive thought category, favored by billions everywhere)

ADVERSITY- The feeling of hardship and the thought that anything opposing you is detrimental rather than a challenge to be overcome

AFFLICTION – The feeling of being distressed with continued suffering

CALAMITY – The feeling that certain events cause great suffering or disaster

DISPLEASURE – The feeling of being annoyed, confused, or outraged

CONTINUAL GRIEF – The chronic feeling of intense sorrow, tribulation, or unrelenting regret

HARM – The feeling of injury or loss

HEAVINESS – The feeling of despondency or depression

HURT – The feeling or fear of being pained or wounded

ILL FAVOR – The feeling or fear of being disliked

MISERY – The feeling of suffering, especially because of poverty or lack

SELF-PITY – The destructive feeling of being sorry for oneself

SORROW – The feeling of distress and pain because of loss

TROUBLE – The feeling or fear of difficulty, unrest, or agitation

WRONG – The feeling of injustice, anything not working properly

Once proficient at clearly, consistently, and quickly recognizing the thoughts on this list, action must be taken to trace back to the source and identify the voice(s) that are speaking the language on this list. I have a no-fly-zone for the voices that evoke the emotions on this list. Part two is to surround and fill your airspace with inoculants and to create an environment of love and abundance. To accomplish that in my life, I use the Good List.

GOOD LIST

BEAUTIFUL – attractive, exquisite, fair, handsome, lovely, or pretty

BOUNTIFUL – abundant, ample, plentiful, or substantial

BETTER – bigger, faster, or stronger

CHEERFUL/GLAD – light-hearted, willing

AT EASE – relaxed, unworried, or unembarrassed

WELL FAVORED – when other folks like you and treat you well

HAPPY WELFARE – health and prosperity

LOVING – expressing goodwill and affection

KIND/USEFUL – helpful

PLEASING/PLEASURE – delighted, fulfilled

SWEET – rich, productive, or possessing winning qualities

READY – available for immediate use

PROSPERITY/WEALTH – success, great abundance, or riches

PRECIOUS/HIGH VALUE – highly priced, of great worth, or excellence

FINEST/BEST – excellent, elegant, refined, or pure (like gold and silver)

Read, feed, listen to, watch, and fill your environment, climate, and airspace with voices whose language and emotion arouses and awakens these things inside you. This way is the easiest: controlling your media consumption by selecting carefully which voices you access via radio, TV, movies, books, magazines, newspapers, online sites, and especially social media. If Facebook, Twitter, Instagram, etc. are arousing emotions from the Evil List inside your environment, you must shut it down and unfollow or block anyone that brings the Evil List inside your family's doorstep. This goes for your child's social media feeds as well.

As part of our loving and abundant environment, our children didn't get cell phones or social media accounts until eighth grade at the earliest. And we consistently limit, monitor, and verify their usage and history. Achieving the environment that produces a Resilient Mindset requires parental commitment, consistency, and vigilance.

Pressures of Social Media

Kiley is about to make the transition from elementary school to middle school. Her mother, Jenn, is feeling apprehensive about Kiley's time in middle school. It was Jenn's most challenging time in all her years growing up. Adding to that apprehension is the all-out stress of the social media phenomenon. The constant bombardment of noise and images, the cyber-bullying and backstabbing, not to mention the predators. Or merely having Kiley unknowingly tagged into a group post, making it appear she is a party to something she is not.

These factors are all reasons that Kimmi and I kept our kids off social media platforms until 8th grade and why we now purposefully monitor their timelines, newsfeeds, who they are following, and who is following them. Taking the time to sit with your kids and view their feeds can be time-consuming, but in the long term teaching your child to spot and block predators will reduce your stress about the minefields these platforms are. This virtual life is an area of the environment that is entirely within the control of us parents.

Use the "Good List" and "Evil List" as guidelines when viewing various platforms. If what is coming across the screen evokes emotions of inferiority, jealousy, hurt, anger, apprehension, depression, agitation, etc., shut down those types of posts – both incoming and outgoing. Creating and maintaining an environment of happy welfare, peace, loving-kindness, and goodwill makes it much more relaxed and enjoyable to navigate parenthood. It is well worth dealing with the "push-back" you will initially receive from your child about a) not being allowed on social media until they are older, and b) having their newsfeeds and timelines monitored and viewed together.

Role Models

This practice goes beyond the environment; it extends to our associations and who we spend our time with. Remember that consciousness is contagious, and so are attitude and mindset. The late, great college basketball coach, John Wooden, said, "You will never outperform your inner circle; if you want to achieve at a higher level, always be improving your inner circle." Commit to upgrade your inner circle. Limit your exposure to neutral and negative people, and then fill that vacuum with constructive role models and mentors. When I was a young lance corporal in the Marine Corps, I would hang out with the senior corporals. Once I was promoted to corporal, I ran with the sergeants and staff sergeants. Once I made sergeant, I would hang around captains and majors.

Our daughter, Michaela, has her sights set on playing on the Duke University women's lacrosse team. She is obsessed with playing lacrosse. She works and trains every day. This past season, she was awarded the JV Offensive Player of the Year Award as an 8th grader. However, her entire lacrosse inner circle has been her local club and school team. These programs, while fantastic, have rarely produced any Division I players. For Michaela to reach the level of play required at Duke, she needed to be around players that were better than she was.

This isn't about dropping her current friends and teammates; it's about adding those influencers that will spur growth in her mindset and performance. Because of that, Kimmi and I have invested heavily in putting her into those circles by taking her to the Duke lacrosse matches and seeing the players. We signed her up for Duke lacrosse camps and took her to clinics put on by the top women's lacrosse players in the country. We encouraged her to follow and engage with constructive role models on social media. Her continued exposure to top-tiered players and coaches has begun to foster mentor/mentee relationships that will help guide Michaela down the path to her target.

I've followed this exact pattern my entire life, but I really started to up my game once I became a federal agent. I had the opportunity to be around the nation's political leaders, and because of those associations, I was able to be around heads of state; the top thinkers in the country; the top business minds; the top artists, storytellers, and musicians; and the top military minds and strategic thinkers. I was like a sponge soaking up as much as I possibly could. I did a lot of listening, spoke only when spoken to, and only offered my opinion when asked for it. Instead of one or two levels above my station, I launched to the highest levels of the economic, intellectual, political, and military fields. What I found astonishing was how many Average-Minded people with average lives were so destructively critical of those top performers. My family did this same thing when I was growing up. My parents and my siblings would lambast and deride anyone who was more successful. "Their success is a fluke. They're not any better than I am. Their family connections got them there. They caught a lucky break."

That reaction is not for us who aspire to be Resilient-Minded parents raising Resilient-Minded children. We choose constructive role models and mentors. We celebrate success and teach our children to do the same. I have continued that very practice of choosing constructive role models and mentors, never being a pest but quietly learning from any master Resilient-Minded role models that will let me into their inner circles to see behind the curtain. I've been privileged enough to protect personally some of the wealthiest families on the planet and hear what they really think (especially after a few glasses of wine). Those experiences were a more valuable education than my Ph.D.

Set your sights on the highest-level role models in your world, and make a commitment to upgrade your associations, beginning with your inner circle. Limit your exposure to neutral and negative people, remembering that consciousness is contagious. Seek out and make friends with some Resilient-Minded thinkers and spend as much time with them as possible. The by-product of hanging with the Resilient-Minded is that you will automatically raise your own level of expectation, confidence, and performance. Teaching your children to upgrade their inner circles and associations will do the same for them.

Attitude

The final part of the mindset upgrade process is to understand that your attitude is yours and yours alone. Back in 2001, I was assigned to provide personal security for Auschwitz survivor and Nobel Peace Prize winner, Elie Wiesel. It was during the Days of Remembrance ceremony at the U.S. Capitol. After the event, I escorted Mr. Wiesel to his limousine. He asked about me – did I have a family; what were the children's ages; etc. It was an amazing experience to be inside his space for that short period of time.

When we arrived at his car, he shook my hand, thanked me, and asked if there was anything he could do for me. Wow! I told him that there was one thing he could do; he could share with me how he made it through the Holocaust and yet was so kind and sincere, without a trace of bitterness.

"No prison, no tyrant, no war criminal, no dictator or persecutor can touch your attitude. They can destroy your body. But your attitude is yours, and that is what defines you." With that, he squeezed my hand and got into the limo, and my time inside his space was over. But the impression he made upon me will last a lifetime. Our attitude is our choice. It is the last bastion of freedom, a fortress that no human can breach, unless we open the gates from the inside.

Every situation doesn't call for a "positive" attitude; for example, in the midst of getting shot at, I have never found myself thinking "sunshine, waterfalls, and unicorns" about those doing the shooting. Use your intellectual power to choose your attitude wisely and deploy it strategically. But whatever you do, don't open the gates to your citadel and abdicate your choice to others or to outside circumstances; don't give anyone or anything that power over you.

Your attitude is your choice. You can choose to change it at any time. My wife and I have a friend who has coined what I call an "Attitude Upgrade Catch Phrase." She says, "Do it like a boss!" My entire family has taken up this mantra whenever we need an attitude upgrade to increase our level of performance.

A few years ago, Michaela, who was 9-years-old at the time, was at tumbling/gymnastics. She was having some performance issues, and her instructors were having a difficult time coaching her through them. During a break, she came over for some water, and my wife told her, "Just do it like a boss!" She went back to the floor, raised the level of her game, and started crushing it. The coaches weren't sure what sparked the change, but they went with it. As the practice session wrapped up, we asked our daughter what made the difference in her performance, and she said, "I just kept saying in my head, 'Do it like a boss!'"

If you find your focus blurring, your self-discipline getting a little loose, or your cutting edge getting dull, get back out there and do it like a boss!

WHAT TO DO:

1) Be vigilant! Remember that consciousness and mindset are contagious; your performance mindset and worldview will be passed on to your children, whether intentionally or not. If you operate from a baseline of fear and scarcity, so will you children.

2) Be intentional and deliberate in adopting the Resilient Mindset. Work from a mentality of love and abundance, espousing the mantra, "I'm the problem, and I'm the solution."

3) Commit! It takes commitment, consistency, and removing all excuses to set your environment and your inner circle to upgrade and maintain a Resilient Mindset.

4) Monitor and co-view social media platforms with your children and use the "Good List" and the "Evil List" as guidelines as to what emotions each post evokes. Then block the "Evil List" posts, protecting and upgrading your environment.

SECRET 4 – MOTIVATIONAL INTELLIGENCE

CHAPTER 8 – Approach or Avoid

Is your child a rule-follower or a rule-breaker? I have found that most rule-followers are the oldest, and the second child tends to be on the other end of the scale. My good friends, Doug and Beth, have two daughters, Ally, six years old and a rule-follower, and Molly, three years old and a rule breaker. Both girls are the sweetest, most loving kids, and so well-behaved that people like to be around them.

However, when it comes to things like brushing their teeth, with Ally, that chore was never a fuss. She just did it because brushing teeth was one of the rules. With Molly, no such luck. As she started to get teeth, she didn't much like having to clean them. And if her parents even mentioned consequences, she doubled-down in her refusal, assumed the duck-and-cover position on the floor, and clamped her mouth shut with no chance of a toothbrush getting near her teeth. Her dad came up with a way to get her to approach brushing her teeth instead of avoiding the task.

One of Molly's favorite animals is the tiger. One night, while getting ready for bed, after a day trip to the zoo and seeing the lions and tigers, Doug told Molly how the zookeepers had to brush the lions' and tigers' teeth. But before they did, they had to get them to smile (accidentally on purpose omitting the part about tranquilizing them first). As Doug and his daughter approached the bathroom for the dreaded brushing of the teeth, he asked her, "Molly, are you a lion or a tiger?"

"I'm a tiger, Daddy!"

"Oh good," he said. "Can I hear your tiger roar, little tiger?" Her face lit up, and she proudly let out a very impressive roar for such a little thing.

"You like my roar, Daddy?" she asked.

"Yes! You have a great roar, Molly. Very impressive!" he said, clapping. Molly's smile beamed from ear to ear.

"Hey, Molly, can I see your tiger teeth?" She of course obliged by displaying them proudly.

"Daddy, you like my tiger teeth?" she asked.

"Yes, Molly. You have great tiger teeth. But they look a little dirty. Can we clean them?" he asked, waiting for her reply, determined not to talk first. Those few seconds seemed like an eternity to Doug. And then, still smiling, Molly nodded in approval, and her teeth were brushed. As time went on, there were a few struggles with the task, but those were quickly overcome with mom or dad saying, "Hey, Molly, show me your tiger teeth!"

One of the great stressors of parenthood is motivating your child to approach those things that nurture growth and development, instead of avoiding those things. For some, it is the stress of daily oral hygiene on toddlers. For others, it is eating vegetables and healthful foods. For others, it is reading or physical activities, and on and on. It is incredible how those stressors are reduced simply by understanding how to motivate your child. I call it Motivational Intelligence.

Logic vs. Emotion (Part 2)

Reasoning with a three-year-old about oral hygiene and the costs and consequences of cavities is not an effective motivator. Not only did Molly not care about the logic behind brushing one's teeth, but she also couldn't grasp the concepts of costs and cavities yet. Parents who attempt to use logic in moving their children to become approachers instead of avoiders are setting themselves up for failure, a fight, and an increase in stress. Doug tapped into Molly's emotions. Emotions that made her feel powerful and in control and therefore allowed her to have her teeth brushed, just like mighty tigers.

Logic is great for steering but makes a horrible engine. If you don't know what you are willing to fight for and why, the chances are incredibly high that you will quit fighting when things get tough. Molly was ready to fight for having power and control over herself. She would not quit. No matter how steep the consequences, she just didn't care. As a toddler, she was tapped into an emotional driver that went well beyond her capacity to comprehend the concept. No amount of logic was going to change her attitude. Logic lacks the power to motivate the human to act.

However, emotion can. The shared Latin root word of emotion and motivation is "movere" (to move). As a Mental Toughness Coach, my primary function is to assist clients in identifying their emotional driver and

164

then remind them of it when the going gets rough. If you use logic as your organic motivation, as most amateurs do, you will quit at the first sign of discomfort and never stay in the fight long enough to overcome even the smallest adversity. When the going gets tough, logic, facts and statistical analysis always tell you to cut your losses. As parents, once we realize this fact, we can begin to "movere" (move) our children to become approachers instead of avoiders.

Understanding the importance of *why* you're doing something is the beginning of Motivational Intelligence. Motivational Intelligence is the capacity to be aware of, tap into, control, and deploy one's motivational drivers to complete an objective, regardless of the obstacles, adversity, or pain. As parents, having high motivational intelligence is vital just for our own sakes in navigating the never-ending stressors of running the household, paying the bills, and dealing with the junk at work, not to mention all the stressors added once you have a child or children. And for the sake of our children, as we learn how to motivate them to want to enjoy success, be fulfilled, and have a happy life.

Bull Riding

I love to watch bull-riding competitions. The cowboy must stay on the wildly bucking bull for eight seconds before the judges score the ride. Most times, the rider gets tossed off the bull before eight seconds, and he often gets trampled by the bull. The trampled bull rider will lie there on the arena floor, in pain and hurt, until Toro the Bull comes around for a second pass. Instantly, the cowboy is healed; he runs across the arena, hops the side wall, collapses into a gurney, and spends the next six months in a body cast. Why did he get up and run to the side? He got up because he feared more pain. The motivation to avoid more pain overrode his current pain.

Humans tend to view a loss to be twice as powerful a motivational factor as a gain. Most of us take great measures to avoid pain and loss. But very few of us tend to take great risks when it comes to pleasure. Most of us are inclined to get up and move to a better place only when we fear that an imminent loss or the current pain reaches unbearable levels.

I informally survey every person I meet and make a tick mark in the Avoid column or Approach column. Over the years, our in-house research shows that well over ninety-five percent of people are in the Avoid column. I don't even have to ask them a question; I just listen to their self-talk about whether they like their job or dislike their job. Whether they like their life or dislike their life. Or more to the point, are they complainers? You locate yourself when you complain. Complainers are avoiders. Approachers will simply go to a better place, a better situation, or they will change their attitude about the situation. Complainers are dissatisfied but will not move off their current spot until the fear of dreadful loss or intolerable pain rises to the level that action must be taken to avoid the impending loss or pain.

As parents, after knowing how to motivate ourselves, one of our biggest challenges is knowing how to motivate our children effectively. And if you have more than one child, like my wife and I do, you know that each child is vastly different in style, approach, personality, and motivational drivers. It's important to assess whether your child is more apt to avoid loss and pain or apt to approach pleasure. Drew and Michaela, like Doug and Beth's daughter, Ally, are both avoiders. Though they were initially easier to motivate, because it's easy to use fear as a motivational driver, they avoid any loss of privileges and avoid the pain they would feel if they disappointed their teachers, coaches, and even their parents. Jack, like Molly, is an approacher. Though he was initially more challenging to motivate, because using fear as a motivational driver had zero effect, he couldn't care less about losing privileges, nor does he care if he suffers pain. He is motivated by the proverbial carrot, and only the carrot. If you use the proverbial stick, he completely shuts down. Realizing these variances has made a world of difference in how we approach, motivate, and deal with each individual child.

The problem with using fear as the motivational driver is that it wears off quickly, and in the long term, it ultimately fails to propel us through adversity, hardship, and seemingly insurmountable obstacles. Once you experience a loss, you no longer fear it. It has already happened, and the leverage of fear no longer holds sway. The reason many managers, coaches, teachers, and parents use fear as a motivational driver is two-fold: 1) It works on most of us, 2) It requires little creativity, inspiration, or cognitive energy or effort (it's the path of least resistance).

Our challenge as parents is to transform our children from avoiders into approachers, as moving toward a target is always more conducive to success, fulfillment, and happiness than sitting still until things become unbearable. Keep reading, as the process of going from avoider (complainer) to approacher will be covered in detail in subsequent chapters.

Will vs. Fear

When Jack was about three years old, he came into the living room and asked his mother and me, "Can I have some gum?"

We answered, "No."

Again, "Can I have some gum?"

"No."

"Can I have some gum?"

"No."

He proceeded to get some gum. He didn't care what the consequences might or might not be. To this day, he demonstrates an ironclad will. If he wants to do something, he just does it. If he doesn't want to do something, he doesn't do it, no matter what. He has no fear of fallout or consequences once he has made up his mind. Our challenge is to teach him to point his will in the right direction, towards the most productive and profitable behaviors.

Making up your mind, being determined, utilizing the mental toughness tool by which you deliberately choose or decide upon a course of action – call it whatever name you want to – it all boils down to the human will. Rosa Parks once said, "I have learned over the years that when one's mind is made up, this diminishes fear; knowing what must be done does away with fear." It has been my observation that weak-willed people, Avoiders, usually are living in fear.

The determined among us usually seem to rise to the top and take the lion's share, or at least get what they want. Ask yourself, "Do I have any fire in my belly?" If it's a no, you will most likely be paralyzed by fear, continually waiting for the other shoe to drop. If you, as a parent, don't have any determination, how will you be able to teach your child to tap into and deploy an approacher-based motivational driver?

Where There's a Will, There's a Way

There many reasons why we do things, why we strive for success, fulfillment, and happiness. There are various motivational theories and models presented in the world of psychology; however, in our extensive work at the Mental Toughness Training Center, we have taken notice of what seem to be the five top motivational drivers. In order of recurrence, they are: 1) Children/Loved Ones/Family, 2) Spiritual/Religious Beliefs, 3) Self-Validation and the desire to prove oneself to oneself, 4) Desire to prove oneself to others, 5) Appreciation/Recognition/Credit.

Congratulations! As a parent, you have a built-in, internal, organic driver. This makes so much easier the task of crossing the threshold from a fear and avoidance-based driver to a determined, approach-based driver, which will yield much greater results. Once you identify and tap into an internal, organic driver, you can much more easily make the decision never to give up, never give in, and to give maximum effort, holding nothing back. Remember the burning house example. Without hesitation, without questions, we don't question a parent who goes into the inferno regardless of the odds because of the internal organic driver of our love for our children.

What if the situation was a little different? You came home from work to find your house engulfed in flames, and there was an antique buffet that belonged to your great-grandmother where you stashed some cash. Same odds as before, a one in a million chance of getting the cash from the buffet. Do you sit on the curb or risk everything and run into the inferno? Of course, you sit on the curb. No sane person would risk everything for a fistful of dollars. Will and determination are inherent in every human being; you just have to locate them and unlock them with the right motivational driver. Once you find your internal, organic driver, once you activate your nature-bending will and determination, every battle is nearly won at the outset.

I remember the first time my oldest son, Drew, crossed the threshold and activated his nature-bending will. I unashamedly had tears of pride and joy streaming down my cheeks. It was a prolific moment, both for the young man who stepped across it and for me.

We were attending a high school wrestling tournament that was stocked with the best teams in the state, teams filled with competitors that would be competing at the collegiate level within a few months. I watched my son, a rookie competitor, go up against the opposing team's captain. The communal expectation was a quick pinning of the rookie.

Drew was in a position of disadvantage almost immediately after the whistle blew to start the contest. He was on his back the entire eternity of those six minutes, but he made the decision not to give up, not to give in. He literally left every ounce of his strength and energy on the mat. He refused to be pinned.

His opponent, who was expecting swift victory, became increasingly frustrated that he couldn't finish the interloper beneath him. The boy could barely stand to his feet when the buzzer sounded. He could scarcely breathe because his windpipe had been flattened out from being in a headlock for the last forty-five seconds of the match (the same hold used by the captain that had choked three other opponents into unconsciousness that day). Being pinned would mean giving up six points instead of three. Drew lost on points but was not pinned, and in the end, his team won the overall match by two points. He lost the battle, and his team won the war.

Drew walked onto the mat an inexperienced rookie and walked off the mat a man and a warrior. Let's flash back to the internal identity statement. Drew had created his own identity statement of who he was and who he aspired to be. I listed his identity statement with the examples in chapter five and repeat it here: "I am a man of greatness who never gives up." Part of Drew's internal identity is that he never gives up. Drawing on his internal identity and his organic driver of proving himself to himself, he dug deep inside. He dug as deeply as any professional warrior I have ever served with, displaying toughness and fortitude beyond his years.

Success in any area of life is now his for the taking. If you don't know what you are willing to fight for and why, you will quit fighting when it gets tough and the discomfort levels turn into pain. If you use avoiding loss and pain as your organic motivation, as most Average-Minded people do, you will quit at the first sign of discomfort and never stay in the fight long enough to overcome adversity.

Emotional Manual Override

All parents of newborn infants know that they can override the desire to stay in bed at 2:45 AM when the baby is colicky. As parents, that is just the beginning of overriding our wants to take care of our child's needs. Vince Lombardi, the legendary Green Bay Packers football coach, said, "I have never known a really successful man who deep in his heart did not understand the grind, the discipline it takes to win."

Until we find and tap into our internal, organic, motivational driver, the will to sustain determined effort can wear off rather quickly. Research has revealed that willpower or self-discipline is like a muscle, in that it can be strengthened and made more enduring. When I first joined the Marine Corps, I was fifty pounds overweight and hated running. It would take twenty minutes for the fat on my legs to stop jiggling after a three-mile platoon run. This condition was not helpful for a successful career in the Marine Corps infantry. After struggling for a year, dreading the morning platoon runs and the weekly company and battalion run, I decided to make running my friend.

I started saying, "I love running, and I love what running does for me. I'm an ultra-marathoner. I love to grind it out, day in and day out." I started running on my own every night. My body would talk to me and say stuff like, "We're exhausted; let's skip the five miles tonight." Oh, so tempting to blow it off.

I would answer my body, out loud (after making sure no one could hear me), "Fine, then we're running ten miles tonight, and every time you try to tempt me out of a run, we are going to double the mileage." And then I ran the ten miles. Guess what? My body stopped whining real fast.

Soon, the morning platoon runs weren't that bad. Within ninety days of grinding it out and being disciplined to run on my own, the morning runs got to be fun. Success in the morning run carried over into success in every other area of my life because I learned to love the grind and love self-discipline. Manually overriding my emotions (***doing*** what I didn't ***feel*** like doing) produced results for me back in 1986, and it has been producing ever since.

Learn to love the grind. Do it for yourself and for your children. The way to love the grind is to have a purpose that is big enough to keep your feet to the fire, especially when you don't feel like it. I ran on my own because my purpose was big enough to get me on the road even when I was exhausted. I was out to prove myself to myself, that I could become more than the crybaby fat kid nicknamed "Beach Ball." Keep on striving to be a Resilient-Minded parent. Your purpose, love of your children, is indeed big enough to continue even when you are exhausted.

Intensity

Back at that same high school wrestling tournament, with over twenty teams competing, my professional curiosity as a Mental Toughness Coach took over. I found myself observing the coaches of the various teams. I watched them all over the course of the event, but I immediately picked out two coaches whose intensity was unmatched by the other coaches. Guess what? Those two teams finished first and second in the overall tournament.

These top two coaches weren't out of control, ranting after a loss or arguing with the refs. They were dialed in tight to every one of their athletes' matches. While most other coaches were standing with their arms crossed, discussing how many points were needed to win the match and calculating the final tournament standings, these guys were completely and utterly concentrating on each individual team member's performance, coaching every second of every match.

Intensity isn't rage; it isn't going berserk. It is laser-focused energy, a channeling of fervency, speed, and earnestness. To illustrate the importance of intensity, I recall the first time that a perpetrator tried to take my gun from me while I was answering a domestic violence call as a police officer. The second you realize, *This guy is trying to kill me,* is the second you become laser-focused; your training kicks in; and you go to work, knowing that failure is not an option and that there will be no rematch, no next time. In this situation, remaining laid back, looking cool, or being anything other than the one who is going to win means that this is the day your life is over. When the stakes are that high, it is much easier to operate with intensity, no question about it. But what if you applied the principle of intensity to becoming a Resilient-Minded parent? You can get good, and even great, at anything if you operate with sustained intensity.

Passion

Being passionate is the root cause of intensity. If you are not passionate about something, you will not sustain the intensity needed to be great long enough to get there.

You must do an honest assessment, dig deep, and find the thing that stokes the furnace of passion within you. When you find that thing, throw fuel on the fire and let it consume your entire being. Or just do what most folks do: tamp it down and self-medicate with food, alcohol, TV, movies, video games, social media, or whatever else is the "drug" of choice for the mediocre.

Most folks seem to be afraid to be passionate about anything, let alone *the thing*. They are afraid that the fire within may burn only hot enough to frustrate; so the unexceptional among us keep the flame as low as possible. Others may opt to redirect the flame onto something safe, never risking their own dreams for fear of disappointment. They are content to be passionate about the performance of others (college teams, professional athletes, contestants on talent shows, political figures, celebrities, etc.), while they sit on the sidelines, elated by a victory earned by others and disappointed at a loss, yet all of it comfortably vicarious. Remember, children learn by imitation.

It all starts with passion; without it, human beings never make the required sacrifices, endure the suffering, or continue through the struggles with the tireless exertions necessary to achieve *the thing*. The genesis of being Resilient Minded is this: passion drives intensity. Passion and sustained intensity are the vehicles which will take us to our potential.

Purpose

Passion and sustained intensity may be the vehicles that will get us to our potential, but they are of little value if we have no planned target destination. No matter how passionate and intense you are about something, be it sports, business, finance, engineering, cooking, sculpting,

176

painting, history, politics, bartending, writing, gardening, teaching, or you-name-it, if you have no planned target destination, you have no purpose. Without a clearly defined purpose, you will falter in your passion and intensity.

This happens to most adults and most parents. When we are young, we are idealistic and have dreams, things that provoke us to feel passion and intensity. However, without a clearly defined purpose, those ideas and dreams begin to wither over time as they are not realized. Eventually, though most people don't know when it happened, they became afraid to be passionate about *the thing*. The fire of their youth, without purpose, burned only hot enough to frustrate them. Ultimately, they succumbed to the "realities" of life and began to keep the flame as low as possible. Having felt early on in life the pain of disappointment, they chose to redirect the flame onto something "safe," fearing to feel that pain ever again, like touching a hot stove. Having learned the hard way, they are content to be passionate about the performance of others sitting on the sidelines, elated by a victory earned by others and disappointed at a loss, yet all of it comfortably secondhand.

I have little tolerance for the parents who live vicariously through their children, forcing them to take the risks and do the work and placing them under enormous pressure to perform. And heaven help the children if they don't measure up! They don't know that in so doing, they allow the pain of secondhand disappointment touch the parent. To bypass this sand trap, Resilient-Minded parents discover and adopt a clearly defined purpose and target of their own and teach their children to do the same. Do we want to doom our children to repeat the same process that hurt us?

One of the biggest hurdles my clients have is clearly defining their purpose in life. Watch the movie *The Wizard of Oz*. When you do, keep in mind this perspective: all the main characters were individually passionate and intense about *their thing*. For Dorothy, her approach-based motivational driver was to go home to her family. For the Scarecrow, he wanted a brain, to be a thinker. The Tin Man wanted a heart, to feel and be human. The Lion wanted courage, to stop living life in fear and anxiety (my own internal organic driver that led me to Parris Island Marine Corps Recruit Depot). Yet, for each of them, their passion and intensity only caused frustration and the fear of the pain of disappointment.

Dorothy did the initial hard work when she faced the seemingly impossible task of going back to the black and white world of 1930s Kansas farmland. Yes, it looked impossible; she wasn't arguing that. But if it were possible, she asked herself and the Munchkins, how would she go about getting home? A musical brainstorming session and a friendly witch later, a solution presented itself. A plan was hatched, and off Dorothy went, following the yellow brick road. As she followed her purpose, she helped the others, each seeking their own individual purpose. Only when they had a clearly defined target destination of the Emerald City did things change. They suddenly had a plan to achieve their purpose. And that purpose plus a clearly defined target caused them to move forward, overcome adversity and hardship, and even escape death to arrive at the Emerald City.

Deep down, humans know what they are passionate about, even if they don't want to allow it to enter their conscious minds for action. To unlock your dormant passion and corresponding intensity, ask yourself, "What and where is my Emerald City?" Envision an ultimate target destination. At the same time, walk your children down this same path. Sit with them while watching the movie, and use it as a vehicle to discuss discovering their own *Emerald City*.

Keep the process deliberately slow and unpressured, and allow your child to explore freely many different *Emerald Cities* before settling on a destination. Allow them to engage several different sports, musical instruments, art, dance, or drama, on a trial basis. Allow them the room to discover which academic subjects they enjoy and which ones fall into the not-so-much column. As they grow and enter the middle school and high school years, the kaleidoscope of dreams, plans, and pursuits will begin to clear and focus. Never belittle or shut down one of their dreams. If you find yourself doing so, check the Mindset Mirror in chapter seven. Naysaying dreams and aspirations is not being Resilient Minded.

WHAT TO DO:

1) Follow Doug's example of Molly and the tiger, using the emotions of being powerful and in control to motivate your child to approach

instead of avoiding those things that nurture growth and development.

2) Take the time and energy to tap into emotions other than fear as a motivator for your child.

3) Watch *The Wizard of Oz*, begin the process and dialogue of helping your children discover their dreams and purpose in life, and allow them to explore freely many options in creating their own *Emerald City*.

CHAPTER 9 – The Ultimate Target

When Drew, my oldest, was about to graduate high school, people would ask him what he was planning to do after graduation. Interestingly, I observed that people asked this of every high school senior. I began taking notes of these interchanges. I noticed that Drew's response was unlike almost every one of his peers, and the adults with which Drew interacted seemed taken aback and even a little shell-shocked.

Most of the graduating seniors could say with clarity if they were either enlisting in the military or attending college, and if so, which college. Many even had a declared major. Almost none could envision what came after that. They had no target other than to graduate college and obtain a degree. Others who had a declared field of study still had no idea what came after completing their baccalaureate. The usual response was to find a job. Popular fields of study included business administration, sports management, exercise science, marketing, finance, and engineering.

My son was crystal clear. His chosen field was mechanical engineering, and adults would respond, "Oh, you mean pre-business?" The conventional wisdom was that most students entered the field of mechanical engineering, discovered the enormous amount of time, energy, and work they would have to put forth, and by the second semester changed their major to business administration.

The reason for this pattern is that Plan B quickly becomes Plan A as soon as things become difficult. These students do not have an ultimate target. The hallmark of Average-Minded people is that they have no clarity of what they want. They only know what they don't want – they don't want to be uncomfortable and be vulnerable. All those Science, Technology, Engineering, and Medical degree programs are difficult and risky, and they come with a high rate of failure. The student must work and grind and sweat.

The most common response I recorded from high school seniors was that they didn't know much of anything beyond what college or university they were attending. The most common response to this statement that I recorded from these kid's parents was, "That's okay. I didn't know what I wanted to do at your age, and I turned out okay." This assurance caused me to shake my head in bewilderment. If you spent any time at all with the parents responding in this fashion, you would hear nothing but complaints about their job, their spouse, their neighbors, the economy, and the world in general. Why on earth would you a) think that's turning out okay, and b) want the next generation of kids to have just an okay life, just like yours, filled with complaints?

After building fantastic memories and guiding your children to discover and adopt an internal identity, the next most important thing for a parent is to help your children envision their ultimate target for life. Most people have no personal ultimate target, vision, or purpose. Worse still, most people are starkly afraid to think about what their lives or their children's lives will look like in five years, ten years, or twenty years, especially if they continue doing what they are currently doing, putting out fires and putting Band-Aids on bullet holes.

However, almost all of the parents I have contact with have no ultimate target for their own lives. They adopt a purpose of taking care of the children, which is fantastic until the children become adults. This is a major reason why parents have a forty-year-old still living in the house not paying rent and with no job. The parents don't want the children to stop depending on them. When that happens, the parents no longer have a purpose.

Once people have kids, discovering their own life's purpose by setting and pursuing an ultimate target becomes an extravagance. I don't agree with that line of thinking; however, do not allow the fact that you feel it's too late for you to pursue an ultimate target keep from you from helping your children discover and set their own. I realize that for you it may be too big a hurdle to discover and pursue your dream, as doing so often requires a massive risk like a transition onto a different career path without the guarantee of a matching income. The Resilient-Minded parent does everything she or he can to pave the way for success, fulfillment, and happiness for their children, and the sooner your children discover their life's purpose and set their ultimate target, the better chance they have of obtaining those things. But just in case you are one of the rare birds that want to find your own success, fulfillment, and happiness, not just relegate those things to your children – buckle up!

Bet on Yourself

Farrah Gray, who became a self-made millionaire by the ripe old age of fifteen, said, "Build your own dreams, or someone else will hire you to build theirs." I spent decades building someone else's dreams, simply because I didn't believe I could build my own. I have a work ethic that is off the charts. But I don't even want to begin to tell you how many years of my life; how much of my mental, emotional, and physical energy and focus; and how many hours of my diligence have been spent on making other people rich and building someone else's dreams.

I settled for what life handed me and tried to make lemonade out of lemons. Adding sugar to sweeten something sour only masks what's sour. No matter how many spoonsful of sugar I added to the mix, the base was still sour lemons. I had to dump the pitcher and go pick some sweeter fruit. I had to change my belief that *I just couldn't accomplish my dream because I had responsibilities*. I had a wife and kids to support; bills to pay; and food, shelter, and clothes to provide. Oh yeah, and I needed those all-important healthcare benefits that come with a good job.

But the real reason I stayed small was that I didn't believe enough in myself to take the risk of flying without a parachute, to risk walking the high wire without a harness and safety net. I wouldn't bet on myself because I wasn't sure what my purpose was. And without knowing my purpose, how could I succeed at doing something I couldn't define? So I settled for no risk, and I substituted making someone else's purpose a reality instead of discovering my own. These people weren't any smarter than I was, no more talented, and no more disciplined. The only difference was ... they had a purpose, an ultimate target, and they bet on themselves to pursue it.

I realized that not betting on myself was the same as betting against myself. I was robbing my wife and kids of a great future and a great life. Once I had this realization, I went to work on changing my belief about myself. It was scary. On many days, it still is. But it's the most exciting and exhilarating experience of my life.

Once you start betting on yourself, you start to win, because losing isn't an option. Once you start winning, you can never go back to betting against yourself, ever! Bet on yourself, and go to work building your own dream! However, you must have a dream first.

The Emerald City

Before we start to set the target, we must be brave enough to see in our mind's eye what our lives will look like in five years, ten years, and twenty years, if we stay on our current track. Think about everything you want your life to be, if it were possible. Don't think about why it can't happen or that it'll never happen. Think only about what you would want your life to be if nothing was impossible. It might not be probable, but it is possible. Take what is probable off the table for this exercise in setting an ultimate target for yourself. This is the very first step toward having a great life in five years, ten years, and twenty years. What does your house look like that you are living in? What is your quality of life? Do you enjoy freedom from reporting to a difficult boss? What kinds of adventures do you and your adult children go on with your grandchildren?

Write a letter to your kids or grandkids about your life and what it looks like ten years into the future, but write it in the past tense. Be sure to tell as much detail as possible, like how great your back patio is with a hot tub, and what it feels like to be with your family and friends and not be stressed about anything. What places did you travel to as a family? What memories did you all build? What does your career look like? How high up the corporate ladder did you climb? Or did you venture out on your own and start a business? What did you give your child as a gift for graduating college?

Envision your own *Emerald City*. Having a great and happy life, chock full of success and fulfillment, is available to each of us in the free world. The truth is that the clear majority of us squander the opportunities that cross our paths because we can't imagine that they will work out. We can't *imagine*.

Very few people, and even fewer parents, have ever taken the time to imagine a great and happy life and then write down what that looks like. Who has the time or energy for that? Work, laundry, cooking, cleaning, making the kids' lunches, dishes in the sink, more laundry, shuttling kids around town from sports to music lessons, school, youth group, and back again, more laundry, the bathrooms need cleaning and the floors vacuumed and mopped, the dusting hasn't been done in weeks, and now the grass needs to be cut and fresh mulch spread in the flower beds, more laundry, more shuttling. I'm stressed out just writing the list. What parent has the time or energy?

Yet, without any idea of what you want your life to look like, you end up with Forrest Gump's Mama's version of life: a box of chocolates. You get whatever fudge they packed in the box at the candy factory.

What is lacking is the willpower, not the time. Time is the great equalizer. Every single living creature on planet Earth has twenty-four hours every day. Whether you are the President of the United States or an eight-year girl living in the Philippines, you have exactly twenty-four hours each day. How you spend it, use it, waste it, or invest it is completely up to you and dictates your results. Can you honestly say you are busier than the President of the United States?

Mindset Reminder

As you imagine your personal *Emerald City*, it is worthy to note that the mindset we have carried with us since our own childhood could possibly hold back the wonders that could make up that city on a hill. Remember, the mindsets are the Defeated (I've lost before I even start), Survival-Minded (I do just enough to have just enough), Average-Minded (I don't want to be rich, just comfortable), the Tyrant (I'm looking out for number one), and Resilient-Minded (I'm the problem, and I'm the solution).

The first time I remember becoming aware that my mindset, programming, and self-limiting beliefs may be hindering the creation of my ultimate target, I was in Honduras. It was early 1990, and I was deployed to perform a counter-terrorist operation. As we were moving from the airfield to our bivouac area, I noticed a remarkable hilltop estate, completely walled and gated. It was adorned with a huge satellite dish. I asked our translator who owned the lavish villa, thinking it was surely a plantation owner, corporate bigwig, or celebrity.

"Huh, that house up there? That's the house of a retired U.S. Navy chief."

"What?"

The mansion and estate were owned by a retired E-7, the same pay-grade as a Marine Corps gunnery sergeant? Full retirement benefits for a gunny, at that time, totaled right at two thousand dollars a month. What is not big, an annual income of twenty-four thousand dollars, was enormous wealth in Honduras. That chief had figured it out, and he was not the first. I ran into several hundreds of those guys in the Philippines. They found a way to make their own *Emerald Cities* a reality.

On the other side of the coin, during the time I was personally protecting one of the richest families in the world, I was assigned to the security detail of the wife (code named "The Missus") during a shopping trip to Manhattan. Ralph Lauren, Prada, Bottega Veneta, and Louis Vuitton were just a few stops on the tour of seemingly endless luxury boutiques.

Places that seemed more like art museums than shops, where the retail clerks wore white cotton gloves to handle the merchandise, gingerly presenting rare and precious items from the display case or off the shelf.

After hours of careful study, inspection, and comparison in more than a dozen such shops, The Missus had finally arrived at a decision on the purchase of a handbag. It was ostrich skin. During checkout, she looked over at me and said, "You know, Andrew, that's probably somebody's mortgage payment."

Let's do a mindset reality check. The price of the handbag is on par with somebody's mortgage payment. How much did the handbag cost?

The purchase price of the ostrich skin handbag was thirty thousand dollars. Yes, you read that right, thirty grand. What figure were you estimating? For many, thirty thousand dollars will buy a decent car. In the circle The Missus travels in, it was the mortgage payment. For her, it was a few hundred dollars.

It's all relative. The business empire built by her husband produces over a thousand dollars every second of every day, and it doesn't take any days off. If anyone in that family drops a hundred-dollar bill on the ground, it would cost them more money to pick it up than to walk off and leave.

Does that reality shock you? Bother you? Did you find yourself saying, "I would never spend that much on a handbag"?

Did the Navy chief's story shock you? Bother you? Here's the thing; the local Hondurans were thinking about the chief's house the same way you were just thinking about The Missus and her handbag.

Most of the entire planet lives on less than two dollars a day; they would most likely be shocked and bothered by your purchases and lifestyle as well. I choose to aspire to be able to buy my wife such a purse instead of decrying the extravagance of it. I know that my two cars and my 3000 square foot house with two flat-screen TVs and indoor plumbing is an extravagance to most of the population of Earth. Keep this relativity in mind while imagining your ultimate target. Get crystal clear on what it is you *do* want. Stop casting aspersions on what those you view as better off than you have, and focus that energy and effort on writing out what you want out of life. However, setting the ultimate target is not enough; you must execute a plan. You must take specific actions to get you there.

Goal Setting Is a Waste of Time

You read that right. Setting goals without an ultimate target, a destination, an *Emerald City,* is a complete waste of time. People are shocked when they hear me say this. Imagine you are going on a family vacation but have no destination. How do you pack? What do you take? You either pack everything or take nothing and buy stuff as you go. This kind of winging it may be a fun adventure, but it is no way to live life.

We have no destination for our trip, no clearly defined target, but we know that conventional wisdom (Average-Mindedness), tells us we

190

should be setting goals. So because we are success-driven parents, we set family goals of getting the best surfboards, skis, fishing rods, and hunting rifles money can buy. We have limited financial resources; so we embark on an extensive *Consumer Reports*-type investigation and bargain hunt. After months of research, searching eBay and Craigslist, we finally negotiate reasonable prices on used equipment in excellent shape from other goal setters. Congratulations! After many hours of effort and hard work, you achieve your goals! Where do we end up going for our trip? Hiking on the Appalachian Trail, we need boots and backpacks.

Now imagine that for our upcoming family vacation, we have the clearly defined target destination of going to Rome, Italy within the next two weeks. What do we need to do? We must get airline tickets, passports, visas, and hotel reservations, and we need to plan what to see and where to eat. We need ground transportation, and we need to pack clothes and toiletries.

When you set a clearly defined target, all the goals self-populate. You don't need to waste time, energy, effort, or money on goals that don't take you closer to your target. You don't need to wonder what goals should be set. Having an Ultimate Target takes care of those decisions for you.

Most Average-Minded parents spend a lifetime of setting goals without a target first, hoping that achieving those goals will take them somewhere that is good but not really knowing where. And those same parents teach their children to follow that way of life. The cycle recurs generation after generation unless someone stops it.

Three-Hundred-Year Plan

I personally have an Ultimate Target that is mind-boggling in scope. In fact, I rarely tell people what it is because they laugh uncomfortably, fearing they are standing in the presence of an insane person. My *Emerald City* is so outlandish that the self-populating goals will require three hundred years to complete. My clearly defined and written Ultimate Target is accompanied by a three-hundred-year completion plan. Most people point out that I won't be around on the planet long enough to complete it and assume how foolish or naïve or ill-informed I am for even entertaining such an idea.

Please allow me to ask you this question: how is it that Paris Hilton can do whatever it is she does? Jet-setting. Parties. Lavish travel. Extravagant clothes, shoes, and accessories. Do you know why Paris Hilton can live such a life? Because her great-grandparents had a three-hundred-year plan.

Have you ever heard of Anderson Cooper, the CNN news anchor? He's a member of the Vanderbilt family. He doesn't need to work; he does his job because he loves it. Why? Because his great-great-great-grandfather had a three-hundred-year plan. I'm kind of mad at my great-great-great-great-grandparents for not coming up with a three-hundred-year plan. My great-great-grandchildren will not have this problem. Will yours?

I began to share my target and corresponding plan with my children in 2007, when Drew, my oldest, was ten years old. He could barely get his head around it. With Jack being seven and Michaela only four when they were first exposed to it, they can't remember a time when there was not a plan in place. I didn't force my children to adopt my target and plan, but instead I taught them the process of discovering and building their own targets and plans. And they have. My children were taught clarity from the get-go. They've spent their short lives setting, focusing, and dialing in on what they *do* want in life. Cultivating this clarity is how Resilient-Minded parents raise their children.

The Process

Drew, being the eldest, grasped the process and began creating his target and plan before the others. He began to clarify and refine his *Emerald City* in the sixth grade. He drew his inspiration from comic book figures, specifically the alter-egos of Batman and Iron Man. If you don't know, those alter-egos are Bruce Wayne, billionaire and critical thinking detective, and Tony Stark, billionaire and inventor and builder of technological wonders. Drew realized early on that being a billionaire gave you options to pursue stuff like crime fighting.

Kim and I bought him a composition notebook, and he began to write out his ideas, a stream of consciousness with never a thought of what

193

was impossible or improbable. He filled page after page with what he wanted his life to look like. He wanted to start and run his own defense contracting firm, inventing and building advanced technological wonders like the exoskeleton suit of Iron Man's, which is currently becoming a reality at places like Georgia Institute of Technology.

My wife and I encouraged Drew, and he continued to flesh out his vision. Sometime during the school year, some self-populated goals began to emerge. One caught me off guard. At the wise old age of twelve, Drew announced that he would be going to The Citadel, The Military College of South Carolina. Kimmi and I looked at each other and said to him, "That's great, honey. Are you sure?" (And amongst ourselves we said, "We'll see.") He said he was sure, that while he didn't want to go on active duty, he needed the military background he would get at The Citadel. He would also need the network of connections he could make there if his business was to flourish in the world of military contracts.

He continued to write in his composition notebook. He decided he needed to be a mechanical engineering major. One hurdle was that The Citadel didn't offer mechanical engineering at the time. Then, in his junior year in high school, with Boeing having moved to Charleston, S.C. and needing mechanical engineers, the state legislature endowed The Citadel with an infusion of funds to establish a mechanical engineering program. Drew never applied anywhere else; he got in and flourished.

Jack, my younger son, found the inspiration for his target and plan in my career and adventures. He, too, has only applied to The Citadel, but for his own reason, namely, wanting to become a U.S. Marine. His vision also involved being on the competitive rifle team, with his field of study in the new construction engineering program. He has always been passionate about building things and being outdoors. He eschewed comic books and fictitious figures and stories and gravitated to non-fiction documentaries and military history.

His plan entails eventually taking over the Mental Toughness Training Center and working to integrate his siblings' ultimate targets into my three-hundred-year plan.

Michaela, to date, is in the eighth grade, and she has complete, laser-focused clarity. She wants to be a pediatrician, go to Duke University, and play on the women's lacrosse team there. Her peers and their parents constantly remind her how hard it is to get into Duke. "They only accept eleven percent of applicants. You have almost no chance of making the team. Why would you set yourself up for disappointment?"

She is undeterred. Her academic grades are stellar. She puts in extra effort in math and science. She's devoted and committed to maximizing her lacrosse skills, practicing daily, year-round. Will she make it? I have no doubt, and neither does she. However, if perchance she does not get into Duke or make the women's lacrosse team, she will play for

UNC Chapel-Hill, win the National Championship, and make Duke wish they had signed her when they had the chance.

Let your child be your child. We made our children play sports but let them choose the sport. Drew started with T-ball, moved to soccer, thought about cross-country, and settled down into wrestling. Jack wanted to play football and did so for several years, wrestled for four years, and moved on to tournament fishing and competitive small-bore rifle. Michaela started with gymnastics, played lacrosse, ran cross-country, and was on swim team for several years before focusing on lacrosse.

Drew loves science fiction and comic books. Jack loves non-fiction and military history. Michaela loves animals, children, and biology and is very competitive. Kimmi and I have encouraged and guided all our children to discover and pursue those things that inspire them and that they are drawn to naturally. We have them write their imaginations and execute a plan to accomplish each benchmark and intermediary goal along the way. We teach them that their Ultimate Target is a living document and can be changed, added to, or subtracted from at any time.

Letting your children go into adulthood without a target destination and a plan is dooming them for many years of expending massive amounts of mental, emotional, and physical energy with no clear direction or purpose. *How many years of their diligence are you willing to let them spend on building someone else's dream instead of teaching them to build their own dream?*

WHAT TO DO:

1) Upgrade your mindset to Resilient Minded, as the Average Minded have no clarity about what they want. They only know what they don't want: they don't want to be uncomfortable and vulnerable.

2) Bet on yourself! Once you start betting on yourself, you start to win, because losing isn't an option. Once you start winning, you can never go back to betting against yourself, ever! Bet on yourself, and go to work building your own dream! However, you must have one first.

3) Write a letter to your kids or grandkids about your life and what it looks like ten years into the future, but write it in the past tense. Be sure to tell as much detail as possible, like how great your back patio is with a hot tub, stone fire pit, waterfall, flat screen TV, full bar, outdoor kitchen, etc.

4) Allow your children to be your children, and have them write their imaginations of their own *Emerald City*. Help them execute a plan to accomplish each benchmark and intermediary goal along the way.

5) Letting your children go into adulthood without a target destination *(Emerald City)* and a plan is dooming them for many years of expending massive amounts of mental, emotional, and physical energy with no clear direction or purpose.

SECRET 5 – TAPPING INTO THE LAWS OF INFLUENCE

CHAPTER 10 – Becoming a Child Whisperer

Layla was fourteen years old when her dad, Eric, passed away. She and Eric were very close. Both talented in the art of impersonations and accents, they would riff off each other seamlessly. To outsiders, it seemed like it had to be a scripted act. It was just Eric and Layla; their connection was that incredible.

The crushing blow of his early departure from the Earth hit her especially hard. A few months after Eric's funeral, dealing with the overwhelming emotions of grief and adding in the hormones of a girl entering womanhood, Layla found her stress boiling over. Layla stood toe-to-toe with her mother, Ruth, shouting, "It's not fair that *he* was the one who had to go!"

Ruth, still working through her own grief, looked loving at her daughter and soothingly said, "You're so right, honey. It's not fair. It's awful. But at least you can draw on the memories of all the good times you and your dad shared. Think of the children of military parents who lost their dad having never even met him. No, it's not fair, but we are so blessed to have had your dad with us for all the time we did."

Imagine that you are in an intense argument with your child. As tensions increase, the situation devolves into a tempest of anger and a stream of hurtful dialogue. The cascade of negative emotions has lasting and cumulative effects on your relationship. As each new conflict arises, the tempest repeats itself, and a pattern begins to form. Bitterness begins to take root, and your child adopts the preconceived assumption and suspicion that you are on his or her case, even when you are not.

Now envision the exact same scenario, except that now you are keeping your cool and sailing through the situation. You are getting what you want, amenability and a behavior change from your child, all without strain or effort.

The parent who displays poise, presence, and composure (a first responder versus an emotional reactor) is the Resilient-Minded parent who decreases the stress levels of the entire household. These parents and kids also smoothly sail through the tense situations of life, all without strain or effort. The solvers of problems instead of the creators of them. The ones who defuse and de-escalate emotionally charged environments and swiftly bring peace to the storm.

As Resilient-Minded parents, we never want to chase our children, causing them to flee from us. Our strategy is always remaining approachable, offering unconditional acceptance, creating an inviting and safe atmosphere, and drawing them to you. The process may take some time. Be patient. Keep the door open, extending an unspoken invitation. When your children do come to you, you are in the position of strength where you are able to wield maximum influence.

Parents who demand that their children love them force their children into submission and compliance and mandate obedience and reverence. Parents who are completely in over their heads find that the toddler is in charge, demanding submission, compliance, and obedience from the parents. Neither of these scenarios is far-fetched, and many of our family dynamics are somewhere in between, each operating from a fear and scarcity mentality.

Whereas the Resilient-Minded Child Whisperer is operating from a love and abundance mentality. Which is not to say that Resilient-Minded Child Whisperers put up with bad behavior. The exact opposite; because we operate out of love, we realize that allowing bad behavior will cause our beloved major heartaches and rob them of success, fulfillment, and happiness if left uncorrected. Child Whisperers simply make course corrections without all the damaging negative emotions, stress, and bad memories.

Awesome Mentor

Think back to someone who has had a major positive impact in your life, an awesome boss, mentor, teacher, or coach. Did that person force you with fear to comply? Or did that person inspire you and draw out your best effort? Your mentor may have been tough on you, but it was tough love from someone who earnestly cared for you. Deep down, you knew it. Observation and study have revealed several key components of why we are drawn to, influenced by, and persuaded by someone. To keep things simple and practical, I break those reasons down as follows:

Character

Consistency

Congruence

Caring

Commitment

Confidence

Chances are high that your awesome boss, mentor, teacher, or coach displayed most, if not all, of the above components. Simply stated, the Law of Influence is this: the more of these components someone perceives in you, the greater the influence you will have on that person.

Let us not confuse influence with manipulation. Tapping into and misusing the laws that govern how influence is wielded over the human machine is what con-artists have been doing since the first one slapped a label on a bottle of snake oil. Manipulation is a weaponized influence that is not for the Resilient Minded. Instead, we operate out of love. We only use our Child Whisperer super-powers for good. I don't teach this stuff until after someone has gone through the first four Secrets of Resilience. Because these traits need to be authentic. Authenticity is only possible once you have already established an internal identity.

Public Life, Private Life, and Secret Life

Being Resilient-Minded is all about character, and character is who you are when you are alone, with nobody else looking. Your reputation is the image that you present or portray to folks when they are looking, like at the PTA meetings, social events, and church.

We all live three lives. We have a **Public Life** (how we act publicly), a **Private Life** (how we act behind closed doors), and a **Secret Life** (how we act inside our heads – also known as thinking). Most people concentrate on managing their Public Life. That's completely backward. To be effective parents and Child Whisperers, we must manage our Secret Life first, and then our Public Life will fall into place. Whatever happens in your Secret Life will come out first in your Private Life and then become part of your Public Life. It's just a matter of time. The casualty list of Secret Lives becoming public is too long to catalog here; just check the #MeToo.

To maximize my ability to have influence in the lives of my children, I hold myself to the highest of standards – not the standard my family, friends, haters, customers, clients, or my employers have for me. My standard for myself is to be the absolute best that I can be. I must meet it, or I can't sleep at night. My inner Child Whisperer won't allow me to become a slacker or to half-step, especially when nobody is looking. If I secretly don't possess character, am not consistent, not congruent, or fake that I care with pretend or selective listening, then I erode my confidence as a parent.

Becoming a Child Whisperer requires the mental toughness to work on your character, not your reputation. If you focus on building your character (*Secret Life*), by becoming the absolute best that you can become and maximizing your own potential, then your reputation (*Public Life*) will match up as a by-product of a great Secret Life. If you are only concerned with your reputation (how they view you at the PTA meeting), your life is a house of cards. And your children will spot it a thousand miles away. You can fake out yourself, but you can't fake out your kids. Focus on building great character, especially when nobody else is looking, and you are on your way to wielding maximum influence in your child's life!

Child Whisperers Aren't Born; They Are Developed

None of us is born a Child Whisperer. The good news is that every parent can become a Child Whisperer. To pull this off and be effective, we must possess five essential characteristics. In no order, they are:

Credibility – the quality of being trusted and believed in

Competence – having the necessary ability, knowledge, or skill to do something successfully

Reliability – a track record and history of stability and consistency

Confidence – the belief that one is reliable and certain of what to do and how and when to do it

Charisma/Presence – compelling personality style inspiring devotion, impressive manner

Some of these characteristics are perceived immediately and can place you firmly in the cornerstone position in every situation. To place themselves instantly in the cornerstone position of influence, Child Whisperers need to assert control of their emotions and bodies (more on this in Chapter Thirteen). Along with superseding their prejudices. The human machine pre-judges by default. Child Whisperers must clean the slate and override any assumptions and prejudices. Both the prejudice that your little angel would never do (insert the unthinkable here). And the second prejudice that of course your juvenile delinquent did (insert the unthinkable here). And finally, Child Whisperers must dominate their fears. Remember: people mirror each other. If you are fearful, your child will sense your fear and become fearful. People are drawn to and positively influenced by whoever is in complete control of themselves, with the mind running the boardroom.

I hate the phrase, "Fake it 'till you make it." Instead, I point to biopsychology. Research clearly indicates that our attitude is influenced by our posture. They are intricately linked together. As a Child Whisperer, you might often find it easier to act your way into good thinking than to think your way into good actions. In other words, Mom was right when she told you to stand up straight and put your shoulders back – your attitude will follow your posture. If you think you are going to come unglued, channel a pose of the calmest and most in control individual you can conjure up. I like to think of the Star Wars Jedi master, Obi-Wan Kenobi, as someone who is poised under pressure, and then mimic his posture. The emotions will follow the body's lead. A reminder of why it is so important to have the mind and body voting together in the boardroom.

The Life-Blood of Influence

Every ounce of influence you have, can have, will have, or hope to have is based on your ability to be credible. Credibility is the ability to be believed and trusted. Without this quality, the Child Whisperer is dead in the water. Think now of the people who have the most sway over you. Are they credible to you? In your eyes, are they to be believed and trusted? Think now of the brand names you hold in esteem, as in you buy their products/services when you have multiple options. Why do you trust the brand? Think now of the media outlets from which you most frequently absorb content and information. Why is it you most frequently watch, listen to, or read their offerings? Do you deem them believable and trusted?

Sans credibility, you are background noise to be ignored, at best, and a scam threat to me at the other end of the scale. Either way, you have zero standing with me. It can take years upon years to build credibility and one instant to destroy it. Ask Brian Williams of NBC News notoriety, who is now relegated to a time-slot that has lower viewer ratings than a teenage girl's YouTube channel.

If you currently haven't built up your own recognized credibility, then during the process of becoming a Child Whisperer, you'll have to grab some the old-fashioned way: borrow it. If your own credibility at this second in time doesn't mean much, you must co-opt some from a source that is recognized outside of your inner circle.

Borrowing credibility is both art and science. The science taps into a psychological phenomenon called schemas and associations. Schemas are the cognitive organizing system that ties bits of information together so that we can make sense of data that would otherwise be random. For example, gold, diamonds, hearts, the number seven, leprechauns, moons, and marshmallows are bits of information that belong to several different schemas. As the list went on, the schemas and associations changed as more bits of data were added. Gold and diamonds started your mind in one direction, but by the time we got to marshmallows, if you are an American, you likely would have been thinking about Lucky Charms breakfast cereal.

Here is where the art comes in. The effective Child Whisperer crafts his or her credibility based on the audience, people, or individuals with whom you are trying to build credibility, namely your child or children. You must choose the most widely recognized and highly thought of ideas and brands (known as social proof) to tie into and create a schema that lends you credibility. My own personal credibility account includes the ideas and brands of U.S. Marine infantry combat veteran; federal agent; and a security contractor with the State Department who trained Navy Seals, Marines, Rangers, and Special Forces. All widely known, recognized, and highly thought of – BOOM! Instantly creating credibility by my association with those ideas, brands and concepts.

None of these ideas or brands meant anything to my children until I trained them to value those ideas and brands. They each were a blank slate when they entered the world. It was up to my wife and me to craft the image of how they viewed these ideas and brands. In our case, Hollywood, news media, and history class helped reinforce the perceptions of each.

As parents, from day one we should be working diligently to craft our credibility with our children if we truly want to have an influence on them. Life is a credibility-based business. Make an effort; put in the work to build your credibility with your children. And then guard it like your life depends on it, because if you want to be a Child Whisperer, it does.

Credibility Sand Traps

There are many things you can do to lose your credibility, especially with your children. First, adopt a poor personal image. Become a slob. Present yourself in an embarrassing manner.

You don't have to wear a suit and tie or a ball gown, but be presentable, and in doing so, show your children you respect them and their social standing. If your child is embarrassed to be seen with you, contrary to conventional delusions, it's not them being teenagers, it's you. **_Action Step_**: Dress and groom yourself in a fashion that will make your kids proud to be seen with you.

The second sand trap is to engage in gossip and rumors. Talk about your in-laws, the jerks at work, and those irritating neighbors. Talk about the other PTA moms, the teachers, the administrators, the coaches of your child's sports team, the den mother and scoutmaster, and everyone in between.

What your children will know instinctively is that, because you gossip, engage in rumors, and talk about others behind their backs, you will do the same thing to them. Why would your teenager ever trust you to keep their confidence and not tell anyone their personal and intimate business? ***Action Step***: Cease gossiping and speaking ill of other people.

Third, use profanity, a lot. And be tasteless, vulgar, and ill-mannered. Nothing screams lack of credibility, command, and control of oneself like an overabundance of F-bombs, along with aggressive, opinionated speech and biased, sexist, racist, or judgmental language. If people are laughing, it's because they're are uncomfortable, untrusting of you, and are looking for a polite and quick exit. ***Action Step***: Think before you speak, and be mindful and diplomatic in the language you use.

Fourth, make excuses. The last thing you want to do if you want to be credible, especially with your kids, is to stop making excuses. ***Action Step***: If you make a mistake or wrong your child, take immediate responsibility for it, and apologize. This act alone will increase your credibility.

Finally, if you want to destroy your credibility, be contemptuous and destructively critical. Being critical of your organization, your boss, your co-workers, your spouse, your child's teachers, your child's coaches, your neighbors, or your child's friends signals to your children that you are also critical of them. Devastating criticism is the most pervasive of credibility stealers, and most people are unaware of it. ***Action Step***: Identify and speak of all the most admirable traits in your child and his or her teacher, coach, school, and friends.

Several years ago when I was deployed to Afghanistan, Drew, my oldest son, was just hitting middle school and feeling his oats. He was giving his mom a hard time, especially in my absence. He was being very critical of how she was running the household. I jumped onto a video chat with him. Did I yell at him? No.

"Hey, Buddy, how's it going?"

"Ok," he said.

"I hear you're giving Mom a hard time. Is that true?"

Sigh. "Yes, sir, I guess so."

"Can I ask you something?"

"Yes, sir."

"Do you pay the mortgage?"

"No, sir."

"Do you pay the light bill?"

"No, sir."

"Do you have any kids that I don't know about?" (These days you have to ask....)

"No, sir."

"Then, have you earned the right to criticize your mom?"

"No, sir."

"When you have kids of your own, you can raise them however you want and then, and only then, will you have earned the right to criticize mom and me about how we have raised you. Of course, it'll be too late by then, but you will have earned the right."

I don't allow a critical thought to set up shop in my head. Criticism quickly sets my one-hundred-twenty-six-bits-of-information-per-second-filter to find everything I don't like about something or someone and discard all the great stuff about them. For example, I don't criticize my wife. I picked her. No one forced me to marry her. If I criticize her, my choice says nothing about her and volumes about my own credibility as a decision maker.

If you criticize your employer, your boss, or your co-workers, I hear volumes about you and your credibility as a decision maker. I must ask; did anyone put a gun to your head and make you work there? No, your job was your choice, and being critical shines a light on your inability to make good choices. Criticizing others only robs you of your credibility and ability to influence others and says nothing about whoever or whatever you are criticizing. As a Child Whisperer who delights in having influence on my children's lives, I don't allow a critical thought to set up shop towards them or their mother. If you are divorced, even if your ex is one hundred percent despicable, that person is still the parent of your child, and being contemptuous and critical of that person robs you of credibility with your child. Remember, you picked your former spouse at some point, and criticizing your ex reflects on you and your decision-making ability.

WHAT TO DO:

1) Display poise, presence, and composure. This way, the Resilient-Minded parent smoothly sails through the tense situations of family life, all without strain or effort.

2) Tapping into the Law of Influence is this simple. The more influential components *(character, consistency, congruence, caring, commitment, confidence)* your children perceive in you, the greater the influence you will have on their lives.

3) Realize that we all live three lives. We have a ***Public Life*** (how we act publicly), a ***Private Life*** (how we act behind closed doors), and a ***Secret Life*** (how we act inside our heads – also known as thinking). FOCUS on your ***Secret Life,*** and the rest will fall into place.

4) Do the work to maintain your credibility as a parent. Life is a credibility-based business, and credibility is, simply stated, the ability to be believed and trusted.

5) Commit to being appreciative and complimentary of other people; shun judgmental and destructive criticism.

CHAPTER 11 – Stress and the Hormone Dump

Elizabeth and Ken had a little more going on than most parents. They had four kids, ages five to eleven. Chaos was routine. On one Saturday morning, Elizabeth packed all the kids up and headed to the local wholesale warehouse club for the bi-weekly grocery shopping. She had completed the list, fought her way through the candy aisles, wrangled her crew through the long checkout line, and managed to load the minivan. She was exhausted, and the kids were just getting started, excited about getting their hands on some of the recently purchased treats.

As Elizabeth was exiting the parking lot, she glanced both ways and proceeded to pull onto the highway. Suddenly a horn blared, and the sound of screeching tires filled her ears. She instinctively slammed on the brakes and looked to her left. The grill of a large four-wheel drive pickup-truck was inches from the driver's side door of the van. Silence filled the van. She quickly checked on the kids, each little face staring back at her in silence. Seconds later, bedlam erupted. Hearts were pounding, and kids were crying. Elizabeth felt sick to her stomach. The thought of what could have just happened was nauseating. She tried to calm everyone down as she pulled onto the highway. Everyone in the minivan felt unsettled the entire trip home, even after having arrived safely.

Stress comes from our internal perception of the facts, events, circumstances, environment, and situation. The way the human machine works is that external events happen around you. You have a short window of time to decide how to interpret and perceive those events. Once your decision is made, the brain produces chemicals called neurotransmitters, many of which are identical to the chemicals created in the endocrine system, i.e., hormones.

Once you interpret the "facts," your brain selects a neurotransmitter to match your chosen response and fires off that signal commanding your endocrine system to flood your bloodstream with massive amounts of the matching chemical. This response is what I call the Hormone Dump. The brain and body work in conjunction to sustain your response (or reaction in most cases). If you have ever been in a near-accident in a car, like Elizabeth and her children, you have experienced this Hormone Dump. Brakes were applied vigorously; horns were honked; but nothing happened. Then, after it was all over and you logically recognized everyone was safe, no harm/no foul, your heart raced, and you felt sick to your stomach.

What you felt is the Hormone Dump. Once the Hormone Dump happens, it takes approximately twenty minutes for the chemical to run its course and the dose to wear off. During this time, a person cannot be rational. You already know all this, as you experienced in the scenario of the near-wreck. You have no rational reason for that nauseous pit in your stomach. You have an emotional seizure. I find it helpful, in becoming a first responder versus an emotional reactor, to view this phenomenon like an epileptic seizure.

If you have been around someone with epilepsy, when that person experiences a seizure, it's a neurological event. We do not try to stop the seizure. We do not try to reason with the person on the floor. We clear the area of hazards and keep the person safe until the seizure ends.

This is what successful Child Whisperers and Resilient-Minded parents do when they recognize an "emotional seizure" that comes from the Hormone Dump. They don't react to the child's Hormone Dump and respond in kind, arguing their point with ever-increasing volume. Oh, and every time you do, you restart the twenty-minute clock, because you cause a new dump. That is why, after an intense and sustained argument with a loved one, you feel completely exhausted and physically drained. Your body drugs itself to sustain your intensity, and when the hormones eventually wear off, you are left to recover.

My wife and I are proactive and not reactive parents. And because we are, we take actions to be aware and regulate our own Hormone Dumps first. Solving anything while we are in the middle of one hurts us, hurts our relationship with our children, and hurts the children, setting an undesirable model of behavior to imitate. Being proactive starts with managing and balancing, as best we can, our own hormonal baseline. This balance decreases your overall stress and sets up your body to help your mind override your emotions.

Most of us are stressed because we are constantly fighting our own biology. Your adrenal glands are the part of the endocrine system that

214

dumps the most powerful of hormones: adrenaline. Adrenaline (epinephrine) surges every time we perceive a threat in order to sustain our strength, energy, and focus and ensure our survival. Minutes later, cortisol (the stress hormone) dumps into your bloodstream, further sustaining your response/reaction to the threat. Handy in the days of hunter/gatherers; however, in our modern society, we have pushed our adrenal glands to the maximum by constantly worrying about negative outcomes.

High levels of cortisol suppress the immune system and increase blood pressure and blood sugar, all clues as to why research shows that over eighty percent of doctor's office visits are stress related and that most heart attacks occur at nine o'clock on Monday mornings. No wonder we have a difficult time remaining calm and collected when our children are pitching a fit to get what they want when they want it.

Kimmi and I were grocery shopping in one of those health-food-type stores, and we had our darling two-year-old Michaela with us. In this store, the staff had set up tasting tables at various points around the aisles, giving away free samples. We stopped at one station and sampled some blue corn tortilla chips. Michaela loved them. Yum!

As we walked away, Michaela wanted more chips. She stood up in the cart and pointed emphatically in the direction of the tasting table, which happened to be behind Kimmi as she was pushing the cart. Michaela, new to verbal skills and proper enunciation of words and

215

demonstrably pointing at what looked like her mother, screamed, "CHIPS! CHIPS!" Only when it came out of her mouth it was, "BITCH! BITCH!" Everyone in the store stopped and stared agape, including us. I scooped Michaela up in my arms, grabbed a chip for her to put into her mouth, and exited the store. We laugh about that incident now, but at the time … it was very stressful and embarrassing.

Stress Control Pyramid

When I coach CEOs, who come to me because of overwhelming stress, the first thing I do is assess their baseline. I have them text me an image of their handwritten journal noting their sleep, nutrition, and fitness activity for each day. If they are unwilling to do so, I don't take them on as a client. Why? Just like you and me, they own their sleep, their nutrition, and their fitness activities.

The human machine is built in such a fashion as to function optimally with six to eight hours of sleep daily. Research records a phenomenon called "Sleep Deficit and Debt." Shortchanging your body of sleep has a cumulative effect, adding up over time and leading to nothing good. Being responsible parents and balancing work, family, and finances, we know that sleep usually goes out the window first. Quickly followed by fitness, because if I don't have time to sleep, I really don't have time to work out. Finally, nutrition goes by the wayside, grabbing whatever is easiest and quickest to keep the hamster wheel turning.

This circle of habits is survival mode, always back on your heels, treading just enough water to keep from drowning. I'm getting stressed just writing about it! Resilient-Minded parents say, "It's impossible to get six hours sleep a night, but if it were possible, how would I do it?" Start with turning off late night television. Read every night for twenty minutes or more. I read every night, and I read books and articles that help me have a good night sleep, not news stories that get me worked up. A great example would be to read some of this book every night before lights out. It will prime your brain to mull over, meditate, and process becoming a resilient parent who raises resilient, successful, fulfilled, and happy children.

You also own your fitness and physical activities. Instead of working through lunch at your desk, go for a walk. You don't have to join a gym, but get moving. Take the stairs as much as possible. Park your car far away instead of as close as possible. Pace around while on the phone (one of my all-time favorites.) Earn your screen time; do as many pushups as you can before you turn on your show. Do squats between shows, and earn the next episode instead of binge-watching three hours of content without getting off the couch except to go to the bathroom.

Finally, you own your food intake and nutrition. If you are having difficulty making good food choices, start hanging around the health nuts at work, the PTA, or church. Remember that consciousness is contagious, and so are obesity and healthfulness. I understand hectic schedules, traveling, and disruption of routine, not to mention your child's extracurricular activities. Many days I wake up unsure of what city I'm in or what time zone. But no one needs to tell you if you are making a nutritionally positive food choice or not. You already know. Some of us are doing the equivalent of putting diesel fuel into a gasoline engine and then wondering why the car won't drive right.

Keeping a handwritten log or journal is an effective way to get control of these pillars of the stress control pyramid. Keep yourself accountable. Your mood, your cognitive processing, your problem-solving skills, your relationships, and your peace of mind and attitude will all improve drastically simply by getting enough sleep, improving your fitness, and eating healthful foods. I cannot overstate the benefits you will reap by making the stress control pyramid your top priority. It is putting the oxygen mask on yourself first on the airplane, and then helping the kids with their masks.

Making Stress Your Rocket Fuel

Stress is a truth, not a fact. It can be positive or negative or both. However, because it is a truth, I can view it any way I chose. It is my choice to view stress as negative or positive. I always choose to view stress not just as good, but great. It is my own personal and legal performance-enhancing drug (PED). It brings into laser-focus what my target and objective is. It brings into laser-focus what needs to be done to hit that target. It brings into laser-focus when it needs to be done (i.e. a deadline) to hit the target. Leaving how to do something (skill) as the only problem to solve.

In the same way that Kaleb practices his basketball skills, I practice my thinking skills (thinking like C.R.A.P.). In the manner of a champion athlete or special operations sniper, I practice applying my cognitive skills until they become second nature. This state is when stress becomes rocket fuel. The stress of a live match or actually going behind enemy lines is exactly what the athlete and sniper have exhaustively trained to do. And as such, they crave to test themselves and their skills at the highest levels. The Resilient-Minded parent takes the same approach to practicing the Secrets of Resilience. When a stressful parenting moment arrives, we love it, craving the opportunity to test our newfound skills when it truly matters.

Pressure-Proofing Yourself

A large part of reducing stress and inoculating yourself against the kind of pressure that stymies performance is being able to see ahead. I'm talking about the skill of anticipation. To anticipate problems or mere course changes, we must raise our perspective to the fifty-thousand-foot level. Wayne Gretzky, hockey great, said, "A good hockey player plays where the puck is. A great hockey player plays where the puck is going to be."

I've been fortunate enough to be trained in vehicle dynamics and evasive/protective driving skills. One of the primary axioms of my driving instructors was, "Keep your eyes up." Effective and proficient drivers must keep their eyes as far into the distance as possible. Taking the long view helps the operator to anticipate problems or mere coursé changes.

One of the training progressions I took was, in fact, a racing school. The instructors taught us some wild, moonshiner-type moves, the kind seen in the movies. They also taught us that during high-speed progressions, if there is a wreck in progress, we drive towards the wreck. At high speeds, when cars collide, they will keep moving beyond the point of impact. In steering toward the point of impact, my vehicle would miss the wreck and make continued evasive/protective action possible.

The same is true for the deer hunter. The rifle must be aimed at the place where the hunted game is going. Shooting where the game is instead of anticipating where it's going to be makes for an empty freezer. It's also true for the Resilient-Minded parent. When you get up out of the weeds and get a bird's eye view of things, you give yourself an enormous vaccination against pressure and stress. Seeing things in the distance gives you tons of reactionary time, so much so that you become proactive instead of reactive.

Consider my three-hundred-year plan. If I have a bad day, in the light of three hundred years, is that bad day a big deal? It's not even a blip on the radar. How about a bad week, month, or year? Compared to three hundred years, it's nothing. I could have a bad decade, and looking at the entire three-hundred-year plan, even a bad ten years has no effect.

Preparation goes hand-in-hand with anticipation. In fact, without preparing for what you anticipate, there is no point in wasting any time or energy "keeping your eyes up" or trying to glimpse that bird's eye view. Why bother to recognize a collision course if you aren't going to take evasive action? Unfortunately, the vast majority of folks do this very thing, and then they cite "how lucky" the ones who avoided the crash were. One of my all-time favorite quotes is from Louis Pasteur, a microbiologist who discovered the principles of vaccination. He said, "Chance favors the prepared mind."

Luck and chance are real. And luck, chance, or happenstance all favor the ones who are prepared. When I was the lead advance agent for Senator Joe Lieberman's security detail, my job was to precede him by two days to every city in which he traveled. This requirement was especially challenging during the lead up to his presidential run. I not only had to anticipate the scheduled events, any contingencies, and all possible threats, but also had to prepare an action plan in the event that exigencies became realities.

I had to learn each city and venue like the back of my hand, or more accurately, like a native of the local area. I remember one trip to a large, Midwestern city that was a last-minute add-on to the senator's itinerary. I landed late in the afternoon, the evening prior to his arrival. I never did go to sleep that night. I advanced each of the event venues first and pushed off the route planning to each site until after midnight. I arranged for marked police escorts to lead the way. But what if the escorts were late or didn't show up, or there was construction along the way, or a wreck? I had to prepare, and the only way to do that was to stay up and learn the routes myself. I spent the graveyard shift driving the primary routes and multiple alternates.

Sure enough, the next morning, the police escort made a wrong turn. I didn't follow. The senator had noticed and asked about it. I reassured him with a calmness that only comes from the confidence of the prepared and drove to the next stop. Can you imagine the pressure I would have felt if I hadn't prepared for that contingency and had just gone to sleep instead? My anticipation of such a turn of events led to my preparation, and boy, was I lucky. Luck favored me because my preparation directly fed into my level of confidence. I had no second-guessing. I wasn't winging it, and therefore, I didn't need luck.

My favorite instant fix when the stress and pressure of the moment get to be too much is laughter and humor. It might sound hackneyed, but finding the hilarity in any situation has been one of my greatest pressure-proofing weapons. Humor is one of my go-to mental toughness and resiliency tools. I love laughing; I love a perspective that finds the funny side of things.

Any professional warrior will tell you the same thing: laughter is a coping mechanism that allows us to perform when we need it most. Some of the hardest belly laughs I've ever experienced (the kind that feels like you just did a thousand sit-ups and leaves you with tears rolling down your aching cheeks), have been had just prior to a mission or coming off one. This feat is usually accomplished by some hilarious one-liner ripping into a fellow team member's idiosyncrasy. The funniest ones are the ones that have been directed at me and pointed out my own ludicrousness. What I call my Clark Griswold moments. The very mention of Clark Griswold makes me laugh.

Laughing at myself has the effect of immediately removing the pressure and stress. It also helps defuse and put my children at ease when we are having a tough and frank discussion. Humor, especially self-deprecating humor, is a fantastic tool to keep yourself and your child from getting upset and experiencing the meltdown moments that come with the Hormone Dump. It always helps in keeping that bird's-eye view perspective. Is it going to matter ten years from now if your middle-schooler didn't take her or his vitamins in the morning? Starting the day with a Hormone Dump over vitamins is ridiculous. It sets the tone for the entire day. Find some humor and some Flintstone Gummies and take them together, laughing about how silly it is for an adult to be taking cartoon gummy vitamins.

Finally, the greatest tool that provides instant stress reduction is gratitude. Be aware: it takes an enormous effort to fire a salvo from this weapon when you are miserable. If you are stuck in the mode of self-pity, complaining, whining, and moaning about your circumstances, your job, your relationships, and life in general, you absolutely will not feel like performing a gratitude bombing run on yourself.

Being grateful is extremely effective. Being thankful and appreciative of all the good things in your life is akin to a nuclear strike on stress, pressure, and any heaviness enveloping you. It's not enough *not* to complain, *not* to whine, and *not* to moan about stuff. To get results, you must speak out loud so that your own ears can hear you in a language that expresses and acknowledges gratitude. It works even better when other people's ears can hear you, too.

Here is the beginning of my gratitude list:

I am so thankful for indoor plumbing, especially hot running water for a shower, and toilets that flush. If you're not thankful for indoor plumbing, spend a few months out in the deserts of Afghanistan or any other location off the grid. It might be good for bears to go in the woods, but that's because they don't know what they are missing.

I am grateful for a warm bed with an actual pillow and mattress. Don't get me wrong. I was grateful to lay my head on my gas mask instead of a rock and to have a poncho liner to cover me up, but the Bed Bath & Beyond stuff is soooooo much nicer.

I am thankful for food that hasn't been dehydrated or flash-frozen and packed in a tin foil toothpaste tube. I appreciate having a meal, any meal, but especially food that wasn't processed three years before I was born.

I am grateful for fresh and clean water, the kind that is safe to drink. Thanks to all the water treatment specialists who spend their lives ensuring that I don't get sick from brushing my teeth in the water that comes out of the faucet. A standing ovation for toothpaste and toothbrushes too, while I'm thinking of it.

Garbage pick-up. Thanks to the all the folks who, in any weather conditions, remove the trash from my home and sanctuary.

And I haven't even started on the important things like my family, friends, and electricity.

Write your own list and read it out loud. Go NUCLEAR on pressure and stress!

WHAT TO DO:

1) Remember, stress comes from our own perception of the facts, events, circumstances, environments, and situations — like beauty, it's in the eye of the beholder. Mind over matter. If you don't mind, it doesn't matter.

2) Be aware: the Hormone Dump, once triggered, takes approximately twenty minutes for the chemical to run its course and wear off. During this time, people cannot be rational; just keep them safe.

3) Use the Stress Control Pyramid daily; remember that it consists of six to eight hours of daily sleep, proper nutrition, and some form of physical activity/fitness.

4) View things from the fifty-thousand feet level. It is an effective way to minimize the negative effects of stress.

5) Use humor and gratitude early and often. These qualities are two of the most powerful weapons to defeat the negative effects of pressure and stress.

CHAPTER 12 – What Are You Saying?

Keith, while a middle school baseball coach, also coaches his daughter Kiley's softball team and son Kaleb's little league team. One of the primary skills Keith teaches all his players is hitting the ball: stance, grip on the bat, dynamics of the swing, timing, and watching the ball leave the pitcher's hand. One of the things that causes Keith frustration and stress is the fact that his kids refuse to receive that information from him because he's their dad. So, every week Keith pays another of his fellow coaches to give hitting lessons to his kids.

"We say the exact same thing! And it costs us $100 a week for them to hear the same exact thing from another coach."

Every communication with your child has three goals: 1) to be understood, 2) to be received, 3) to be acted upon. For example, as Michaela entered middle school, I communicated that I strongly prefer she did not apply makeup to her beautiful twelve-year-old face. Let's check if I hit my intermediary targets. 1) Did she understand me? Check. 2) Did she receive it? Um, not so much. She didn't receive the message from her dear old dad that she was so gorgeous she didn't need make-up. She may have received this message from a cute boy at school, but not from me. 3) Did she act upon my message? Not the way I wanted. Make-up was applied whenever I wasn't around to see it.

This response brings up the only three possible responses to any communication. No matter what message is communicated, via whatever platform, in whatever form, the human machine will have one of three reactions. The response will be either a negative reaction, a neutral reaction, or a positive reaction. Or as I like to say in our corporate training, the response will either produce **conflict, compliance,** or **commitment.** Most Average-Minded parents, if they had to choose which they prefer, would say some form of compliance because they just want to avoid conflict.

I prefer commitment. Commitment means that my child buys into my message, acting upon its content not only in my presence, but also when nobody else is looking. If I can't secure commitment, I prefer conflict. Yes, conflict. Conflict allows both parties to uncover areas of disagreement that can be worked on and negotiated. The absolute worst response, for me as a parent, is compliance. Compliance means the child understands the message, does not receive the message, and merely acts upon it in my presence. Compliance hides the conflict and is a disaster waiting to happen. Only conflict can shine a light on those things that need to be worked through to secure commitment.

Understanding the process of communication allows us to embrace conflict as the vehicle to guide our children to adopt the principles of resilience, critical thinking, and the ethics and morals we as parents wish to instill. You are now armed with the knowledge of the only possible responses to your messaging. That leaves us with the more complex process of messaging.

Noted psychologist Albert Mehrabian said, "Communication is 7% Verbal, 38% Vocal, and 55% Visual ... when dealing with communication of feelings and attitudes." Note that he refers to communications of feelings and attitudes. Can you think of any communication with your child where feelings and attitudes do not enter play? Other than factual exchanges of information like what time school starts or ends, I can think of very few instances. And upon further review of these factual exchanges, either or both parties often spice the factual gumbo with a little attitudinal salt, pepper, or Tabasco.

As a Child Whisperer and Resilient-Minded parent, I find Mehrabian's observation about communication being seven percent verbal (the words and language we use), thirty-eight percent tone of voice (it's not what you say but how you say it), and fifty-five percent visual (body language, gestures, facial expressions, posture, and presence) to be vital. Clearly the element of largest impact of every face-to-face communication is our visual presentation. The least impactful element is the words we say, which carry even less weight than the way we say those words. Yet most of us only concentrate on that least impactful element, the words we say, and discard conscious thought of ninety-three percent of our message.

To be effective, we must focus, think, and concentrate on our own body language and nonverbal communication. Reading other people's body language is an opinion at best, and trying to decipher someone else's non-verbal messaging is an exercise in assumption. As in, I'm placing my truth and my perception ahead of the facts of the message. However, all those you encounter, including your kids, will perceive your body language and non-verbal habits and make assumptions of what they think you mean before you even speak the words of your message.

The research coming out of Princeton reveals that a first impression is formed in one-tenth of one second. Whenever you walk into a room, other people form their opinion about you instantly, and they anchor everything that comes after based on that truth. It's called the Law of Primacy: we remember and anchor our attitudes and actions based on what we perceive first. And others' first impression is registered every time you reappear. You instinctively know this and base your perception of the "new" first impression on past interactions. That is why when your spouse walks in the door from work, you immediately judge whether they've had a good day or a bad day. When we string together the 7/38/55 communication concept with the Law of Primacy and the findings on first impressions, we as parents face the question, "What are you 'saying' to your kids before you say anything?"

Have you ever been pulled over for speeding? What if the officer that stopped you was three hundred pounds overweight, and he waddled up to your window in a wrinkled uniform with donut crumbs on his shirt? What is that officer saying before he says anything?

Now imagine a state trooper pulled you over. The sun reflecting off his spit-shined boot blinds you in your review mirror as he steps out of his car. He smartly places his Smokey-the-Bear hat squarely on his high-and-tight haircut. He marches to your vehicle with precision and confidence. His uniform, pressed with military creases, is immaculately tucked and cleaned. What is that officer saying before he says anything?

You are the adult. The parent. You set the climate, the atmosphere, the tone, and the attitude. Recall from the first chapter the phenomenon of neural coupling where human brains, when in the same space, time, and interaction, sync up. Our brains literally begin to mind-meld, and the same regions of the brain fire in the same sequence, based on the leader-follower distinction in the neural coupling. As in, the leader's brain dictates what is to be mirrored and imitated, and the follower's brain(s) hook in, match up, and fall in line. This fact cannot be overstated. Your children will mirror you, as you are the leader. Make sure you are presenting something you want them to mirror. If you don't like your children's attitude, tone, facial gestures, and body language, assess your own. Course correct your own visual presentation, your tone and attitude, and give your kids what you want to receive back from them.

Mirror My Movement

As a young Marine grunt, I remember one of my first commanders standing in front of the formation of one hundred fifty Marines after a five-mile run, holding his hands in front of him, and commanding his Marines, "Mirror my movement." He would randomly clap his hands, and all of us were to mirror his clap, in unison. We were tired, hot, sweaty, and out of breath, yet we had to muster the discipline to mirror our leader. I remember being in awe of him. He didn't look tired, hot, sweaty, or out of breath, and even though all the rest of us did, he didn't mirror us. He made us mirror him.

This front position is the space we parents must occupy. I've long said that you can't hide weak leadership in a crisis. No matter rank, pay, title, or seniority, humans will always look to the person who is in complete self-control for leadership. I realize it's popular in sales, negotiating, and networking circles to "connect" with others by mirroring them. This practice is a recipe for disaster, and cognitive neuroscience proves that out. To communicate, influence, and persuade others effectively, we must be in complete control of ourselves first (mind running the boardroom) and then let those we seek to influence (like our children) mirror us. This dynamic is where success happens.

Think about this for a second: if you mirror someone whose emotions are running the boardroom, who then is leading and directing attitudes and course of action? I see this situation in law enforcement every day. The officers and the suspects both end up acting out of fear, distrust, and anxiety. They end up mirroring each other, and things spiral quickly. I also have observed this phenomenon during sporting events, where a team's coach has a meltdown over an official's call, and I can see the entire team's attitude and performance nose-dive. Then there is the parent and the unruly toddler or the hormone-charged teenager. The human brain will either set the agenda or adopt someone else's.

Mirror my movements, because I'm not going to mirror yours. What if two Resilient-Minded individuals enter the same space? Perfect! We've got two critical thinkers in comprehensive control of their thoughts, feelings, and attitudes, with their minds running the boardroom. Now that's a perfect scenario for neural coupling. Imagine how smooth communication with your child will be when you both are in control of your critical-thinking minds, which are running your respective boardrooms.

To See and Decide

If you aren't setting the agenda and the targets (the outcomes you *do* want, not what you *don't* want), then by default you are letting someone else set the agenda and the targets. For every interaction with your child that you as the Resilient-Minded Child Whisperer have, you must set a target, an outcome that you want. Average parents struggle with communicating with their children because they have not clearly identified the target of the communication. Do you want a commitment from your child or mere compliance? Are you avoiding conflict? Is that your target? What are you attempting to accomplish? Is your target to strengthen the relationship continually? Is it to set your child up for success? Or is it to get your kid to stop an irritating behavior that subconsciously reminds you of your own shortcomings or those of someone you despise?

Setting your communication agenda is only the starting point; without a clearly defined target, interaction with a child will be frustrating for both of you. Once the target is established, the challenge to obtain commitment becomes the main issue. Herein is the magic. The Child Whisperer always presents that agenda in terms of the child's perspective, in the child's world, not in the parent's world, from the parent's perspective.

As the lead advance agent for Senator Joe Lieberman, I was tasked with setting up and coordinating all security, transportation, and medical contingency and emergency tactical response resources in every city in which the senator traveled. In each city, my special agent siblings in the Secret Service had left behind a reputation of forcefully demanding cooperation and one of commandeering state and local resources. This arrogance left a bad taste in the mouths of the state and local officials. By the time I showed up, the locals were extremely defensive and uncooperative from the get-go. To get their assistance and hit my target successfully, I had to present that target and agenda in terms of their perspective. I had to operate as a guest in their world, not force them as hostages into mine.

Police chiefs, sheriffs, and state police commanders were each shown respect and given liberal amounts of courtesy when I framed my target and agenda in their world. Instead of a target that involved taking over their departments and resources, as my siblings did, my new target would be to get them **to see and decide** that helping me would help them fulfill their purpose of public safety and job security. If they helped me, I would make sure they got all the credit for a safe and enjoyable visit by the Senator. If they didn't help me (and whether they chose to help me or not was totally up to them) and anything "bad" happened, I would also help them get the credit.

As a father, I want my children to get good grades in school. However, I set that agenda in their world, not mine. It's not about me having bragging rights that my kids are so smart, on the honor roll, and are better performers than the neighbors' kids. No, I set the target of good grades in school by framing the issue around what they would like to achieve and accomplish. Yes, they need excellent science and math scores to be engineers and doctors. The fact that you are going into fields of science doesn't mean that you can blow off English class. They will need excellent English, grammar, composition, and language skills because the most successful engineers and doctors can write well and have more credibility than someone who gets "two," "to," and "too" mixed up.

To maximize the influence I have in my child's life, I set the agendas and targets, acting as a guest and adopting that child's perspective, not taking the child's viewpoint hostage and forcing my child to see from my perspective. Every interaction should have the target and agenda of getting others **to see and decide** that we add value to their worlds. **To see and decide** that we can be the solution to the problems

235

they are facing. **To see and decide** that we are helping them fulfill their own purpose, hit their targets, and accomplish their agenda.

Empathy

Strategic empathy should be part of who you are, your internal identity. My partner, Harold "Dutch" Coleman, Jr., has an identity statement that includes the phrase: "who loves people." I've watched him consistently demonstrate fundamental compassion for people and a love that doesn't change, regardless of circumstances. He is a sports-talk broadcaster, and I've seen him in action, loving people who call into his show, even when they are the furthest thing from lovable.

Strategic empathy is a lifestyle, an underlying, internal characteristic that genuinely loves people. It is having a fundamental compassion for others and the human condition that sees shortcomings in others and thinks: *I could just as easily fall prey to that same thing.* That does not mean that Dutch puts up with bad behavior. I find it helpful to understand strategic empathy as an overarching understanding that we are all fallible human beings. However, strategic empathy is not meant to deal with localized conditions of specific behaviors by moving people out of their own way for their own good and hitting our own target.

This is where tactical empathy enters the scene. As a Child Whisperer moving my child, persuading my child, and influencing my child, I must remember the number one need of my child. My child, above all else, needs to feel accepted, safe from the fear of rejection, judgment, and negative criticism. This is easily accomplished by deploying tactical empathy.

Creating a space where my child feels safe and accepted, even when we are discussing an emotionally charged issue (sex, alcohol consumption, partying, or drug usage), takes enormous energy on my part: mental, emotional, and physical energy. Mentally, I must box up my agenda, my thoughts, and my opinions and put them on the shelf of the back closet of my mind. Emotionally, I must see, hear, and feel, as best I can, from my child's point of view. No judgment, no problem-solving, no advice, just understanding. Physically, I must communicate visually that I accept you (displaying open and welcoming body language) and am giving you my full attention (leaning in, toes/knees pointed to the speaker, slight and rhythmic head nods). At this point, I have fulfilled my child's number one need and removed my child's number one fear. Now we can have a real conversation without the negative emotional spiral.

Now you are ready to tap into neural coupling and get your child's brain in sync with your own without mirroring your child's distress. The fastest and most effective way to connect and get both your brains in sync without delving into the abyss of the pubescent hormone-triggered mood swings is to mirror the last critical words the child says. And only mirror the words. Remember: fifty-five percent of communication is visual (body language, gestures, etc.); thirty-eight percent of communication is the tone of voice; and only seven percent of communication is the words we say.

Mirror the seven percent (the words), not the other ninety-three percent (the attitude). While maintaining a presence, charisma, and a soothing tone (I like to channel Barry White), mirror the last 1-3 critical words, asked in the form of a question. In so doing, you guide and direct the course of the conversation without the child even realizing what's happening.

It looks like this:

"Hey Kiddo, how's it going?"

"Fine."

"Fine?"

"Well, it's actually been a rough couple of days."

"A rough couple of days?"

"Yeah, I have a huge project due on Friday in Social Studies; I got a seventy-two on a Math quiz; and practice this week has been a nightmare."

"Practice has been a nightmare?"

"Yeah, the coaches are making us do extra conditioning because we lost."

(At this point, hearing that the coach is giving the team extra work reveals an opportunity to transition from mirroring words to taking the lead and redirecting us toward the target of a shift in attitude.)

"What a great opportunity to crush it!"

"Crush it?" (Notice the switch; the child is now mirroring my words.)

"Yeah! Imagine how you will dominate all the other teams who didn't do extra conditioning. Crush it!"

And the neural coupling has taken place. Notice, I didn't mirror the attitude. I didn't mirror the tone of voice. I only mirrored the words. Once neural coupling takes place, I can begin to maximize my influence in the direction of the conversation, the attitude, the mindset, and the course of action. Mirror the words, not the attitude, and then take the lead.

Creative Ways to Open Communication

Consider creative ways to keep open lines of communication with your children. One of our favorite ways of spurring discussion is to watch movies and television shows together as a family. It's been our practice since the kids were watching *Mickey Mouse Clubhouse* and *Sesame Street*. As Kimmi and I watched their shows, we could talk about things from their perspective. We have continued this practice throughout the years.

Each of my kids has favorite shows, movies, and even genres. I make it a priority to sit with each and watch the movies and shows each child enjoys; doing so gives us a starting point for in-depth discussions on a variety of issues, opening the door to teachable moments about difficult subjects. For example, talking through a character's actions or decisions and using that backdrop to speak unemotionally about how to handle a moral dilemma, allowing for a proactive, teachable moment. Critical thinking and decision-making can be practiced with the safety net of a what-if scenario with no real-world consequences at stake.

The years of watching content together have had an interesting consequence. It has created a catalog of instant illustrations of teachable moments from which to draw in real time. Aiding in the quick recall of those safely well-thought out responses when faced with similar dilemmas in the real world. And having the effect of creating our own language and form of messaging based on the recall and the repeating of a plethora of one-liners. And with it the ability to perform a comedic recall, instantly infusing humor and laughter into any conversation, soothing any negative emotional buildup.

Kimmi and Michaela have created their own special "shared journal." Ever since Michaela leaned to write, they have been jotting notes in the journal and leaving it for the other to respond. It's a running conversation of whatever they are feeling, both positive and negative, presented in a format that allows the other party to process the offered information as a first responder versus an emotional reactor. This tool has been extremely effective in keeping communication lines open without inducing the feeling of rejection or conditional acceptance. It's a simple and effective emotional work around, giving the mind the best possible chance of retaining control of the boardroom.

Another tool my entire family utilizes is the Snap Chat social media app. Michaela finally got a cell phone starting this year, eighth grade. (She was the last to come online – we were in no hurry to thrust her into the cesspool of social media.) We all snap each other and celebrate our streaks with each family member. The app has the benefit of a picture along with text, adding the visual component to words sent. It helps us extrapolate the missing thirty-eight percent of the tone of voice. We've added Bitmojis, cartoon caricatures of ourselves, to add to the fun. Bottom line is that anything you can do as a parent to foster clear, present, and effective communication should be done. It can only help. Remember this: no news is not good news. Good news is good news. No news is miscommunication.

WHAT TO DO:

1) Have a clearly defined target for your communication. In general, the target is three-fold: 1) to be understood, 2) to be received, 3) to be acted upon.

2) Be aware that the only three possible responses to any communication are: *conflict*, *compliance*, or *commitment*.

3) Remember: when feelings and attitudes are in play, all communication is seven percent verbal (the words and language we use), thirty-eight percent tone of voice (it's not what you say but how you say it), and fifty-five percent visual (body language, gestures, facial expressions, posture, and presence).

4) Be mindful and purposeful about what are you 'saying' to your kids before you say anything.

5) Do anything and everything you can as a parent to foster clear, present, and effective communication. Remember this: no news is not good news. Good news is good news. No news is miscommunication.

SECRET 6 – COURSE CORRECTIONS

CHAPTER 13 – From Resistance to Harmony

Hank is a proud alumnus of the Corps of Cadets at Texas A&M. He is involved in booster activities and financially supports the university. He credits what success he has enjoyed in life as a direct result of the military environment of his college days. Since the birth of his son, Robert, Hank has had his heart set on little Robert following in his footsteps and graduating from the military program at Texas A&M. During Robert's last year in high school, he made the mistake of saying he wanted to go to college where his friends were going, Eastern Carolina University. Hank exploded. The only option in his mind was for Robert to follow in his footsteps or else … "Don't ever come to me and ask for anything. You are a complete disappointment!"

On average, a child's perception of parental relationships begins to decline consistently starting at age eleven. But what if you could completely change the dynamic of your strained or difficult relationship with your child? Most parents do not relish it when their children act in resistance to the parent's expectations. Most would prefer a harmonious relationship with their children, but harmony can only begin to exist when we remove the emotional barriers, expectations, and predetermined plans that cause relational deterioration.

The target is harmony, not unity. Unity is the state of not being multiple; it takes away individual identity. Whereas harmony is a pleasing arrangement of different parts. Parents who find themselves in a relationship decline with their children tend unconsciously to demand complete agreement from the children and are inclined to withhold acceptance when that demand is not met. A harmonious relationship allows for disagreement and divergence yet still affords unconditional acceptance.

Primacy and Recency

The way the human machine works is that we tend to remember not what was said, nor the facts of what happened during in an external event, but how we felt. We tend to remember the first thing and the last thing of any interaction, and what happens in the middle becomes fuzzy. Further, humans tend to remember how we felt after an interface, not the content of the communication. When an interaction ends with either or both participants feeling badly, that negative feeling becomes an anchor and is recalled to the conscious mind (the one hundred twenty-six bits per second) at the beginning of the next contact. The tone is set. Defensiveness and resistance become the default mode of the relationship.

Once this pattern of defensiveness becomes a habit, the relationship deteriorates without the participants even realizing it. Derogatory derision, hurtful tones, and an argumentative spirit become the new normal, a state in which all parties become desensitized to the hurts they are causing, all the while nursing the offenses they perceive into bitterness and resentment, eventually leading to contempt. As a Child Whisperer, you must act to stop the cycle of resistance and create a new cycle of harmony. By way of reminder to all of us Resilient-Minded parents, our mantra is, "I'm the problem, and I'm the solution." Therefore, we have nowhere to lay blame or responsibility for moving our children from resistance to harmony, outside of ourselves.

State Change

Before beginning any communication with your child, before a word comes out of your mouth, you must assess and address the child's emotional state. The Child Whisperer focuses on the child's emotion first and foremost, realizing that if the child is experiencing a Hormone Dump, that child cannot hear you or rationally process any information you convey.

It's similar to the first time you're pulled over by a police officer for speeding. The marked patrol car speeds up behind you and attaches itself to your bumper. Suddenly the flashing blue and red lights are activated, and the siren whelps and chirps. As a newbie driver, you are flooded with hormones and enter an emotional seizure. Thinking back, you most likely will not be able to recall everything the officer said to you accurately, in the order it was said, but you do recall how you felt. If your child is not in the emotional state to receive from you, you are fighting against biology and nature. Not much hope of success.

Once you identify your child's emotional state, think clearly about what emotional state would be most conducive to facilitating effective communication. Your intermediary target is to move your child to that conducive state prior to conveying your message. If your child is already eleven years old and your relationship has already started the decline revealed in the empirical data, you have some work to do. Going from resistance to harmony requires a strategic mindset. This is an ongoing process that requires a long-game mentality. If damage has already been done, do not despair; it will, however, take a little more work and persistence.

For every interaction with your children, they need to be happy to see you and happy that they saw you. Happy to talk to you and happy that they talked to you. Concerning having a harmonious relationship with your child, your target is to condition the child to have an emotional state change to happiness when they see you or talk to you. This requires that you never end an interaction on a bad note.

When I was living in Hawaii as a young Marine corporal, I wanted to learn to surf. I made some local friends who were teaching me. Their number one rule was never to end a surf session, no matter what, on a wipeout. Why? Because that's the last thing you remember, and it sets up how you feel about the next time out. I have adopted this same principle in cultivating harmonious relationships with my kids. I never end an interaction with my kids on a wipeout. We need to end in an emotional state that we were glad to have interacted with the other. Happy to be in each other's airspace, happy to have been in each other's airspace, and looking forward to the next time we get to be in each other's airspace. Remember me sharing about how whenever a family member walks in the door from school, work, or anywhere, we all jump up, meet that person, and greet the new arrival with hugs and kisses? We continually reinforce and condition an emotional state change of happiness to see each other.

The science behind this training is called classical conditioning. You have most likely heard of this concept by way of Pavlov's dogs. Pavlov would wait to feed his dogs until they were hungry, and just as he brought the salivating dogs their food, he rang a bell. He continued to do this: wait until hunger, ring the bell, and bring the food. Eventually, the dogs would salivate every time the bell was rung, regardless of whether they were hungry or not. The dogs were conditioned to salivate when they heard the bell. Day or night. Hungry or full. Ring. Salivate.

Dad's home. Happy. Dad's calling. Happy. Run errands with Dad. Happy. Got a bad grade in school. Bummer. Dad's home. Happy. Tell Dad about the grade, we talk about it, and make course corrections. Happy. Got in a wreck with Dad's truck. Yikes! Tell Dad about the wreck, we discuss it, and take corrective action. Happy. I've conditioned my kids that no matter what, once they get to me, happy. I'm the bell ring.

Compliment Formula

If you were to receive a compliment, any compliment, what would you most like it to be? Grab a pen and paper, and write it down. Is it an internal or external compliment? If it's not internal (work ethic, integrity, honesty, honorable, loving, etc.), choose one now.

Looking at the internal compliment that you would most like to receive, ask yourself, "Would anyone like to receive this compliment? Would anyone be mad if they were given the compliment I just wrote down?" I would offer that no human would be mad at receiving a sincere compliment about an internal quality of character. A sincere, heartfelt compliment of character positively changes the human emotional state. It moves a person from resistance to harmony. It's extremely difficult for any person to resist the fulfillment of the number one human need for acceptance, validation, and love.

The simple process of expressing acceptance, validation, and love is something I call the compliment formula. It will change the dynamic of the most strained relationships in an instant. Prepare the compliment beforehand. This is your child; surely you have a long list of great things to say about your child's character. If not, give the compliment as a faith statement. Dale Carnegie said that if you give someone a reputation to live up to, they usually will rise to it. Kimmi and I compliment our kids on all the things we want them to develop and espouse. Their kindness, good attitude, patience, endurance, fortitude, generous spirit, honor, courage, work ethic, diligence, attention to detail, preparation, study habits, organizational skills, spirits of being teachable and coachable, humility, and willingness to stand up for what is right.

To produce a state change in your child, perform these three steps:

1) Give the child the specific, internal compliment.

2) Tell the child how observing that quality made you feel.

3) Ask the child, "How do you do it?"

I learned this method from Senator Joseph Lieberman when he gave me the greatest compliment of my life. It was the spring of 2002. After the September 11, 2001 terrorist attacks, I was assigned to the Dignitary Protection Division of the United States Capitol Police. Every officer and agent in law enforcement was working crazy hours for months on end. As Joe Lieberman's lead advance agent, I preceded his arrival anywhere at any time, and as such, I was away from home quite a bit. When I was in town, I would often not arrive at home prior to midnight, and I would leave the next morning in the wee hours before dawn, usually by 4:30 AM.

By April 2002, my oldest son, Drew, who was four years old at the time, asked me one day, "Daddy, how come you don't live with us anymore?" My first reaction was, "I still live here," but after seeing it from his point of view, my heart fell. I asked to be transferred temporarily back to uniform duty for a few weeks to reassure my son. The U.S. Capitol

Police operates as a family. They take care of each other, and they are family-oriented. My superiors immediately granted my request, and to do so, they had to do all kinds of scheduling gymnastics to make it happen, for which I am eternally grateful.

I reported for uniform duty the next morning. A week or so later, I was assigned to secure the back stairwell of one of the Senate office buildings when Benjamin Netanyahu, the Prime Minister of Israel, was visiting Capitol Hill. I took my post facing the stairwell with my back to the hallway; I was far from the media circus and entourage parading to the committee room reception for Mr. Netanyahu. I heard the commotion at the far end of the corridor and continued to focus my attention on my sector, the stairwell. At first I didn't realize it, but the commotion was increasing in volume. The cacophony of voices became footsteps, camera clicks, and distinguishable words. The entire train had changed tracks and was headed straight for me, a dead-end.

As I sensed the imminent arrival of the procession of press, staffers, protective agents, and police escorts, I felt a hand on my shoulder. I turned to see Senator Joe Lieberman standing there with the Prime Minister, surrounded by the throng. The senator introduced me to Prime Minister Benjamin "Bibi" Netanyahu. He said, "Bibi, this is Andrew; you can have no greater friend. I always feel safe with him. Andrew, how do you do it?"

As I stood there, mouth agape, I finally found my voice and muttered some nonsense like, "That's just how we roll, Senator." I shook hands with Bibi, and we exchanged greetings. What happened to my emotional state? What was the dynamic of my relationship with Senator Lieberman? Could I ever be mad at him? Ever? Not after that. He publicly gave me the greatest compliment I could ever receive. In one phrase, he summed up and encompassed the best internal character traits that exist. He said I was the greatest friend you could have and that I made him feel safe. And to seal the deal, he asked me how I managed to pull that off.

Imagine, instead of embarrassing your children in front of their friends with a public meltdown, that you deployed the compliment formula in the same fashion as Senator Lieberman. What would that practice do for the dynamic of your relationship with your child? What would that do to resistance? And further, what if you made it a practice, a new pattern of behavior, a habit of having a harmonious relationship?

Bridge the Gap

As a Resilient-Minded parent and Child Whisperer, I know that it is always my job to figure out how to bridge any gap between my child and me, not the other way around. I meet my children where they are and where they want to be. I do not force them to be in my space and come to me on my terms, doing only things I enjoy. Each of my children is different, with different preferences, and they enjoy different activities, content genres, and even different personality styles. As my target is a

251

harmonious, close-knit, and enjoyable relationship with all of my kids, I enter their airspace. I pursue them.

During Jack's, my youngest son's, junior year in high school, I felt we were subtly drifting apart. Nothing major, but I sensed my level of influence was waning. I felt the clock ticking; I only had another eighteen months before he was off to college. He spent a lot of time fishing, both with his buddies and alone. Kim and I bought him a kayak when he joined the high school fishing team, and he used it often. I have never enjoyed fishing. I didn't do it much as a kid, and those few times had produced memories that lacked a certain fondness.

Instead of nagging Jack that he wasn't spending enough time at home or with the family and threatening to curtail his time on the lake, I decided to bridge the gap. I asked him if he would help me research and get a kayak and fishing gear of my own and if he could teach me how to fish. He lit up like the Christmas tree at Rockefeller Center in New York! We spent many hours researching kayaks. We ended up purchasing a boat matching the model we had gotten for him. We researched, discussed, and tested several rods and reels. Scoured the shelves of the outdoor and adventure stores and shops for tackle, paddles, and life vests. We designed a rigging system to load, transport, and unload the boats. We planned trips and got fishing licenses and boating permits. And we enjoyed paddling on the lake, casting, and even catching and releasing bass. Jack became the teacher and me the student. We have had some grand times and will have many more to come. And most importantly, I have bridged the gap.

Contrast this paradigm with the relationship I have had with my own father. In order to spend time with my father, I had to be doing what he was doing. We spent time fixing the car, painting the house, growing vegetables in the family garden, producing his weekly radio sermon, and studying the ancient Greek language of the Byzantine texts of the New Testament. I learned a great many things and occasionally had fun, but unless I was inside of his airspace, acting in accordance with his credo that "children should be seen and not heard," there was no relationship. I don't remember him going to many of his kids' little league games, concerts, or school plays, and forget about hunting, fishing, or playing ball or board games. The only time he will spend with his children or grandchildren is according to his parameters, doing what interests him, and he doesn't want to hear you. The result is that he has missed out knowing and enjoying his children and grandchildren, is lonely, and has a difficult time understanding why his relationships are not smooth and harmonious. I still love and admire my father, but for the most part, I don't feel happy when I spend time with him.

That kind of relationship is not for us Resilient-Minded parents. We bridge the gap. We know what to do and how to move from resistance to harmony.

WHAT TO DO:

1) Recognize that on average, a child's perception of the parental relationship begins to decline consistently starting at age eleven. Commit to making the effort be an exception.

2) Children tend to remember how you make them feel more than what you say to them. Start and end every interaction with a sincere effort to make them feel unconditionally loved.

3) As a Child Whisperer, utilize classical conditioning continually with your child to reinforce and condition an emotional state change of being happy to see each other.

4) Liberally use the compliment formula. A sincere, heartfelt compliment moves a child from resistance to harmony. It's extremely difficult for any child to resist the fulfillment of the number one human need for acceptance, validation, and love.

5) Bridge the gap. The target is a harmonious, close-knit, enjoyable relationship with your child. Enter the child's airspace, and pursue the child instead of making the child cater to you.

CHAPTER 14 – Resolving Conflict: Defuse and De-escalate

"The coach is a complete jerk! I hate her! I'm not going to practice today!"

"I'm not eating these vegetables! I don't like them! I'm not eating them!"

"I am wearing those tennis shoes! I like them, and they are comfortable! I don't care what you say!"

Before we attempt to resolve a conflict, we must first diagnose and assess the root cause of it. Most people, I have observed, seem inclined to avoid confrontation as their default method of dealing with conflict. This avoidance inevitably worsens the situation until frustration, anger, fear, and hurt feelings boil over into a massive mess. Not to worry, that won't happen to us. We are Resilient-Minded parents with the mind running the boardroom, and we are in complete control of ourselves.

No matter the shape or form of any conflict in the history of humanity, there are only five root causes. Once you understand them and can readily identify them when you see them, they are child's play to manage. Here they are:

1)   Information & Facts

2)   Methodologies

3)   Priorities

4)   Targets/Destinations

5)   Values

A conflict over ***information and facts*** is the easiest to resolve. An example is a sister and brother, when asked what time it is, arguing whether it's 2:58 PM or 2:59 PM Eastern Time.

"Get a watch that works!"

"You get a watch that works!"

Do an internet search for the atomic clock. Go to the website and check the atomic clock. Problem solved.

Conflicts over ***methodology*** are a little more difficult, but the critical thinker knows that there is more than one way to bake a cake. We all believe that our way of doing things is the best way, otherwise we'd do it a different way. However, once we are exposed to and taught a different method, we may adopt it as more efficient or simply preferable for us. Or we may choose to continue using the original method. "My way is the best way" and "If you want something done right," etc., are truths, not facts. You like your method, and it works for you. Simply allow others that same consideration, problem solved.

Admittedly, this was a little difficult for my OCD-recovering self. Once the boys were old enough to cut the grass, I turned over the chore to them to free up my time. I liked to mow the lawn in such a manner that it looked like the outfield of a major league baseball field. Crisscrossing lines at a diagonal angle with carpet-like knap patterns displayed. The lads simply cut the grass. No lines. No diagonals. No knap. In fact, sometimes they missed some stalks of grass, with the final product looking like the yard had a mohawk. Early on, I tended to get uptight, and my inner dialogue may have said something like: *If you want something done right...*

Cool your jets, Andrew. Take two minutes, and move into the first responder column and out of the emotional reactor column. Alas, the lawn was mowed; the boys were just learning how to cut the grass. I didn't do all that great cutting the grass as I was growing up, and I didn't spend any of my current time doing it. Further food for thought: does it really matter, considering my three-hundred-year plan? Conflict over methodology solved.

When folks who are occupying the same space have different **priorities**, resolution to conflict gets a little more difficult. When I was a special agent, on almost every trip I took, I would buy a pair of cowboy boots. Over the course of one year, I amassed a collection of over ten pairs. My priority was the acquisition of snipped-toe, exotic-skinned boots with a riding heel.

Guess whose priority wasn't the acquisition of snipped-toe, exotic skinned boots with a riding heel? My wife. The conflict began to brew, simmer and eventually bubble up. So, being the Resilient-Minded individual that I am, knowing that I'm the problem and I'm the solution, I began buying a very nice piece of jewelry for her and a pair of snipped-toe, exotic-skinned boots with a riding heel for me on each trip. It took some re-budgeting, but in meeting the priorities of each party, the problem was solved.

This is the conflict Doug and Molly had over the brushing of her teeth. Doug's priority was Molly's oral health and hygiene. Molly's priority was feeling powerful and in control. Doug tapped into the example of how powerful tigers were in control by allowing the zoo keepers to brush their teeth.

The minute a conflict occurs between people that have different *targets* in life, we must realize that the conflict cannot be resolved unless one or both parties change their target to match the other. If you and I were in Washington, D.C. for a two-week visit, and when the trip was over, you were going to New York while I was going to Miami, how far could we travel together? Most likely as far as the airport. At some point, we must separate, unless one of us abandons our own target destination and changes it to match the other's, or we both choose a new and mutual target destination.

This kind of conflict happens most often when a child decides he isn't going to your alma mater (remember Hank and Robert and Texas A&M vs. Eastern Carolina). Or your daughter enlists in the Marine Corps, and you're an Army family. Or your son enlists in the Marine Corps instead of going into the ministry. Any number of divergent target destinations can create a trying and emotionally-charged strain on the relationship. As a Resilient-Minded parent, I have given guidance and attempted to maximize my influence in helping my kids set their target destinations, but ultimately, it's their decision and their life. I refuse to allow this conflict a place in our relationship. If they are going to New York and I'm going to Miami, we make sure to meet each other in Washington, D.C. as often as possible. No strain. No conflict. No problem.

Finally, you may have a conflict of **values**. The instant you recognize a conflict of values rising, remove yourself immediately and withdraw. It is impossible to resolve this type of conflict without war. Never engage in a conflict over values unless you are prepared for that war and the costs that come with it. I never argue politics, religion, or sports. There can be no winner, only losers. Even if you eventually win the war, your losses will be great. No war was ever won without cost.

Understand that you have a limited window of opportunity to instill and pass down your set of values to your children. Once that window is closed and they have adopted their own values, you can either accept that they have different values than you do, or you cannot. If you cannot, either war will break out, or you will feel the necessity to cut off contact. Both outcomes are extremely costly to everyone involved.

As a Resilient-Minded parent, I have vetted every single one of my beliefs, giving special attention to those beliefs that make up my values. I know what I believe and why I believe it. Sadly, most people have not vetted their beliefs, and kids can spot that gap a mile away. For instance, a parent proclaims unconditional love and acceptance of a child

259

and then places conditions on that acceptance that entails the child adopting a certain value system.

For example, I am firmly pro-life. If my daughter happens to come to a different conclusion and actively adopts the belief in the right to have an abortion, I would never cut her off, nor would we have a heated argument over the issue. It may seem that it is easy to say, as this situation is currently hypothetical. However, it is accurate, as evidenced by the fact that I have several relatives and friends who are staunchly pro-choice, while a few are actively pro-abortion. We agree to disagree on the issue. We do steadfastly agree that we appreciate each other and our relationship with one another. And because I exponentially value my relationship with Michaela far and beyond any of those folks, I can honestly say that if Mick doesn't adopt my pro-life value system, our value disagreement will not affect my unconditional acceptance and love of her.

Defuse and De-escalate

Once you have identified the root cause of conflict, you can formulate a plan for resolution. Regardless of the cause, as a Resilient-Minded parent, your first task is to assess and address the emotional state of your child. Be mindful of the Hormone Dump/emotional seizure and mentally prepare yourself for several rounds of twenty-minute time blocks. Take your time. Slow down. Allow the hormones sustaining the emotional reaction to dissipate. Start running the clock by asking, "What's bothering you, Honey?" Allow the child to express what is inside. Don't interrupt your child. Let your child get it all out. Once the child stops speaking, ask, "Is there anything else?" Repeat the cycle. Don't interrupt; let the child get it all out. Once the child stops speaking, ask again, "Is there anything else?" Repeat until the child tells you there is nothing else. This tactic serves as a delaying action, and it will also help to uncover the real issues causing turmoil.

This approach necessitates, first and foremost, that you do not take personally anything the child says during the emotional seizure. Second, work as hard as you possibly can (i.e. maximum effort), to empathize with and understand the child's situation, and more importantly, the child's feelings. **Never argue!** Read that again. **Never argue!** Write it down. Memorize it. Practice it. When you argue, the brain perceives the argument as a precursor to rejection, causing fear of physical pain to be avoided like avoiding touching a hot stove. The child's defensive shields will be immediately raised; internal red alert klaxons will sound; and psychological battle stations will be taken up. Replace argument and disagreement with alignment followed by a pivot. Here are some of my favorite alignment statements:

"I'm with you …"

"I hear you …"

"I know …"

"I'm not saying I'm right …"

"I'm not saying I'm opposed to that …"

"I'm not saying I disagree ..." (I'm also not saying I agree, but that's not what the child hears.)

"I'm not saying you're wrong ..." (I'm also not saying the child is right, but that's not what the child hears.)

These alignment statements should be immediately followed by the pivot, pointing towards the target, the outcome that I want. It may look something like this:

"The coach is a complete jerk! I hate her! I'm not going to practice today, Mom!"

"I don't disagree with you, Honey ... let's get your gear in the car and grab your water bottle."

Notice what Mom did say and what Mom didn't say. Mom didn't say, "Well, you're going! You made a commitment, and you just need to deal with it!" Nor did she say, "Aw, Honey. I know; that coach is so mean. All the other moms say she's the worst person ever. You don't have to go today if you don't want to go." However, Mom did say, "I don't disagree with you," validating her daughter's right to feel that way, and then she merely pivoted to loading up the car to go to practice. No argument, only acknowledgment of the child's feelings about the coach and then movement forward. Let's try another one.

"I'm not eating vegetables! I don't like them! I'm not eating them, Dad!"

"I'm not saying you're wrong, buddy … eat them first, and all that's left is stuff you like."

Notice what Dad did say and what Dad didn't say. Dad didn't engage in an argument, resist the child's stated opinion, threaten the child with consequences, offer a bribe to coax the child, or open negotiations. Dad did acknowledge and even validate the child's current feelings about vegetables, pivoting to eating the vegetables.

Finally, to defuse and de-escalate, always let your child save face. Cheryl, a 7th grader, was caught in class looking at her phone. The teacher, who was having a bad day, exploded into a rant, berating Cheryl in front of the entire class and demanding that Cheryl give her the phone. Embarrassed and feeling threatened, Cheryl's endocrine system launched an emotional seizure. She shouted back to the teacher in no uncertain terms that she was not giving up her phone. The teacher, feeling her authority being disrespected, launched into her own emotional seizure.

Eventually, the teacher called the vice principal to the classroom. Within minutes, the vice principal, having confronted a noncompliant Cheryl amidst a Hormone Dump, felt disrespected and experienced his own Hormone Dump. He called the school resource officer, a police officer assigned to provide security to the school. Instead of defusing and de-escalating the situation, he, too, feeling embarrassed at having a thirteen-year-old girl defy him, entered his own emotional seizure, grabbed Cheryl around the neck and shoulders, and threw her across the room, out of her desk and chair. All captured on video from the other students on the scene. The police officer was fired for excessive use of force.

All this could have been avoided if anyone in positions of authority had allowed Cheryl to save face in front of her friends. Instead, as each higher power entered the scene, the new adult exacerbated Cheryl's embarrassment and humiliation. No human being enjoys being embarrassed, humiliated, shamed, or made to feel awkward. As class was wholly disrupted anyway, the teacher, vice principal, or police officer could have cleared the classroom of all the other students. Had anyone proceeded to deal with Cheryl in a private setting and waited for the twenty minutes of her emotional seizure to dissipate, no one would have ever seen or heard this story that made the national news. If your child is in the unfortunate position of experiencing an emotional seizure in public, do everything thing you possibly can to protect your child from humiliation, especially in front of peers. Smooth things over and get your child out of there as inconspicuously and discreetly as possible.

When I was seven or eight years old, I remember being in a church service when my father was preaching the sermon. It was an evening service, and my younger brother and I were trying to survive the hard, wooden benches in the sanctuary. Apparently, I was squirming around too much for Dad's liking because he stopped his sermon in mid-sentence and sternly said, "Andrew, sit up straight, and be still." The entire congregation turned and looked at me. I promised myself to avoid embarrassing my own children in that manner. Always, always, always allow your child to save face. Make course corrections privately, and your child will make you proud publicly.

Elements of the Exchange

Congratulations! You have successfully waited out the Hormone Dump. The emotional seizure, having ended, returns your child's biology to a state that allows reasonable and rational dialogue. As a Resilient-Minded parent, you know that it's not what you say that carries the most weight (only seven percent of the message), it's how you say it (thirty-eight percent of the message) and how you present yourself visually (fifty-five percent of the message). Equipped with this knowledge, you show respect, courtesy, and empathy.

One of the most powerful psychological phenomena in human interactions is called reciprocity. Reciprocity is the social norm of responding to action in kind. In other words, treating others the same way we want to be treated. If you want your child to show you respect, you must first show your child respect. If you want to be treated with courtesy and consideration, you must first treat your child with courtesy and consideration. If you would like your child to see your point of view, you must first see your child's point of view. If you would like for your feelings to be acknowledged, you must first acknowledge your child's feelings.

You can tap into reciprocity to resolve conflict, or you can tap into reciprocity to intensify conflict. If you escalate the war, go out of your way to belittle your child, or show your child disrespect, contempt, and disregard for his/her feelings, the child will be inclined to respond in kind. That kind of escalation is not for us. We utilize reciprocity to bring soothing resolution.

Recognizing your child's feelings goes a long way towards the acknowledgment of them. The most effective way to pull this off is to label your child's feelings in the form of a question. This method allows a child either to affirm or correct what you are sensing, while taking the sting out of it.

"It seems like you are frustrated with me because I embarrassed you."

If the child affirms your action to be the crux of the issue, the child needs a heartfelt apology and plea for forgiveness, followed by the question, "What can I do to make sure I don't embarrass you again?"

When the child responds, bring the truths you hear around to facts. For example, the child says, "Well, just don't disrespect me in front of everyone." Disrespect is a truth. To turn this truth into a fact, ask the child to tell you exactly what you did that felt disrespectful. "Well, when you called my name from the pulpit and told me in front of the entire congregation to sit up straight and be still. That made me feel disrespected." Now, we know exactly what will keep you from embarrassing the child again.

Finally, always end the conversation on a note of gratitude. An attitude of gratitude will instantly defuse your own emotions, and it has the side effect of finishing on a good note instead of a wipeout. Recall the Law of Recency: we remember the last thing and carry that feeling into the next interaction.

Dealing with Complaints

We don't do complaining in our house. We know from neuroscience that complaining begets complaining and that the neurons that fire together wire together and that you're creating a superhighway that creates the habit of only seeing things that make you unhappy. We prefer to replace complaints with gratitude. However, we aren't so uptight that we don't allow the kids to express themselves. For example, if the kids say, "It's so hot outside," when in fact it is a hundred degrees Fahrenheit, I don't take that comment as a complaint; it requires no response. Although, chances are I'll say something like, "I'm with you."

There are other times when a complaint may simply be bringing attention to a valid issue that needs to be addressed. When this happens, I encourage you to listen with an open mind, ask clarifying questions, and finally ask what solution is being proposed. Some time ago, my oldest son, Drew, brought to my attention that I tend to delegate a task and then take it over, or hover over his shoulder and give him obvious step-by-step instructions. Like asking him to find and set up streaming a movie, only to take over the job or give ridiculous commands, ("Hit the play button." Are you sure, Dad?)

I listened to his "complaint," which was not a complaint at all but a statement of fact. Ouch! When he finished his accusatory and frustration-laden statement, I asked clarifying questions, "How do you mean, buddy?" Allowing further articulation of my control-freak-ness.

Finally, I said, "I'm with you; how can we fix it?"

He said, "You can stop doing that."

I said, "Okay, but how do we make that work?"

He said, "Well, whenever you start doing it again, I'll just tell you that you're doing it again and to stop."

I said, "Perfect. I'm so sorry. I didn't even realize I was doing that, but you're right. Please forgive me and call me on it right away if it happens again."

WHAT TO DO:

1) Recognize that there are only five root causes of conflict:

    a. Information & Facts

    b. Methodologies

    c. Priorities

    d. Targets/Destinations

    e. Values

2) Realize you have a limited window of opportunity to instill and pass down your set of values to your children. Once that

window is closed and they have adopted their own values, either you can accept that they have different values than you do, or you cannot.

3) **Never argue!** Replace argument and disagreement with a statement of alignment followed by a pivot towards your target resolution.

4) Tapping into reciprocity! Defuse and de-escalate by showing your child respect, courtesy, and empathy.

5) Listen to your child's complaints with an open mind, ask clarifying questions, and finally ask what solution is being proposed.

CHAPTER 15 – Dealing with Change

Ben and Elizabeth, a couple in their mid-forties and the parents of four children aged twelve to eighteen, could see the light at the end of the parenting tunnel. Their first child was graduating high school, while the two middle children were in high school and the baby was halfway through middle school. The kids were mostly on autopilot and didn't require the constant care and energy they had when they were younger. Then the couple was blindsided! SURPRISE! Elizabeth was pregnant. She and Ben were in total shock and having a hard time processing the news. The children, on the other hand, were over-the-moon excited about it.

We've all heard that kids are resilient. What happened to us parents? It seems that kids adapt to change quicker than their parents. Somewhere between childhood and adulthood, we seem to misplace our grasp on our innate resilience. Major changes in life present the most intense stress. Getting married. Starting a new job. Moving. Parenthood. And having a surprise bundle of joy late in life. How do you react to change? What is your response to emotionally challenging information? To navigate the stress of parenthood and life in general, if we do not learn to manage and even embrace change, we face an uphill climb of constant struggle. Heraclitus, an ancient Greek philosopher, said, "No man ever steps in the same river twice, for it's not the same river and he's not the same man. The only thing that is constant is change."

We all instinctively know this truth, yet most adults seem to have difficulty dealing with change. Our thoughts are often flooded with fear of discomfort, fear of loss of control, the uncertainty that we possess the necessary skills to negotiate the new river, or simply resistance to the prospect of having to expand our current levels of mental, emotional, and physical energy and effort. The mantra of the Average Minded is, "I just want to be comfortable and have security." This mindset loathes change and does everything it can to avoid it. And when change is unavoidable, the Average Minded will act like a drowning victim, thrashing and flailing against the currents of change, expending their energy on resisting the river's current, confused as to why life is so difficult.

Instead, imagine the Resilient-Minded parent calmly embracing the current and flow of the water, channeling and directing responses into surfing the torrent and using the river's energy to power inner efforts. This illustration shows the crux of resilience, adroitly and skillfully using change to power our journey down the road to success, fulfillment, and happiness. Master this concept, and the world becomes your oyster, waiting to be shucked. Teach your children to master this concept, and success, fulfillment, and happiness cannot be withheld from them.

Human beings are creatures of habit. That is how we are designed to operate. Remember: our brains function by taking in eleven million bits per second and filtering out one hundred twenty-six bits per second to the conscious mind for action. Leaving over ninety-nine percent of what's happening outside of our conscious minds. We are creatures of habit. I'm not saying it's good. I'm not saying it's bad. It just is. The question becomes: how can I use that fact to my advantage?

How long does it take to make a habit? I ask this question to our corporate audiences during resilience training workshops. Most will shout out three weeks or twenty-one days – the prevailing conventional wisdom. I contend that it takes the human being exactly one time of doing something to make a habit. Imagine that you are in the audience at my workshop, and it is a two-day event. Where will you sit in the room on the second day of training? Chances are very high that you will sit in the exact same chair as on day one. You will look to park your car in the same spot, and if it is taken, you will not be happy and will find a parking spot nearby. The key to creating a habit has nothing to do with time and everything to do with comfort. The faster the human becomes comfortable, the faster the human repeats the behavior. Habits are easy to make but hard to break. The trick to making something a habit is to become comfortable doing that thing as quickly as possible. Comfort is also the trick to surfing the river of change. When new things are sprung on you, the quicker you become comfortable with change, the quicker you adapt and overcome.

Adapt and Overcome

One of the greatest skills the U.S. Marine Corps taught was dealing with change. This concept was immortalized in the film by Clint

Eastwood, *Heartbreak Ridge*. Eastwood played Gunny Highway, and his mantra was, "Adapt and overcome."

When we were preparing and training for combat in the Corps, our superiors all the way up the chain of command to the commandant would never seem to be able to make their minds up about what they wanted us lowly foot soldiers to do. The troops would joke that there would be an average of twenty-two changes to any given order before it was executed. Things changed so often that it seemed impossible even to make dinner plans. It was constant turmoil.

It wasn't until years later that I began to realize, as I progressed through the ranks, the fact that this chaos occurred by design. It was a calculated strategy and deliberately done not to torture the grunts on the ground, but to prepare us for the turmoil that was certain to come in combat. People call it the "fog of war." In battle, there is no comfort and no security other than each Marine's own ability to be comfortable being uncomfortable and to know that the only security is that all Marines can handle anything that is thrown their way. Marines can adapt to and overcome anything; they've been doing it their entire careers.

During Drew's freshman (knob) year at the Citadel, this same strategy was in full effect. The powers that be seemed not to be able to make up their minds. As I watched the students, their parents, and even the alumni freak out over each new change, I was ecstatic for my son. I was happy that they kept changing the instructions, changing roommates,

273

changing schedules, changing traditions, changing, changing, and more changing. Because that is the exact reason for going to the Citadel or any military college or service academy. They were teaching the students how to deal with change. Unfortunately, it doesn't take for most people, even those in the military. They never catch on and resist each new iteration. Fear of change is not for us! And it is not for our children.

Each time Drew was tempted to get upset by a new change (and how could he not be? He is surrounded by cadets who freak out at change, and consciousness is contagious), he would facetime me as soon as he was able. He wanted to point his one hundred twenty-six bits of information in a direction that would help him instead of hurting him. I reminded him of what was really going on and walked him through the phases of adapting to change. He became very good at it and quickly became a respected leader and rank holder. Resilient parents teach our children to surf the river of change, quickly surpassing those who refuse to adapt and overcome.

Phases of Adaptation

The human machine, when faced with change, goes through a series of phases in the process of adapting to the new situation. The quicker one progresses through the phases, the quicker one adapts and overcomes. It is important to know what the phases are so that you can become self-aware of what phase you are in the middle of dealing with and then move quickly to the next phase to the end of the progression.

Think of it like a board game in which you move your piece from the start point to the end as quickly and efficiently as possible.

When we are confronted with the news of change, the first thing we meet is **resistance**. Resistance is a result of a fear and scarcity mentality and is accompanied by shock, denial, and even blame. This was the first stop for Ben and Elizabeth when they first discovered her pregnancy. Initially, shock. Then denial. *There's no way. How could this be? Ben had the operation twelve years ago.* And let's not even think about blame. After it was confirmed by a doctor that indeed Elizabeth was pregnant, Ben high-tailed it to his doctor to get tested himself. Sure enough, Ben needed a re-do procedure. Resistance was futile, and they moved on in the process.

Next stop is **confusion.** The uncertainty of the future carries distress and worry about how the change will affect our lives. We simply don't know how to proceed. For Ben and Elizabeth, the questions of how to proceed swirled around them. *How will we tell the kids? What effect will this have on Elizabeth's career? Or should Ben become a stay-at-home dad? What new baby stuff do we need? Crib? Diapers? Formula or nursing? How does Elizabeth's age factor in?* As the new reality sets in, we progress to the next phase.

Welcome to **integration**. New routines begin emerging as experimentation with the new reality begins. Mistakes are made, but so are course corrections, learning how to overcome. Fortunately for Ben and

Elizabeth, they had seven more months to plan and integrate the new arrival. Decisions were made. The older siblings would pitch in with baby care, and in a big way. Plus, they were excited to do it. Elizabeth and Ben would return to work after maternity and paternity leave periods, leaving minimal gaps in coverage for day care. And because it had been so long, Lamaze class! Yay!

Finally, **commitment**. The new reality becomes the new normal, and we become comfortable once again. I say commitment, because once you get comfortable with the new reality, you become committed to it. You develop an emotional attachment and are invested. And now you will fight to keep it. Ben and Elizabeth can't even imagine what life would be like without little Jonathan. Neither can his older siblings. None of this family would ever trade their new reality for the old. The old one somehow seems so unfulfilling now.

WHAT TO DO:

1) Be aware that the only constant is change. Adapt and overcome, and you will increase your success, fulfillment, and happiness.

2) To navigate the stress of parenthood and life in general, learn to embrace change and to see it as an opportunity to make your family's life ever better.

3) Recognize that when you face change, you will go through a series of phases in the process of adapting to the new situation. The phases are resistance, confusion, integration, and

commitment. The faster you progress through each stage, the quicker the new reality becomes normal.

CHAPTER 16 – Making Course Corrections

Everyone within earshot of the commotion at the little league baseball complex turned to see what the ruckus was all about. There stood a mother facing off with her three-year-old son in front of the concessions stand. The crowd couldn't tell you the exact product the boy was demanding, but he was demanding it at the top of his lungs. The mother was working her way through a steadily increasing progression of volume and intensity. What started with, "Not right now, honey," moved into a negotiation, then pleading, and onto begging. These failing, she turned to threats of various punishments, trying to find the right leverage to get him to comply. No dice. Her frustration rose to the level where she lost her self-control and grabbed the child by the arm. A wrestling match ensued that turned into an MMA match. They were striking each other. The mother, not knowing what else to do, stood up, straightened her clothes and her posture, and walked away, leaving the child on center stage.

The crowd began to turn their attention back to the games being played, shaking their heads. One person muttered, "If that's what it's like in public, imagine what goes on behind closed doors."

"The reason that happened in public is that the kid is in complete charge behind closed doors," another replied.

A friend's father, a retired U.S. Army colonel, put it perfectly, "Remember that when dealing with small children, course corrections are a management issue; when they progress to pre-teen years and beyond, course corrections become a leadership issue." The child's brain does not fully develop rational maturity until approximately age twenty-five. Even the teenager's brain processes most information via the emotion-centric amygdala. Whereas the fully mature adult brain processes information via the rational prefrontal cortex. I say mature, because there are many forty-year-old "seventh -graders" walking among us.

If parents have not trained themselves to operate with the mind (logic and reason) running the boardroom, how can we expect the children to do so? And the pattern continues, with each new generation imitating the previous. If you have made it this far into this book and have committed to implementing the principles herein contained, you will have created a new pattern for your offspring to imitate. We as parents must display mental and emotional maturity, course correcting our own bad behavior before we can credibly and effectively course-correct our children.

Arguing or reasoning with a small child is an exercise in futility. There is no reasoning with, negotiating with, nor persuading a two-year-old. Their brains are not developed to process those higher executive, cognitive functions. That's why course corrections are a management issue. To manage means to be in charge and control. A manager makes the trains run on time. The manager doesn't ask the conductor and engineer what they think about the schedule, how they feel about the job, if they have any suggestions about the schedule, and if they feel like they even need a schedule. The manager makes the schedule and ensures the schedule is carried out.

Good managers also model the behavior they want to see in their employees. A research team from the Max Planck Institute for Evolutionary Anthropology in Leipzig, Germany, developed a series of learning tests they called the Primate Cognition Test Battery, in which they compared chimpanzees and orangutans with two-and half-year-old children. All three groups performed equally well in performing physical learning skills (finding hidden objects, discovering the source of noise, etc.). The children, however, out-performed the primates in social learning skills (watching others solve a problem and imitating the solution). In one test, researchers demonstrated how to open the ends of a plastic tube to get to a treat. The children imitated the demonstrated solution, while the primates did not, digressing instead to chewing on the plastic tube.

Notice that the research team did not explain, reason, or negotiate with the children in teaching them problem-solving. They demonstrated and modeled the behavior. Neither primates nor children had demonstrated higher executive cognitive functions. Resilient-Minded parents deliberately model critical thinking, being a first responder versus an emotional reactor, having asserted control of their thoughts, feelings, attitudes, and actions. This is the beginning of training children to enjoy a successful, fulfilled, and happy life. Yes, training. That is how the human machine learns and adopts patterns of behavior and habits.

Operant Conditioning

Kimmi and I began training our children immediately, modeling the behaviors we wanted them to adopt. We made immediate and consistent course corrections whenever the kids strayed from those behaviors, never allowed those behaviors to set up shop, and never allowed the kids to think the bad behavior was acceptable. In psychology, this concept is called operant conditioning, when an association is formed between a behavior and a result. This differs from classical conditioning (Pavlov's Dogs), which pairs two stimuli, in that operant conditioning pairs a behavior with an outcome.

Imagine you go for a job interview, and when you arrive, the receptionist greets you, collects your phone for security purposes, and escorts you to a room to wait for your appointment to start. The room contains a table, a single chair, three blank walls, and a mirror on the fourth wall. In the center of the table is a big, red button, like an Easy Button from those old office supply television advertisements. What do you do? Do you sit down? Do you stand? Do you check yourself out in the mirror? Many minutes pass. And many more pass by without contact from the outside world, nothing at all. How long before you sit in the lone chair? Or have you already? How long before you decide to press the big red button? Let's pretend you are tired of waiting and take the plunge and press the red button. As soon as your hand depresses the button, you feel the *click,* the door opens, and the receptionist hands you a twenty-dollar bill. He immediately leaves without saying a word. *What is going on?* you ask yourself.

More time passes, and nothing. You decide to hit that button again. As soon as you do, the receptionist instantly enters again, hands you another twenty-dollar bill, and exits without saying a word. You mash the button a third time. The receptionist enters on cue and hands you yet another twenty-dollar bill. You figure you are being punked, but, hey, you've got sixty bucks in hand. You mash the button again and again in rapid succession. Alas, there is no additional money, but you've been conditioned to repeat the behavior because it was initially rewarded.

The next day, your friend has a job interview at the same place. You have told her about the setup with the button and the money. She enters the same room, same setup, no phone, checks the mirror, sits down, and presses the red button. The receptionist immediately enters the room and dumps a bucket of ice cold water over your friend's head. WHAT the WHAT! Pop Quiz: Does your friend press the red button again? Ummmm ... No.

Behavior tied to a result, either reward or discomfort, equals training. Rewarding a behavior conditions the repeating of the behavior, even after the reward ceases to pour forth. Behavior that results in discomfort conditions the cessation of the behavior, course correcting the action from taking place again.

All parents use operant conditioning. However, the majority use it to their detriment and to the detriment of the child. Without immediate course corrective action of undesirable behavior (as in the child receives no consequence of discomfort), the parent by default is conditioning the behavior to be repeated. Even with warnings to "stop hitting your sister." Threats of "don't do that again or else." Declarations of "I'm not going to tell you again." Because, as the child knows, you are going to tell them again, and several more times after that, and still no consequence is coming. Congratulations! You have just conditioned your child to keep hitting his sister.

Kimmi and I "Barney Fife" bad behavior. Barney Fife was the deputy on *The Andy Griffith Show*, an old television show from the 1960s. Barney Fife regularly enforced the smallest of ordinances to "nip" crime in the bud. Well, that's exactly what Resilient-Minded parents do; they "Nip it! Nip it! Nip it!" whenever it comes to undesirable behavior. What you think is no big-deal at two or three, like kids throwing a temper tantrum over not getting their way at the Little League concession stand, is a huge problem at sixteen, still throwing temper tantrums over not getting their own way.

I'm not talking about inflicting pain on your children to make a course correction. However, they do need to experience a level of discomfort that they don't wish to experience again anytime soon. I'm also not talking about having your children live in fear of you. However, they do need to have such a healthy level of respect and esteem for you that they dread letting you down. Each child is different in what is an effective *consequence of discomfort*. For example, my oldest son, Drew, reached that level with a mere look from Kimmi or me of stern displeasure in his behavior. Notice, I said displeasure with his behavior, not in him. This difference is a subtle but enormous one. As a Resilient-Minded parent who continually offers unconditional acceptance, I am never disappointed in my children, ever. If their behavior is unacceptable, that is where I place my displeasure, on the behavior. We should never be critical of people, only of behavior. My children have never heard me say, "I'm disappointed in you." They have heard me say, "That behavior is disappointing and unacceptable; let's fix it."

For Jack, my youngest son, he couldn't care less about consequences or stern looks, nor does he care about being sent to his room. At some point in his young life, someone gave him some chewing gum to soothe him from being upset. It worked so well (operant conditioning - the behavior of chewing gum brought the result of soothed calmness), that he became a chewing gum devotee. He loves chewing gum so much that all Kimmi and I had to do was take it away from him one time as a *consequence of discomfort,* and the mere threat of losing gum enacted course correction.

For my daughter, Michaela, she hates being "yelled at." I merely had to don my Marine Corps drill instructor tone with her, and that was more than enough. To this day, she hates being yelled at, which has spurred her year-round practice of lacrosse fundamentals, all on her own, simply not have to hear the coach yell at her during the season. The Marine Corps Officer Selection Officer at the Citadel tried recruiting her to go into the Corps, and Michaela looked her dead in the eye and said, "Why would anybody want to join the Marine Corps and get yelled at? No, thank you."

Not to say these *consequences of discomfort* were always enough. Several times, the children have been so deep in an emotional seizure, hormones raging, that I would course correct by making them stand at the position of attention, which entails bringing the left heel against the right; turning the feet out equally to form an angle of forty-five degrees with the heels on the same line and touching; keeping the legs straight but not stiff at the knees; making hips and shoulders level and the chest lifted; leaving arms hanging naturally, thumbs along the trouser seams, with palms facing inward toward the legs, fingers joined in their natural curl, and elbows in; lifting head and body erect with eyes straight ahead, mouth closed, and chin pulled in slightly; standing completely still; and not talking. Do you realize how agonizing it is for a four-year-old to stand completely still for sixty seconds? No fidgeting, no movement at all? A minute seems like an eternity of discomfort.

If you properly condition your child from the earliest possible age (beginning no later than two-and-a-half-years-old according to the Primate Cognition study), then you will have to make far fewer course corrections as the child matures. It is a rare occasion that we have had to course correct bad behavior drastically as our children have reached their teenage years. Because Kimmi and I took immediate and consistent action to correct undesirable behavior from the earliest of ages, we have reaped the rewards of a close-knit, inseparable relationship with each of our children individually and matching enjoyment as a family unit.

At this stage, course corrections have become a leadership issue. We perform daily, after-action reviews of significant events in each of our kids' lives. We discuss, guide, coach, and advise our children in their thought processes and decision-making matrixes and in their critical thinking and emotional intelligence skills. As parents, Kimmi and I enjoy almost unheard-of influence in our children's lives. We ask questions and point the kids in the direction we believe will most likely help them; however, the decisions they make are theirs. We will help them walk through the process of dealing with the consequences of their decision and actions, but we don't act for them, fix consequences for them, or clean up their messes. For these teenagers who will soon become adults, Kimmi and I have acted as their safety-net but allowed them to make low-risk decisions and feel the brunt of the consequences of those decisions (good and bad). In doing so, we allow them to learn and grow. Teaching them that there is no such thing as failure as long as you learn from what happened and adjust going forward, making course corrections.

The ultimate training and conditioning target is, indeed, teaching your children to make their own course corrections. Once you condition your children never to waste a "failure," they cannot help but enjoy success, fulfillment, and happiness. Baseball great, Babe Ruth, had a lifetime batting average of .342. Translation: He only produced a hit about one-third of the time he went to the plate. He struck out one thousand three hundred and thirty times and hit seven hundred fourteen home runs. Wow! Here was one of the all-time greatest performers in any field, and he struck out (*failed*) almost twice as many times as he hit home runs. Looking at these numbers and Babe's huge lifetime success takes some of the pressure off to hit it out of the park every time. As Babe once told a reporter who mentioned his failure rate of strikeouts, "Every strike brings me closer to the next home run." This attitude is the self-adjusting, course-correction conditioning that we parents need to instill in our children.

Greatest Coaching Job of All Time

Parenting is the greatest and most vital of all the head coaching jobs in all the world. Eddie Robinson, legendary head coach at Grambling State University, said, "Coaching is a profession of love. You can't coach people unless you love them." Of course, every parent loves their kids more than words can express. That's the first requisite of any coach, loving the folks you coach; so it's a good start. Congratulations, Mom and Dad, you made the cut … you're a coach! Like it or not. Let's take a minute to look at a few thoughts on coaching from a parenting point of view.

Ara Parasheghian, who guided the University of Notre Dame's 1966 and 1973 national championship football teams, said, "A good coach will make his or her players see what they can be rather than what they are." As Resilient-Minded parents, let's help our children see what they can be rather than telling them where they are falling short or not meeting our expectations. We have all experienced how exhausting it feels trying to measure up while simultaneously being told you're not measuring up.

John Wooden, who won ten NCAA national championships in a 12-year period as head coach at UCLA, including a record seven in a row, said, "A coach is someone who can give correction without causing resentment." Our greatest challenge as parents is to help our charges make course corrections without planting the seeds of bitterness, embarrassment, or belittlement. What's even worse is to give no correction at all. Lack of course corrections is setting up your child for failure. And showing disappointment or disgust or simply turning your back on a performance that we deemed not up to par causes extreme long-term damage to those under our tutelage. Immediate adjustments are the best. And in private, if possible.

Ricky Williams, a professional football player, said, "A team takes on the personality of the head coach." If you don't like the way your team of little darlings is acting, look in the mirror. In most cases, they got it honestly. There's no overnight fix, but if you personally work on developing better habits in the areas you don't like to see in your children, they'll take

288

the cue and work on those habits as well. (Just *telling them* to fix it ain't gonna get it done.)

WHAT TO DO:

1) When dealing with small children, course corrections are a management issue; when they progress to pre-teen years and beyond, course corrections become a leadership issue.

2) Take Control. As a parent, you are in charge. You control the family's airspace. The buck stops with you. There is no reasoning with, negotiating with, or persuading a two-year-old. Their brains are not developed to process those higher executive, cognitive functions.

3) Apply operant conditioning, an association formed between a behavior and a result, dispensing child-specific, effective consequences of discomfort and rewards in order to condition desirable behaviors and banish undesirable behaviors.

4) The ultimate training and conditioning target is to teach your child the process of making self-adjustments and making their own course corrections. Never wasting a failure, using it to learn and grow.

5) Parenting is the greatest head coaching job in all the world. Teams take on the personality of the coach. If you don't like the way your team of little darlings is acting, look in the mirror.

Make course corrections in your behavior first, then lead the children.

SECRET 7 – BALANCE

CHAPTER 17 – Life on All Eight Cylinders

Just wanting a great life for your child isn't enough. Otherwise, every child would grow up and enjoy a happy, successful, and fulfilled life. A life filled with harmonious relationships, not ones frayed by hurtful wrongdoings, drama, and embitterment. A life filled with thriving abundance, not struggling to survive or simply overcoming lack. The enjoyment of a purposeful and fulfilling vocation they love, not grinding out a job they hate. No, it is not enough to love your children. Not enough to want the best for them. Not enough.

Resilience is the ingredient necessary in yourself and in your children that will lead to a happy, successful, and fulfilled life. Resilience gives you:

- The capability to take complete control of your thoughts, feelings, attitudes, and actions, especially under pressure

- The skillset to handle anything life throws your way

- The mindset that says, "I'm the problem, and I'm the solution. If I have a problem, it's me, but the good news is that I'm also the solution. I cannot fail, as long as I learn and grow."

- The habit of operating from a foundation of love, not fear, turning negative stress into rocket fuel

- The ability to tap into internal emotional drivers that enable you to push past obstacles, difficulties, loss, or pain and complete any worthy accomplishment.

Resilience knows who you are, where you are going, and why you are going there. It is being rooted and grounded, with the fortitude of an inner citadel that weathers any storm. Only one thing remains for us to pass on to our legacy in our great quest as parents: balance.

One of the greatest compliments I continue to receive about my children is that they are well-rounded and balanced. I have studied the lives of many of history's greatest success stories, only to find that they were super-successful in one area of life and a dumpster fire in virtually every other area of life. I have observed that our greatest strengths can often be exploited as our greatest weakness. Think about Superman. His greatest strength is that he comes from the planet Krypton. That strength is also exploited as his greatest weakness. In my own life, my intensity has served me extremely well in achieving success. That intensity, left unchecked and unbalanced, has at times become a weakness that has robbed me of fulfillment and happiness. My oldest son, Drew, never quits. It gives him an enormous advantage, especially during a wrestling match. However, unchecked and unbalanced, his strength was exploited and left him with a broken forearm, requiring surgery, and a dislocated hip, requiring years of rehabilitation. A great military commander I personally know, beloved by his troops, is strong because of his loyalty to them.

Unchecked and unbalanced, his loyalty to his troops has at times superseded his relationship with his own family. I aspire for myself and my children that our greatest strength is that of balance.

Growing up in the era of the great American muscle cars with huge, gas-guzzling, horse-power-laden, V-8 engines, I remember when I first became aware of the concept of the car losing performance when it was out of balance because not every one of its eight cylinders was firing properly. My family had a used 1970 Dodge Polara, complete with 440 cubic inches and a V-8 engine, the same ones used in the police packages. My dream was to inherit that car, once I got my license. It began to have some problems; not all eight cylinders were firing properly. It wasn't a big deal until you wanted to travel on the highway. The faster you drove, the more pronounced the unbalance became, and the performance suffered.

My obsession has been to have my life running on all eight cylinders and for my kids to experience a high-powered, high-performance, balanced life. One that can smoothly handle the curves, road hazards, and circumstances beyond their control. My highest hope is for you and your children to enjoy the same life. A life that is strong, durable, and has the horsepower to achieve success, fulfillment, and happiness.

We are all born with a high-powered, V-8 engine; each of us is our own version of the muscle car. The problem is that most of us aren't running on all eight cylinders. Some of us are sputtering through life with only one or two cylinders firing, leaving us with diminished horse-power to handle the curves, road hazards, and hills.

Here are the eight cylinders of the human machine:

1) Spiritual Health

2) Physical Health

3) Mental Health

4) Emotional Health

5) Social Health

6) Professional Health

7) Financial Health

8) Cultural Health

When our lives and the lives of our children are balanced, tuned up, and firing consistently in each of these areas, life is so sweet. Let's look under the hood and explore each cylinder. I have listed them in the order of importance, starting at the epicenter of the human machine. Each building upon the next, no skipping.

Spiritual Health Cylinder

This Spiritual Health cylinder is about our internal identity. Your spirit is the real you. You are not your resume or a role that you play. Being spiritually healthy takes work; you actually have to come to terms with who you truly are and who you want to be. Not externally, not taking on the label others give you, not labeling yourself. Even though taking on a label based on externals is much easier, it isn't healthy.

Take the time to get alone and ask yourself:

Who am I, and what is my internal identity?

Who do I want to be?

What are the qualities by which I want to define myself?

Is your identity a person of character, integrity, honor, selflessness, love, and abundance-based consciousness? Are you a person of gratitude? Are you full of life and your very presence a salve to others?

Spiritual Health is the foundational cylinder of all the others; without it, your life is a house of cards built not on a rock, but on shifting sand. Modeling Spiritual Health for your children is essential. "Do as I say and not as I do," won't fly with the kiddos.

Physical Health Cylinder

Having personally spent many years with some of the world's wealthiest people, many will tell you that all the money in the world cannot buy good physical health. I realize that this statement is a no-brainer, that money can't buy good health, but we sure can invest in eating nutritiously and in our fitness. The funny thing is, we know that cakes, pies, ice cream, cookies, and fast food aren't nutritious, yet we don't think twice about consuming that junk. We also know that exercise does a body good, yet we find ten thousand excuses to avoid it.

If you owned a Ferrari, you would never put diesel in the tank for fuel. You wouldn't dream of putting the cheap, low-octane, water-laced, no-name-brand gasoline in it. Why? It would ruin the engine, and the car would either not run at all or sputter and cough its way down the street. Nevertheless, we do that very thing to our bodies, which cannot be replaced.

Most folks don't even realize that the reason they are exhausted and have no energy is directly related to their Physical Health Cylinder. When you don't feel physically good, it's hard to do anything, accomplish anything, or even find the energy to feel fulfilled and happy, even when you do accomplish something. It's a fight just to get up. Have you ever had the flu? If you have … forget about it.

A balanced life requires good physical health, and it's the easiest cylinder to tune up. Can disease and illness strike even the healthiest of people? Yes, but the odds of beating those things can be drastically increased in your favor by eating right, getting enough sleep, and working out (not to mention laying off the liquor, smokes, and sugar). If you want a high-performance, high-powered life filled with success, fulfillment, and happiness, get your nutrition and fitness on the right track and stick with it. In doing so, you are giving your child the blueprint for the same. Remember: *knowing and doing* are completely different animals.

Mental Health Cylinder

We are transformed by the renewing of the mind. A complete mental renovation is a necessary start. In fact, that is the entire purpose of this book, the remodeling of your mindset, mentality, and perspective.

However, in the same way, that new avocado-colored kitchen remodel on your parents' house when you were growing up is now outdated, worn, and old. Our Mental Health Cylinder is the same; one remodel is a good start but not enough. Our minds require maintenance and upkeep.

I read for an hour every night before lights out, usually a business book, science journal, biography, history, or as my wife likes to joke, some random academic textbook. Each morning, I scour the news websites, read *The Wall Street Journal*, and scan a plethora of business, economic, political, and current event periodicals. Feeding my mind, practicing my critical thinking skills, verifying and vetting new information, upgrading old beliefs and opinions when new evidence and facts are discovered.

If I'm not mentally sharp, every other cylinder tends to suffer. I have modeled a thirst for life-long learning for my children by craving fresh knowledge and endeavoring to put into practice and assimilate that knowledge. It's amazing how little time there is for worry, anxiety, and stress when you get your brain out of neutral, open the engine of your mind, and engage your mental horsepower. What are you actively doing to grow, develop, and learn? How are you directing your thoughts and attitudes? What are you feeding on? The answers directly affect how you think your thoughts and the very thoughts you think.

Emotional Health Cylinder

Ralph Waldo Emerson said, "Nothing external to you has any power over you." Most of us seem to be living on an emotional roller coaster. We tend to get sucked into the drama of the office, neighborhood, PTA, church, civic club, and most intensely, our family relationships. When things don't go the way we expect or want, that is the exact time to be in control of our emotions.

I always work to keep things in the center of the highway concerning my emotions. I have worked diligently to do the same for my children. Often talking them off the emotional ledge after a particularly rough day. The reason I work so hard to keep things on an even emotional keel is that I have learned the hard way how allowing my emotions to run free has put my *muscle car* in the ditch on the side of the road, either the "blissful waterfalls and rainbows" ditch or the "frustrated, angry, and fearful" ditch.

When you find yourself starting on the emotional roller coaster and begin to feel as though you can't handle whatever is happening, ask yourself this question: *What are the **facts** here?* As in, "Where is the actual, factual evidence that I can't stand this situation?" or "Where is the actual, factual evidence that this is 100% bad?" or "Where's the actual, factual evidence that this is the zombie apocalypse happening?"

We humans tend to exaggerate and to deal in truths instead of facts, especially when our emotions run wild. We use words like "everything," "nothing," "always," and "never." If you find yourself using this verbiage, red flag yourself; your Emotional Health cylinder needs attention.

Ask yourself: *What are the **facts** that can be entered into evidence that so-and-so always or never does this or that?*

Whatever happens in life, whatever drama or disappointments, or even whatever successes, you are the only one that can control your response(s). No one else can make you feel and react in any way. No one can "push your buttons" without your permission. You aren't going to get control of your emotions simply by reading this book. You have to practice mental toughness and resilience regularly before they, too, become habit. If you feel like your life is out of control and you feel helpless to right the ship, get in contact with us at the Mental Toughness Training Center. We've got a long track record of helping thousands of folks get their lives running on all eight cylinders. Remember: monkey-see-monkey-do; imitation is how we learn. Are you modeling Emotional Health for your child to imitate, or are you on the emotional roller coaster?

Social Health Cylinder

This year, my wife and I are celebrating our thirtieth wedding anniversary. Nobody gave us much of a chance of making it when we got married; we were told ad nauseam that we were too young for it to last. Enjoying harmony in any relationship comes down to that four-letter word: W-O-R-K!

Kimmi and I waited nine years before we started having children. Why? It takes hard work to control yourself and your emotional responses during real or perceived offenses from those around you. We first had to

299

"burn the boats" and commit to each other, no matter what. We made it a priority to enjoy a harmonious relationship with each other. We decided, long before the birth of our children, that we would deliberately create and foster harmonious relationships with each child that would last the span of our lifetime.

Kimmi and I each had to start with loving and accepting ourselves. Most folks don't love and accept themselves, and so it is impossible for them to love and accept others. Once Kim and I got over our own faults, it freed us up not to judge or blame the other for their faults. We also learned (mostly the hard way) always to be honest and open. When you assume anything in any relationship, it can only go badly. Being honest isn't about being mean, but it does require clarity, relevance, accuracy, and precision.

My wife and I have applied these same principles to all our relationships, inside and outside the home. Modelling for our children how to deal with the customer/client, boss, co-worker, employee, teacher, or little league parent that gets under your skin. Once you accept your own faults, work on accepting the fact that everyone else is just like you ... not perfect, a fallible human being. Remember: you don't like to be judged or blamed, and others are just like you ... they don't enjoy it much, either. You're not a fan of people assuming things about you ... they aren't either. So stop assuming things about them.

It's amazing how much our family enjoys being together. The unbreakable bonds of love and trust with our children started with the commitment to build those bonds. Social Health is a top priority that we can only achieve through building and balancing the preceding cylinders. You are the most difficult person you have to deal with. Once you stop being a difficult person, an amazing thing happens: so does everyone else.

Professional Health Cylinder

Imagine if you spend an extra hour every day of studying your chosen profession. What level of expertise would you achieve with that kind of dedication, learning, and development? If you want your Professional Health Cylinder firing with maximum horsepower, you must show yourself to be, at the very least, competent. Look around – legitimately competent performers are extremely rare. How many customer service calls to your cable or cell phone provider were filled with awesomeness? Or how many times has the order at the drive-through gotten messed up? Let's not even mention the hail-storm-chasing home repair contractors.

If you just show up on time, don't call in sick, and have a half-decent attitude, you have already made it into the top twenty percent of the professional world. If you want to be at the top of your field, here's the secret: hit the off-button on the remote and begin reading and studying for one hour every day. If you find it boring to study in your chosen field, it's time to change fields.

What do you think about when you don't have to think about anything? What do you think about when you're driving home, going for a stroll, lying out at the pool, or while you're in the shower? Go study that thing grabs your interest. You might be surprised to find that one hour turns into two or three, and after five years, you'll be getting calls from headhunters, the media, and new clients. Focus for one hour each day on activities that increase your competency. Of course, if you hate your job, you'll be spending every waking hour trying to distract yourself from the misery of your professional life. Imagine if your child learned to imitate this penchant for competence from the ripe old age of twelve? What would that do for their professional careers?

The funny thing is, a by-product of Professional Health is an increase in Financial Health.

Financial Health Cylinder

Financial Health has more to do with your relationship, thinking, and beliefs about finances than it has to do with your net worth or account balance(s). If money is your target, you doom yourself to a life of misery. Money is a tool and vehicle to help you live your life, hit your targets, and enjoy it all along the way. Having money is like having food. Imagine that your pantry is full, but amassing food is your target. You only eat just enough to survive and stockpile the rest. Every time you check the pantry, you feel awful that even though it's full, it's not enough. You need a bigger pantry. And you would never have a holiday family dinner because that would cut into your stockpile of food.

On the other hand, the folks that barely have enough to eat are constantly thinking about food and where they can get some. Everything in their life is geared toward finding the next meal, which could be days away. The instant we have some extra, we squirrel it away. But no matter how much we try, the pantry never gets full. Often the next step is to complain that people with full pantries are crooked, corrupt, greedy, and insincere and that it's not fair they don't care about people. Besides, food won't make you happy, and the love of food is the root of all evil.

The third option is to gorge yourself on sumptuous fare. Overindulge. Become a glutton and someone who wastes food, keeping so much to yourself that it spoils. You see, Financial Health is more about mindset than the amount in your account.

I've been both, in lack and in abundance. I can tell you that having money is much better than having none and that having more makes life easier, more enjoyable, and less stressful than less money. Saving more is not the answer. Living the draconian, spartan lifestyle of doing more with less is for the Survival Minded. The answer is to focus on earning more. Focus on your Professional Health; become an expert talent in your field and earn more money. Take an honest inventory of what you think and believe about money. If you catch yourself talking about what you'd do if you won the lottery, you do not have Financial Health. Chasing riches and wealth at the expense of the other cylinders and your family is equally unbalanced and unhealthy.

303

Cultural Health Cylinder

We all have heard that we shouldn't criticize and judge someone until we have walked a mile in their shoes. Growing up as a missionary's kid came with a steaming hot cup of culture shock. I learned quickly that I had a very low level of awareness when it came to just how vast and diverse the world is. I remember how stunned I was when I learned that *football* means different things to different folks, as do the *bathroom, napkins,* and *bum* ... amongst seemingly infinite other words, phrases, customs, and norms.

Living life on all eight cylinders requires Cultural Health. A good place to start is with awareness. I'm not talking about giving up your culture so that it doesn't offend others; I'm talking about gaining some understanding about others in order to connect with them. It's amazing what you can learn, both in similarities and differences. And it isn't all religion-based, ethnic, or even transnational. New Jersey has a completely different culture than South Carolina or Georgia. And West Texas is different from California and Wisconsin, etc.

Cultural Health encompasses more than conventional wisdom suggests. Plumbers have a different culture than insurance agents, and bankers have a different culture than engineers, and on and on. You can be exponentially vaulted to unbelievable heights simply by being able to bridge the gaps between cultures. Imagine how smoothly your culturally-healthy children can move within various socioeconomic, religious, and ethnic groups because you modeled Cultural Health to them. Take the time at least to imagine what it would be like to walk a mile in another person's shoes. Learning even a little bit about someone's culture goes beyond courtesy; it demonstrates respect. It costs you nothing, but the return on investment is incredible. Implementing this one thing has the potential to unlock undreamt-of levels of success, fulfillment, and happiness.

CONCLUSION

You don't have to join an elite military unit to be resilient and mentally tough. You don't have to be in combat or a fire fight or almost get killed in a war. If you're a parent, you have resilience within you; you need only learn how to tap into it, deploy it, and then teach it to your children. This book is less a parenting book and more a mental toughness manual for parents in leading their children to be resilient. It is a field guide that lays out time-tested, proven, science-based, duplicable processes for imitating, learning, and modeling resilience and mental toughness. Hopefully it has also demonstrated how to lead and persuade your children to adopt a Resilient-Minded mentality by revealing the Seven Secrets of Resilience.

The Seven Secrets of Resilience for Parents are:

1) CRITICAL THINKING & THE BRAIN

2) INTERNAL IDENTITY

3) MINDSET MASTERY

4) MOTIVATIONAL INTELLIGENCE

5) TAPPING INTO THE LAWS OF INFLUENCE

6) COURSE CORRECTIONS

7) BALANCE

NOTES AND RESOURCES
Introduction

Larsen, Linda. *12 Secrets to High Self-Esteem.* Mission, KS: SkillPath, 2001.Audiobook.

McGraw, Phillip C. *Self-Matters: Creating Your Life from the Inside Out.* New York, NY: Free Press, 2002.

Maslow, A. H. *Motivation and Personality.* New York, NY: Harper, 1954.

Croston, Glenn, Ph.D. "The Thing We Fear More Than Death: Why Predators are Responsible for Our Fear of Public Speaking." *Psychology Today.* Nov. 29, 2012. https://www.psychologytoday.com/blog/the-real-story-risk/201211/the-thing-we-fear-more-death.

University of Michigan Research Team. "Sticks and Stones: Brain Releases Natural Painkillers During Social Rejection, U-M study finds." Michigan Medicine: University of Michigan. Oct. 10, 2013. http://www.uofmhealth.org/news/archive/201310/opioid-social?tidrss=research.

Pinker, Susan. "Watching Terror and Other Traumas Can Deeply Hurt Teenagers." *Wall Street Journal.* Feb. 8, 2017. https://www.wsj.com/articles/watching-terror-and-other-traumas-can-deeply-hurt-teenagers-1486567986.

Patel, Ushma. "Hasson Brings Real Life into the Lab to Examine Cognitive Processing." Princeton University. Dec. 5, 2011. https://www.princeton.edu/main/news/archive/S32/27/76E76/index.xml?section=featured.

Hasson, Uri, and Chris D. Frith. "Mirroring and Beyond: Coupled Dynamics as a Generalized Framework for Modelling Social Interactions." The Royal Society Publishing. Apr. 11, 2016. http://rstb.royalsocietypublishing.org/content/371/1693/20150366

Konvalinka, Ivana, and Markus Bauer, Carsten Stahlhut, Lars Kai Hansen, Andreas Roepstorff, and Chris D. Frith. "Frontal Alpha Oscillations Distinguish Leaders from Followers: Multivariate Decoding of Mutually Interacting Brains." ScienceDirect. Mar. 12, 2014. http://www.sciencedirect.com/science/article/pii/S105381191400144X.

Chapter 1

Brown, Rebel. *The Influential Leader: Using the Technology of Your Mind to Create Excellence in Yourself and Your Teams*. eBook by Rebel Brown, 2013. http://switchandshift.com/wp-content/uploads/2013/12/The-Influential-Leader-FINAL-FREE.pdf.

Chabris, Christopher, and Daniel Simons. *The Invisible Gorilla: and Other Ways Our Intuitions Deceive Us*. New York, NY: Random House, 2010.

Chopra, Deepak, and Rudolph E. Tanzi. *Super Brain: Unleashing the Explosive Power of Your Mind to Maximize Health, Happiness, and Spiritual Well-Being*. New York, NY: Random House, 2012.

Gladwell, Malcolm. *Blink: The Power of Thinking without Thinking*. New York, NY: Little, Brown and Company, 2005.

Kahneman, Daniel. *Thinking, Fast and Slow*. New York, NY: Farrar, Straus and Giroux, 2011.

Pillay, Srinivasan S. *Your Brain and Business: The Neuroscience of Great Leaders*. Upper Saddle River, NJ: Pearson Education, 2011.

Wilson, Timothy D. *Strangers to Ourselves: Discovering the Adaptive Unconscious*. Cambridge, MA: Harvard University Press, 2002.

Pillay, Srinivasan S. *Life Unlocked: 7 Revolutionary Lessons to Overcome Fear*. New York, NY: Rodale, Inc., 2010.

Cuddy, Amy. "Your Body Language Shapes Who You Are." TEDGlobal. 21 min., 02 sec.; streamed. Filmed Jun. 2012. https://www.ted.com/talks.

Dweck, Carol. "The Power of Believing that You Can Improve." TEDxNorrkoping. 10 min., 20 sec.; streamed. Filmed Nov. 2014. https://www.ted.com/talks.

Dean, Jeremy, Ph.D. "Cognitive Biases: Why We Make Irrational Decisions." PsyBlog. Feb. 2013. http://www.spring.org.uk/2013/02/cognitive-biases-why-we-make-irrational-decisions.php.

LiveScience.com. "Everyone Thinks They Are Above Average." CBS News. Feb. 7, 2013. http://www.cbsnews.com/news/everyone-thinks-they-are-above-average/.

LaBar, Kevin S., and Roberto Cabeza. "Cognitive Neuroscience of Emotional Memory." Nature Reviews Neuroscience. Jan. 1, 2006. http://www.nature.com/nrn/journal/v7/n1/full/nrn1825.html.

Bergland, Christopher. "The Neuroscience of Recalling Old Memories." *Psychology Today.* Jul. 3, 2015. https://www.psychologytoday.com/blog/the-athletes-way/201507/the-neuroscience-recalling-old-memories.

Mercola, Joseph. "Neuroplasticity Studies Reveal Your Brain's Amazing Malleability." Mercola.com. Jan. 15, 2015. https://articles.mercola.com/sites/articles/archive/2015/01/15/neuroplasticity-brain-health.aspx.

Reference.com, s.v. "What Is a Schema in Psychology?" https://www.reference.com/world-view/schema-psychology-1645cd0847eb3b81 (accessed June 18, 2018).

Chapter 2

Heminway, John. *Stress: Portrait of a Killer,* Documentary DVD. Written and Directed by John Heminway. National Geographic Television. Los Angeles, CA: 20th Century Fox, 2008.

Goleman, Daniel. *Focus: The Hidden Driver of Excellence*. New York, NY: HarperCollins, 2013.

Ariely, Dan. "Are We in Control of Our Own Decisions?" EG 2008. 17 min., 26 sec.; streamed. Filmed Dec. 2008. https://www.ted.com/talks.

Bandura, A. "Self-efficacy: Toward a Unifying Theory of Behavioral Change." *Psychological Review* 84 (1977): 191-215.

Bandura, A. "Exercise of Personal Agency through the Self-efficacy Mechanisms." In *Self-efficacy: Thought Control of Action*, edited by R. Schwarzer. Washington, DC: Hemisphere, 1992.

Bandura, A. "Self-efficacy." In *Encyclopedia of Human Behavior, 4*, edited by V. S. Ramachaudran, 71-81. New York: Academic Press, 1994.

Bandura, A. *Self-Efficacy in Changing Societies*. Cambridge, UK: Cambridge University Press, 1995.

Fuemmeler, B. F., and C. A. Lovelady, N. L. Zucker, and T. Østbye. "Parental Obesity Moderates the Relationship between Childhood Appetitive Traits and Weight." *Obesity* 21 (2013): 815–823.

Healthy Schools. "Childhood Obesity Facts." Centers for Disease Control and Prevention. cdc.gov. https://www.cdc.gov/healthyschools/obesity/facts.htm (accessed Jun. 18, 2018).

Chapter 3

Minto, William. *Logic, Inductive and Deductive.* London: University of Aberdeen, 1915.

Paul, Richard W., and Linda Elder. *Critical Thinking: Tools for Taking Charge of Your Professional and Personal Life.* Upper Saddle River, NJ: Pearson Education, Inc., 2002.

Wittman, Andrew. *Ground Zero Leadership: CEO of You.* 1st ed. Greenville, SC: Get Warrior Tough Media, 2016.

Chapter 4

Amen, Daniel, M.D. *Change Your Brain Change Your Life.* New York, NY: Harmony Books, 1998.

Larsen, Linda. *12 Secrets to High Self-Esteem.* Mission, KS: SkillPath, 2001.Audiobook.

McGraw, Phillip C. *Self-Matters: Creating Your Life from the Inside Out.* New York, NY: Free Press, 2002.

Myers, David G. *Psychology.* 10th ed. Hope College, Holland, MI: Worth Publishers, 2013.

Chapter 5

Maslow, A. H. *Motivation and Personality.* New York, NY: Harper, 1954.

Croston, Glenn, Ph.D. "The Thing We Fear More Than Death: Why Predators are Responsible for Our Fear of Public Speaking." *Psychology Today.* Nov. 29, 2012. https://www.psychologytoday.com/blog/the-real-story-risk/201211/the-thing-we-fear-more-death.

University of Michigan Research Team. "Sticks and Stones: Brain Releases Natural Painkillers During Social Rejection, U-M study finds." Michigan Medicine: University of Michigan. Oct. 10, 2013. http://www.uofmhealth.org/news/archive/201310/opioid-social?tidrss=research.

Wikiversity, s.v. "Motivation and Emotion/Book/2013/Avoidance Motivation." https://en.wikiversity.org/wiki/Motivation_and_emotion/Book/2013/Avoidance_motivation (accessed Jun. 18, 2018).

Covey, Stephen R. *The 7 Habits of Highly Effective People.* New York, NY: Free Press, 1989.

Myers, David G. *Psychology*. 10th ed. Hope College, Holland, MI: Worth Publishers, 2013.

Chapter 6

Laule, Sara, M.D., rev. "Sibling Rivalry." C.S. Mott Children's Hospital: Michigan Medicine. University of Michigan Health System. Jun. 2009, updated Mar. 2017. http://www.med.umich.edu/yourchild/topics/sibriv.htm.

Pickhardt, Carl, Ph.D. "Adolescence and Parental Favoritism." *Psychology Today*. Mar. 7, 2011. https://www.psychologytoday.com/us/blog/surviving-your-childs-adolescence/201103/adolescence-and-parental-favoritism.

Kalman, Izzy. "The Myth of the 'Normal' Sibling Rivalry." *Psychology Today*. Aug. 5, 2013. https://www.psychologytoday.com/blog/resilience-bullying/201308/the-myth-the-normal-sibling-rivalry.

Marston, William M. *Emotions of Normal People*. London: K. Paul, Trench, Trubner & Co. Ltd., 1928.

Ekstrand, D.W. *The Four Human Temperaments*. eBook by D.W. Elkstrand. 2012. http://www.thetransformedsoul.com/additional-studies/miscellaneous-studies/the-four-human-temperaments.

Wolfe, Ira. "Why DISC Doesn't Work for Employee Screening." Toolbox:HR. Oct 31, 2011. http://hr.toolbox.com/blogs/ira-wolfe/why-disc-doesnt-work-for-employee-screening-49119.

Jacobi, Jolande. *The Psychology of C. G. Jung*. New Haven, CT: Yale University Press, 1973.

Harris, M. A., and C. E. Brett, W. Johnson, and I. J. Deary. . "Personality Stability from Age 14 to Age 77 Years." *Psychology and Aging* 31(8) (2016): 862-874. http://dx.doi.org/10.1037/pag0000133.

Chapter 7

Dweck, Carol S. *Mindset: The New Psychology of Success*. New York, NY: Random House, 2006.

Siebold, Steve. *177 Mental Toughness Secrets of the World Class: The Thought Processes, Habits and Philosophies of the Great Ones*. Montgomery County, OH: London House, 2010.

Christakis, Nicholas A. and James H. Fowler. *The Spread of Obesity in a Large Social Network over 32 Years*. New England Journal of

Medicine 357 (2007):370-379. DOI: 10.1056/NEJMsa066082 http://www.nejm.org/doi/full/10.1056/NEJMsa066082.

"Cortés Burns His Boats." PBS. https://www.pbs.org/conquistadors/cortes/cortes_d00.html (accessed Jun. 18, 2018).

"Surround Babies with Protection." Centers for Disease Control and Prevention. cdc.gov. Jun. 27, 2017. https://www.cdc.gov/pertussis/pregnant/mom/protection.html.

Encyclopedia Britannica, s.v. "Sumerian language." Gelb, Ignace J. https://www.britannica.com/topic/Sumerian-language

Strong, James. *Strong's Exhaustive Concordance of the Bible.* 1st ed. Peabody, MA: Hendrickson Publishers, 1988.

Gladwell, Malcolm. *Outliers: The Story of Success.* New York, NY: Little, Brown and Company, 2008.

Chapter 8

Pink, Daniel H. *Drive: The Surprising Truth About What Motivates Us.* New York, NY: Riverhead Books, 2009.

Selk, Jason. *10-Minute Toughness: The Mental Training Program for Winning the Before the Game Begins.* New York: McGraw Hill, 2009.

Myers, David G. *Psychology.* 10th ed. Hope College, Holland, MI: Worth Publishers, 2013.

Kahneman, D., and A. Tversky. "Choices, Values, and Frames." *American Psychologist* 39 (4) (1984): 341–350. doi:10.1037/0003-066x.39.4.341.

Duckworth, Angela Lee. "The Key to Success? Grit." TED Talks Education. 06 min., 12 sec.; streamed. Filmed Apr. 2013. https://www.ted.com/talks.

"What You Need to Know about Willpower: The Psychological Science of Self-Control." American Psychological Association. http://www.apa.org/helpcenter/willpower.aspx (accessed Jun. 18, 2018).

Chapter 9

Pillay, Srinivasan S. *Life Unlocked: 7 Revolutionary Lessons to Overcome Fear.* New York, NY: Rodale, Inc., 2010.

"Teen Millionaire Farrah Gray: 'Reallionaire.'" *The Tavis Smiley Show.* National Public Radio. npr.org. Dec. 8, 2004. https://www.npr.org/templates/story/story.php?storyId=4208767.

Helmstetter, Shad. *What to Say When You Talk to Yourself.* Scottsdale, AZ: Grindle Press, 1982.

Siebold, Steve. *177 Mental Toughness Secrets of the World Class: The Thought Processes, Habits and Philosophies of the Great Ones.* Montgomery County, OH: London House, 2010.

Myers, David G. *Psychology.* 10th ed. Hope College, Holland, MI: Worth Publishers, 2013.

Proctor, Bob. *You Were Born Rich.* Scottsdale, AZ: Lifesuccess Productions, 1994.

Wittman, Andrew. *Ground Zero Leadership: CEO of You.* 1st ed. Greenville, SC: Get Warrior Tough Media, 2016.

Chapter 10

Kolenda, Nick. *Methods of Persuasion: How to Use Psychology to Influence Human Behavior.* Boston, MA: Kolenda Entertainment, LLC, 2013.

Cialdini, Robert B., Ph.D. *Influence: The Psychology of Persuasion.* New York, NY: Harper Collins, 2007.

Schaffer, Jack, Ph.D. *The Like Switch.* New York, NY: Simon & Schuster, 2015.

Golson, Hodge. "The Laws of Influence." Management Psychology. http://www.managementpsychology.com/articles/the-laws-of-influence/ (accessed Jun. 18, 2018).

Brinol, Pablo, Petty, Richard, and Wagner, Benjamin. "Body Posture Effects on Self-evaluation: A Self-validation Approach." Ohio State University. Feb. 25, 2009. http://www.psy.ohio-state.edu/petty/documents/2009EJSPBrinolPettyWagner.pdf.

Chapter 11

Myers, David G. *Psychology.* 10th ed. Hope College, Holland, MI: Worth Publishers, 2013.

Lee, John R., M.D. *Hormone Balance Made Simple.* New York, NY: Hachette Book Group USA, 2006.

Zodkoy, Steven M. DC, CNS, DACBN, DCBCN. *Misdiagnosed: The Adrenal Fatigue Link*. Waitsfield, VT: Babypie Publishing, 2014.

Amen, Daniel, M.D. *Change Your Brain Change Your Life*. New York, NY: Harmony Books, 1998.

Hoffman, John. *Sleepless in America*, Documentary DVD. Directed by John Hoffman. National Geographic Television. Los Angeles, CA: 20th Century Fox, 2015.

Iliff, Jeff. "One More Reason to Get a Good Night's Sleep." TEDMED 2014. 11 min., 41 sec.; streamed. Filmed Sept. 2014. https://www.ted.com/talks.

Patel, Ushma. "Hasson Brings Real Life into the Lab to Examine Cognitive Processing." Princeton University. Dec. 5, 2011. https://www.princeton.edu/main/news/archive/S32/27/76E76/index.xml?section=featured.

Hasson, Uri, and Chris D. Frith. "Mirroring and Beyond: Coupled Dynamics as a Generalized Framework for Modelling Social Interactions." The Royal Society Publishing. Apr. 11, 2016. http://rstb.royalsocietypublishing.org/content/371/1693/20150366

Konvalinka, Ivana, and Markus Bauer, Carsten Stahlhut, Lars Kai Hansen, Andreas Roepstorff, and Chris D. Frith. "Frontal Alpha Oscillations Distinguish Leaders from Followers: Multivariate Decoding of Mutually Interacting Brains." ScienceDirect. Mar. 12, 2014. http://www.sciencedirect.com/science/article/pii/S105381191400144X.

Chapter 12

Mehrabian, Albert, Ph.D. *Silent Messages: Implicit Communication of Emotions and Attitudes*. Belmont, CA: Wadsworth Publishing Co., 1972.

Wargo, Eric. "How Many Seconds to a First Impression?" Association for Psychological Science. Jul. 1, 2006. http://www.psychologicalscience.org/index.php/publications/observer/2006/july-06/how-many-seconds-to-a-first-impression.html.

Stone, Vernon A. "A Primacy Effect in Decision-Making by Jurors," *Journal of Communication* 19 (3) (1969): 239–247. doi:10.1111/j.1460-2466.1969.tb00846.x.

Strack, F., and LL Martin and S. Stepper. "Inhibiting and Facilitating Conditions of the Human Smile: A Nonobtrusive Test of the Facial Feedback Hypothesis." National Center for Biotechnology Information.

Journal of Personality and Social Psychology 54 (5) (1988):768-77. http://www.ncbi.nlm.nih.gov/pubmed?term=Strack%2C%20Martin%20%26%20Stepper%20back%20in%201988%20(Inhibiting%20and%20facilitating%20conditions%20of%20the%20human%20smile (accessed Jun 18, 2018).

Kleiman, Karen, MSW, LCSW. "Try Some Smile Therapy." *Psychology Today.* Aug 1, 2012. https://www.psychologytoday.com/blog/isnt-what-i-expected/201207/try-some-smile-therapy.

Golle, Jessika, and Fred W. Mast and Janek S. Lobmaier. "Something to Smile About: The Interrelationship between Attractiveness and Emotional Expression." Taylor & Francis Online. Jul. 22, 2013. http://www.tandfonline.com/doi/abs/10.1080/02699931.2013.817383.

Holloway, Pam. "The Secret to Likeability." About People. Jan. 13, 2015. http://www.aboutpeople.com/Articles/Likeability.php.

Cialdini, Robert B., Ph.D. *Influence: The Psychology of Persuasion.* New York, NY: Harper Collins, 2007.

Chapter 13

Lerner, Richard M., Laurence Steinberg, eds. *Handbook of Adolescent Psychology.* Hoboken, NJ: John Wiley & Sons, Inc., 2009.

Weaver, C.M., and D.S. Shaw, J.L. Crossan, T.J. Dishion, and M.N. Wilson. "Parent-child Conflict and Early Childhood Adjustment in Two-parent Low-income Families: Parallel Developmental Processes." National Center for Biotechnology Information. *Child Psychiatry and Human Development* 46 (1) (2015): 94–107. doi:10.1007/s10578-014-0455-5. https://www.ncbi.nlm.nih.gov/pubmed/24610382.

Developmental Psychology. The American Psychological Association. Vol. 41, No. 6, 971–984. 0012-1649/05/$12.00 DOI: 10.1037/0012-1649.41.6.971, 2005.

McLeod, Saul. "Pavlov's Dogs." *Simply Psychology.* 2007, updated 2013. https://www.simplypsychology.org/pavlov.html.

Cialdini, Robert B., Ph.D. *Influence: The Psychology of Persuasion.* New York, NY: Harper Collins, 2007.

Kolenda, Nick. *Methods of Persuasion: How to Use Psychology to Influence Human Behavior.* Boston, MA: Kolenda Entertainment, LLC, 2013.

Schaffer, Jack, Ph.D. *The Like Switch*. New York, NY: Simon & Schuster, 2015.

Chapter 14

Voss, Chris, and Tahl Raz. *Never Split the Difference: Negotiating as if Your Life Depended on It*. New York, NY: Harper Business, Harper Collins Publishers, 2016.

Camp, Jim. *Start with No*. New York, NY: Crown Publishing Group, a division of Random House, Inc., 2002.

Golson, Hodge. "The Laws of Influence." Management Psychology. http://www.managementpsychology.com/articles/the-laws-of-influence/ (accessed Jun. 18, 2018).

Cialdini, Robert B., Ph.D. *Influence: The Psychology of Persuasion*. New York, NY: Harper Collins, 2007.

Brosnan, Sarah F., and Frans B.M. de Waal. "Monkeys Reject Unequal Pay." *Nature: International Journal of Science* 425 (2003): 297–299. Sept.18, 2003. http://www.nature.com/nature/journal/v425/n6955/full/nature01963.html

Fehra, Ernst, and Klaus M. Schmidt. "Theories of Fairness and Reciprocity - Evidence and Economic Applications." Massachusetts Institute of Technology. Oct. 2003. http://web.mit.edu/14.193/www/WorldCongress-IEW-Version6Oct03.pdf.

Loewenstein, George F., and Leigh Thompson, and Max H. Bazerman. Interpersonal Relations and Group Processes: Social Utility and Decision Making in Interpersonal Contexts. Journal of Personality and Social Psychology 57 (3) (1989): 426-441. http://www.anderson.ucla.edu/faculty/keith.chen/negot.%20papers/Loew ThompBazer_SocUtilDecMake89.pdf (accessed Jun. 18, 2018).

Blake, P.R., and others. "The Ontogeny of Fairness in Seven Societies." *Nature: International Journal of Science* 528 (2015): 258–261. December10, 2015. http://www.nature.com/nature/journal/vaop/ncurrent/full/nature15703.html

Konnikova, Maria. "How We Learn Fairness." *The New Yorker*. Jan. 7, 2016. http://www.newyorker.com/science/maria-konnikova/how-we-learn-fairness

Chapter 15

Tasler, Nick. "How to Get Better at Dealing with Change." *Harvard Business Review.* Sept. 21, 2016. https://hbr.org/2016/09/how-to-get-better-at-dealing-with-change.

University of Sydney. "How Kids Cope with Change: New Findings on Adaptability." Medical Xpress. Oct. 31 2013. https://medicalxpress.com/news/2013-10-kids-cope.html.

Kübler-Ross, Elisabeth, Ph.D. *On Death & Dying*, 1969. *The Stages of Acceptance.* Interpretation by Alan Chapman, 2008. http://www2.bakersfieldcollege.edu/jkirst/spst48/stages_of_acceptance.pdf

The Men Who Built America. Television Show; streaming. The History Channel. 2012. http://www.history.com/shows/men-who-built-america (accessed Jun. 18, 2018).

Chapter 16

Staddon, J. E. R and D. T Cerutti. "Operant Conditioning." *Annual Review of Psychology* 54 (1) (2003): 115–144. doi:10.1146/annurev.psych.54.101601.145124. March 23, 2013. http://www.annualreviews.org/doi/abs/10.1146/annurev.psych.54.101601.145124?journalCode=psych.

Sather, Rita, R.N., and Amit Shelat, M.D., rev. "Understanding the Teen Brain." University of Rochester Medical Center. https://www.urmc.rochester.edu/encyclopedia/content.aspx?ContentTypeID=1&ContentID=3051 (accessed Jun. 18, 2018).

DeLong, M.R. "Activity of Pallidal Neurons during Movement." *Journal of Neurophysiology* 34 (1971): 414–27. http://jn.physiology.org/content/34/3/414 (accessed Jun. 18, 2018).

Richardson R.T., and M.R. DeLong: "Electrophysiological Studies of the Function of the Nucleus Basalis in Primates.". In Napier, T.C., and P. Kalivas and I. Hamin, eds. "The Basal Forebrain: Anatomy to Function." *Advances in Experimental Medicine and Biology* vol. 295 (1991): 232–252. New York, Plenum, 1991.

Frank, Michael J., and Lauren C. Seeberger, and Randall C. O'Reilly. "By Carrot or by Stick: Cognitive Reinforcement Learning in Parkinsonism." *Science* 4 (2004).

Chapter 17

Gilbert, Daniel. *Stumbling on Happiness*. New York, NY: Random House, 2006.

Myers, David G. *Psychology*. 10th ed. Hope College, Holland, MI: Worth Publishers, 2013.

Ross, Will. *A Guide to Shameless Happiness: A Rational Emotive Behavior Therapy Booklet Book 1*. eBook by Will Ross, 2012. Kindle ed.